LIFE ON THE LINE IN CONTEMPORARY MANUFACTURING

D1193733

LIFE ON THE LINE
IN CONTEMPORARY
MANUFACTURING

*The Workplace Experience of Lean Production and
the 'Japanese' Model*

RICK DELBRIDGE

OXFORD
UNIVERSITY PRESS

*This book has been printed digitally and produced in a standard specification
in order to ensure its continuing availability*

OXFORD
UNIVERSITY PRESS

Great Clarendon Street, Oxford OX2 6DP

Oxford University Press is a department of the University of Oxford.
It furthers the University's objective of excellence in research, scholarship,
and education by publishing worldwide in

Oxford New York

Auckland Bangkok Buenos Aires Cape Town Chennai
Dar es Salaam Delhi Hong Kong Istanbul Karachi Kolkata
Kuala Lumpur Madrid Melbourne Mexico City Mumbai Nairobi
São Paulo Shanghai Taipei Tokyo Toronto

Oxford is a registered trade mark of Oxford University Press
in the UK and in certain other countries

Published in the United States
by Oxford University Press Inc., New York

© Rick Delbridge 1998

ISBN 0-19-924043-4

For Jared

Always look at the whole of a thing. Find what it is that makes its impression on you, then open it up and dissect it into cause, matter, purpose, and the length of time before it must end.

Marcus Aurelius, *Meditations* (1995: 83).

PREFACE

Before I started this project I had never worked in a factory. Like most people, I suppose, I understood that factory work was mundane, repetitive, hard work. I thought I knew what to expect when I entered the plant and in a way I did. But it was more mundane, more repetitive, and harder than I had expected, more soul-destroying to work on a line in a dreary factory for hour after hour, day after day, than I can really articulate. You have to be there. And that is the experience of millions of people, year after year. My time with the workers of Valleyco and Nippon CTV was an education in the true sense and when I left them my admiration and respect for those people and my despair at the systematic wasting of their talents was complete.

This book is about the working lives and experiences of those people and their social relations on the shop-floor in the changing world of manufacturing. The data that are presented here were gathered during two periods of participant observation working on the shop-floor at the plants. This research approach allows an 'up close and personal' account of these workplace relations. The objective at the start of this project was to understand more about the complexities and dynamics of a particular social situation, namely the shop-floor experience under 'new manufacturing techniques'. It is my intention that in writing this book the true nature of this shop-floor situation will be understood more widely. In particular, this book addresses debates over the role of workers in modern manufacturing, the nature of new management techniques, and the influence of Japanese management on the 'new' workplace.

In writing this book I have been fortunate to have the support of many people. I would like to thank my past and present colleagues at Cardiff Business School. In particular, I am grateful to Barry Wilkinson who was the inspiration and guiding light for the project, and to Mike Bresnen, Jim Lowe, Nick Oliver, Peter Turnbull, and Syd Weston for their friendship, support, and guidance. I am grateful to Ed Heery and Professor Paul Edwards of Warwick Business School for their comments on drafts of the manuscript and to David Musson of Oxford University Press for his faith and patience. Thanks also to Wendy Brown for her help in preparing the book for publication.

Closer to home, my thanks and love to my parents and sister Rachel. And most importantly, of all the people to whom I am indebted, the biggest 'thank you' is to Susan and Steffan for their love, support, and understanding during the long time that this book has been in the writing.

It is appropriate that I am writing this preface on the first of May since this book is for workers everywhere. However, I would like to take this opportunity to dedicate the book to one very special little worker of the future—my beautiful baby son, Jared—in the hope that the world that awaits him is rather fairer and more equitable than the one he has entered.

Rick Delbridge
Radyr
1 May 1997

CONTENTS

FIGURES

ACRONYMS

ACAS	Advisory, Conciliation, and Arbitration Service
AEEU	Amalgamated Engineering and Electrical Union
AEU	Amalgamated Engineering Union (now the AEEU)
APC	Automated Parts Checker
ASTMS	Association of Scientific, Technical and Managerial Staffs (now the MSF)
AV	Audio-visual
CAB	Company Advisory Board
CTV	Colour Television
EETPU	Electrical, Electronic, Telecommunications and Plumbing Union (now the AEEU)
GMB	General, Municipal, Boilermakers trade union (formerly the General, Municipal, Boilermakers' and Allied Trades Union)
HNC	Higher National Certificate
HRM	Human Resource Management
IDN	Identification Number
IMVP	International Motor Vehicle Program
JIT	Just-in-Time
MD	Managing Director
MSF	Manufacturing, Science and Finance Union
NAF	No Actual Fault
NDC	Nippon Denki Corporation
PA	Public Announcement
PCB	Printed Circuit Board
PI	Performance Index
PIP	Productivity Improvement Programme
QC	Quality Control(ler)
SMV	Single Minute Value
SPC	Statistical Process Control
STS	Socio-Technical System
TA	Technical Assistant
TP	Total Productivity
TQC	Total Quality Control
TQM	Total Quality Management
TUC	Trades Union Congress

1

Contemporary Manufacturing and Workplace Relations

INTRODUCTION

What's New about the 'New' Workplace?

For Eric Hobsbawm, the 'Short Twentieth Century' (1914–91) has resulted in a qualitatively different world from that which existed at the turn of the century in three respects. First, it is no longer Eurocentric and the USA of the 1990s looks back on 'The American Century'. Second, 'the globe has become far more of a single operational unit' and, 'Perhaps the most striking characteristic of the end of the twentieth century is the tension between this accelerating process of globalization and the inability of both public institutions and the collective behaviour of human beings to come to terms with it'. Third, 'the disintegration of the old patterns of human social relationships' and the 'snapping of links between past and present' (Hobsbawm 1994: 14–15).

Arguably, these shifts are mirrored in the development of business and the economic world of the twentieth century. Certainly during most of this period the USA has been the major economic force in world trade and it has been the 'society-in-dominance', that is, the society which has generated and diffused its version of 'best practice' in business and management (Smith and Meiksins 1995). 'The American Century' has seen the propagation of Scientific Management, Fordism, the MBA, business schools, and management consultancy; what Jacques (1996) describes as the 'colonization of the world by American management theories and institutions'. That this diffusion of American management knowledge has taken place in an increasingly global market is conventional wisdom. Certainly the 'world characteristics' noted by Hobsbawm are consistent with the increasingly international nature of markets and capital, with intensifying competition between ever larger transnational corporations, and with heightening concern over the role and significance of the nation-state within this global economy. What have these developments meant for the 'human social relationships' of work?

My concern in this book is at the level of the workplace and with particular reference to the nature of workplace relations. 'The American Century' and the global market-place are the context of this arena and inform my observations—but what of the 'snapping of links between past and present'?

Continuity and Change

It is commonplace for researchers of work organizations and business to talk of the contemporary period as one of radical change and discontinuity. Management theorists proclaim a 'revolution' (Hammer and Champy 1993; Kanter 1989; Peters 1987); trade union researchers speak in terms of 'the transformation of industrial relations' (Kochan *et al.* 1986), of 'new industrial relations' (Kelly and Kelly 1991), and of the 'new workplace' (Ackers *et al.* 1996); and students of business organizations discuss 'new forms of work organization' and 'new work structures' (Geary 1995), 'post-bureaucratic organizations' (Hecksher and Donnellon, 1994), and 'transformations in the buyer-supplier relationship' (Morris and Imrie 1992).

The discussion of radical change in these areas of study has prompted an overarching debate over whether these changes are representative of fundamental shifts in the social and economic relations of society or whether there is an essential continuity over time. Notions of 'post-industrial society' (Bell 1974; Handy 1984), 'postmodernism' (Clegg 1990), and 'postfordism' (Kenney and Florida 1988) represent arguments for a fundamental discontinuity in the history of economic development and organization.

However, Dastmalchian *et al.* (1991: 11) reflect that, 'Academic researchers appear to pay more heed to change than continuity . . . Thus in the study of work organization, just as in other areas of social science, warning bells should ring when all the talk is of the new and excludes what remains from before'. Roy Jacques's 'discursive history' of the origins and development of American 'management knowledge' begins by pointing out that many of the characteristics of 'post-industrial management' proposed for the 1990s were actually observed and reported sixty years or more ago (Jacques 1996). Jacques notes that, 'Perhaps we are in the throes of a revolution, but we should remind ourselves that it appears to be a condition of modernity for every generation to believe it is in the midst of revolutionary change' (Jacques 1996: 18–19). Jacques's concern is to present a discursive history of the development of 'knowledge *about* organizations' so that he may illustrate the way that 'industrial thinking' has shaped ' "post-industrial" rhetoric' (Jacques 1996: 10–20). For Jacques the universal 'common sense' of contemporary management knowledge is historically and culturally bound to the context of its development and is consequently inappropriate for the twenty-first century. Jacques offers his analysis as 'a history of the present'.

In reviewing the current dynamics of employee relations, Blyton and Turnbull (1994: 10) reflect that '*all* periods are characterised by elements of change and continuity'. While researching different aspects of change in the world of work, both Jacques and Blyton and Turnbull are critical of considering time as 'linear' and 'progressive'. Blyton and Turnbull are mindful of the need to find an approach which 'adequately encapsulates both continuity and change' and turn to the conceptualization of time moving along a 'spiral' and thus involving elements of progression, continuity, and reversal (1994: 11). Here they draw on the work of Filipcova and Filipec (1986) and on that of Burrell (1992), who applied the notion of 'spiral time' in organizational analysis. Blyton and Turnbull (1994) use the concept to survey the changing nature of employee relations and conclude that the lesson of the last fifteen years in the UK is that, 'Nothing changes yet everything is different: as we twist around the spiral of capitalist economic development we experience progression and return, never a return to exactly the same point but always to a point that is familiar' (p. 298).

Legge (1995) recognizes the approach of Blyton and Turnbull as an example of the 'synthesising orthodoxy' that has emerged, that is, that all periods are characterized by *both* change and continuity. For Blyton and Turnbull then, the *form* of employee relations had broadly remained intact in the majority of workplaces but at the same time the *content* had changed. In this book I present the findings of a detailed empirical study of the form and content of workplace relations in two manufacturing organizations. There has been considerable discussion of a fundamental shift in the organization and management of manufacturing operations, especially regarding 'flexible' and 'lean' production (Piore and Sabel 1984; Womack *et al.* 1990; MacDuffie 1995). This book considers the impact of so-called new management techniques—notably just-in-time and total quality management (JIT and TQM), human resource management (HRM) and team working, and lean production and the 'Japanese model' of manufacturing management. In introducing these issues in this chapter, I will outline the key research questions and explain the structure of the book.

FORM AND CONTENT IN CONTEMPORARY MANUFACTURING

Manufacturing organizations are complex combinations of social and technical features and contemporary research into the management of these organizations has increasingly emphasized the need to find a 'fit' between the social and the technical or technological aspects. Much of the discussion surrounding the technical aspects of manufacturing has been incorporated into discussion of JIT and TQM production.

JIT and TQM

Just-in-time production is closely associated with the Japanese motor industry and particularly Toyota. This approach to the management of stocks and material flow was popularized in the West by business writers such as Richard Schonberger (1982; 1986) and began to receive widespread attention, particularly in the USA, as the Japanese car makers gained a share of the market and then set up overseas operations. Knowledge about the technical aspects of the JIT system was also provided by Japanese writers who had their work published in English (Monden 1983; Ohno 1988; Shingo 1988). These authors concentrated their attention on the Toyota production system and this became largely synonymous in the West with JIT and 'Japanese' manufacturing management.

According to Taiichi Ohno, a Toyota production engineer widely regarded as the founder of JIT, 'the fundamental doctrine of the Toyota production system is the total elimination of waste' (Ohno 1988: 1). Ohno directly contrasts this with his view of the American mass production model and seeks to demonstrate the various benefits of JIT. Under the JIT system, production is driven by market requirements as information regarding demand *pulls* production through the processes. This may be compared to the *push* approach to production scheduling under traditional western manufacturing in which output plans are developed on the basis of historic information and production is decoupled from demand. The intention is to reduce the amount of stock, labour, and time (and hence cost) in the system. This in turn reduces the amount of 'buffering' between processes and hence production quality must be right-first-time.

The reduction in buffers has placed considerable stress on labour and suppliers to provide what is required when it is required and at acceptable quality levels. Oliver and Wilkinson (1992) have argued that the essence of understanding JIT lies in the recognition that these production systems 'dramatically increase the interdependencies between the actors involved in the whole production process, and that these heightened dependencies demand a whole set of supporting conditions if they are to be managed successfully' (p. 68).

Since JIT places a considerable emphasis on reliable production quality, discussion of JIT is regularly bracketed with that of total quality management. TQM is typically characterized as a set of ideas that was developed by Americans but implemented by the Japanese. The American 'quality gurus' such as Crosby and Juran were particularly interested in the 'hard' production management perspective of quality and hence their influence is largely on the technical aspects of manufacturing. However, others, particularly Deming and Feigenbaum, also stressed the significance of the workforce in the management of quality.

Wilkinson *et al.* (1992) identify three approaches to 'quality'. One focuses on the 'hard' production aspects of quality design and conformance to specification with the use of statistical process control to monitor quality and control standards. A second approach concentrates on the 'soft' qualitative aspects involving employees with customer responsiveness and service. The third approach emphasizes a mixture of 'hard' and 'soft' which recognizes the need for process control *and* employee participation.

This third view of quality in manufacturing has become predominant as the need to combine efficacious and mutually supportive technical and social aspects of management has been emphasized. In particular, the notions of a 'fit' between these technical aspects of production and the management of the workforce have centred on issues within the debates surrounding human resource management (HRM) and team working.

Human Resource Management and Team Working

Discussion of HRM originated in the USA during the 1980s (Guest and Hoque 1996). There are various views on what HRM 'is' and in the UK in particular much of the debate has surrounded the question of whether HRM actually exists at all, either as an ideology or as a set of management techniques that is identifiable and distinct (see Legge 1995). In the USA the debate has been more normative and prescriptive, particularly in linking business strategy and human resource strategy (for example, Miles and Snow 1984) and in presenting HRM as an approach which is concerned with the full integration and utilization of the workforce (for example, Lawler 1992). Walton (1985) contrasts an old 'control' philosophy with a preferred new philosophy of 'high commitment' in managing workers. Legge outlines Walton's position thus:

The new HRM model is composed of policies that promote mutuality—mutual goals, mutual influence, mutual respect, mutual rewards, mutual responsibility. The theory is that policies of mutuality will elicit commitment which in turn will yield better economic performance and greater human development. (Legge 1995: 64.)

It is this view of HRM that has been most influential in the debates over the high-performance manufacturing organization. The predominant discourse in this literature is founded on the apparent success of certain manufacturers in combining these social aspects with the technical features of JIT and TQM in the 'lean production' model of manufacturing management.

'High-commitment' HR practices and 'team-based work systems' are central to the argument of MacDuffie (1995) that 'flexible production' plants consistently outperform 'mass production' plants. MacDuffie's work stems from his involvement in the International Motor Vehicle Program (IMVP) which initially led to the publication of the most influential manufacturing management book of the early 1990s—*The Machine that Changed the World* (Womack *et al.* 1990). MacDuffie's arguments are consistent with the lean production model of Womack *et al.* but seek to emphasize the integrated nature of HR practices within the production system and to demonstrate the interrelated and mutually reinforcing 'organizational logic' of low buffers, team working, and high commitment HRM.

'Lean' production or 'flexible' production is readily recognizable as the Toyota production system outlined by Ohno and others and discussed above. MacDuffie (1995) comments that a 'flexible production plant reduces inventory levels and other "buffers", increasing interdependence in the production process' (p. 198). Lean production proponents argue that this system successfully combines the social and technical aspects of efficient manufacturing to provide a universal model of best practice. While lean production is resonant of socio-technical systems research of the 1950s in the emphasis on the relationship between the social system and the technical features of production, MacDuffie (1995: 199) identifies a fundamental distinction:

STS theory characterizes autonomous work teams as an alternative to Taylorist approaches to work organization that is superior in any technical setting. STS organizational designs thus seek to maximize the autonomy of work teams from the constraints of the technical system, often by adding buffers to the technical system. In contrast, this paper explores the integration of HR practices that seek to expand employee skill and involvement with production processes that *minimize* buffers.

Thus the dominant argument, particularly in the USA, is that the successful management of contemporary manufacturing organizations requires the integration of low buffered and tightly controlled technical systems with flexible, high-commitment, team-based social systems that incorporate increased worker skill and involvement. There is no doubt that the major influence on this view of high-performance manufacturing management is the 'Japanese' model.

The 'Japanese' Model

While we may be in 'The American Century', the most noteworthy development and influence in business and management over the past twenty years has been the advent of Japan and the newly industrialized economies of South Korea, Taiwan, Hong Kong, and Singapore. Biggart and Hamilton (1997: 33) comment that 'The leading business success story of the past two decades cannot be disputed: the tremendous growth and economic development of the East Asian economies.' This success has led to an increasing interest in the management of the major companies in these economies, particularly the management practices associated with large Japanese corporations.

The debate surrounding the 'Japanese' model has progressed through various stages since the 1950s. Initially the literature attempted to expand on the limited knowledge of Japan and its developing post-war industrial system in the West. These works were often descriptive and were couched in terms of the industrialization thesis propounded by Kerr *et al.* (1960). In exploring evidence for convergence this research concentrated on the nature of Japanese employment relations. The three most influential authors from this period until the late 1970s were James Abegglen (1958), Robert Cole (1971), and Ronald Dore (1973). In setting the agenda for research and debate in the English-speaking world these three have had an influence that can barely be overstated.

During the 1960s and 1970s, Japan's economic growth prompted writers to seek explanations for the country's success and to begin to recommend the adoption of what had come to be seen as 'Japanese' methods in the West. These management methods, following the emphasis on employment relations of the earlier literature, were deemed to have their basis in personnel practices and relations between workers and managers. During the early 1980s, perhaps because of the focus of Abegglen and Dore on Japan's culture and institutions, authors such as Pascale and Athos (1982) and Ouchi (1981) placed great emphasis on Japanese culture and traditions in explaining management practices and business performance. The emphasis in the literature was on demonstrating the explanations for Japanese corporate success and on applying the lessons to western business.

However, as we have discussed above, the translation of the work of Japanese engineers such as Ohno (1988) and Shingo (1988) emphasized the significance of the technical aspects of production and attention has focused more recently on the effective combination of social and technical aspects of manufacturing management. In conjunction with this perspective, the manner in which the Japanese manage their supplier relations has come under close scrutiny. Thus the 'Japanese' model is seen as incorporating aspects of operations management, HRM, and supply chain management including team working, high-commitment HR policies, and employee involvement as well as JIT, TQM, and long-term 'trust-based' buyer-supplier relations (see Kenney and Florida 1993; Oliver and Wilkinson 1992; Sako 1992).

Much of the recent debate over the 'Japanese' model has centred on the opportunities for, and desirability of, the transfer of Japanese management practices to western contexts. Elger and Smith (1994) recognize two approaches to the transfer of the 'Japanese' model: 'universalistic models' which argue that the model can and should be transposed regardless of setting (Kenney and Florida 1993; Womack *et al.* 1990) and discussions which consider the extent of the 'diffusion' of the model (Abo *et al.* 1994; Oliver and Wilkinson 1992).

It is not my intention to review the debates surrounding the accuracy of this depiction of Japanese corporate practice, nor to reflect on the evidence for or against the 'Japanization' of western industry. Rather the purpose has been to explain the background to the development of current 'best practice' in management thinking with regard to managing manufacturing operations. The research data presented in this book provide various opportunities to comment on the flaws and misconceptions inherent in the conventional wisdom surrounding the 'Japanese' model and its transfer but carry wider significance regarding the nature of capitalist workplace relations and the role of labour on the new shop-floor.

Workers in Contemporary Manufacturing

The role of labour is central in these outlines of contemporary manufacturing practice. For commentators such as Womack *et al.* (1990) and MacDuffie (1995), workers are multiskilled problem solvers working in teams to both make products and improve processes. As Kenney and Florida (1993) emphasize, the key difference between the stereotypical description of Taylorist techniques and new management practices is with regard to the recombination of planning and execution so that the workers who carry out the production tasks also have input into the design, development, and improvement of product and process technology. Thus the Taylorist principle of rigid standardization and minutely detailed job cycles and timings may still be in place but there is an assumption that practices *can and will* be improved. Put simply, the satisficing mentality of

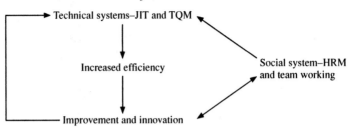

FIG. 1 A Model of Contemporary Manufacturing 'Best Practice'
Source: Adapted from Delbridge and Turnbull (1993).

traditional manufacturing is replaced by a maximizing attitude that demands a constant search for improvements, that is, the principle of *kaizen*.

In *Beyond Mass Production*, Kenney and Florida (1993) describe five dimensions to the new model of 'innovation-mediated production': a transition from physical skill and manual labour to intellectual capabilities or 'mental labour'; the increasing importance of social or collective intelligence as opposed to individual knowledge or skill; an acceleration of the pace of technological innovation; the increasing importance of continuous process improvement on the factory floor; and the blurring of the lines between the research and development (R&D) laboratory and the factory. Thus innovation-mediated production is 'a concept we advance to refer to the integration of innovation and production, of intellectual and physical labor' (Kenney and Florida 1993: 14).

These social processes of innovation and improvement are supported by structures in the organization such as problem-solving groups, suggestion schemes, and appraisal schemes that systematically measure and reward individual input to quality improvements. The formalization of this aspect of the labour process incorporates workers' ideas into the management process. The system recognizes that to separate the planning and design of tasks from those who execute the tasks is *technically* inefficient. One of the intentions of this study was to explore this aspect of the role of labour and to consider the implications that this recombination of activities may have for the *social* efficiency of the system since the division of labour and fragmentation of tasks represents a fundamental principle of traditional capitalist control (Braverman 1974; Edwards 1979). (See Figure 1.)

While there has been increasing consensus regarding contemporary manufacturing in the management literature, there has been little empirical research which explores the nature of these new techniques in practice and, in particular, the experience of the workforce. In fact, much of the qualitative research that has been conducted is critical of the management literature regarding the 'Japanese' model with respect to team working and employee involvement in Japanese transplant car assembly operations (Fucini and Fucini 1990; Garrahan and Stewart 1992; Graham 1995; Parker and Slaughter 1988). This research has questioned the rhetoric of team working and high-commitment HR practices and reported a tight and oppressive factory regime under which there is little autonomy or opportunity for worker discretion. These empirical research findings have prompted considerable debate regarding these new management techniques, the nature of the 'new' shop-floor, and the experience for workers (Delbridge *et al.* 1992; Elger 1990; Turnbull 1988). Here I reflect on these issues with regard to the content and form of shop-floor practices and the experiences of workers in two plants outside the car assembly sector.

THIS STUDY

In this book I report the findings from two periods of study as a participant observer working on the shop-floor. The intention in this research was to gain a close-up view of the impact of new manufacturing techniques on the experiences of workers and on workplace relations between management and labour. I wanted to go beyond the management rhetoric and explore workers' reality.

For this research I spent three months working in a European-owned automotive components supplier and one month working in a Japanese-owned consumer electronics plant. In researching a supplier to the car assemblers I was able to contrast my findings with those who have researched the car makers themselves, and also to witness and record the influence exerted by the customers on the component supplier's operations. By researching a Japanese transplant I was able to establish at first hand the evidence for the transfer of a distinct 'model' of manufacturing practice and consider the effects of these practices on the shop-floor.

In both cases I am indebted to management for the opportunity to research their operations and to the workforce for their time, help, trust, and friendship. The names of the two plants have been changed, as have the names of all the people, but otherwise the findings reported here are as I observed and recorded them.

The detailed findings of the research are presented in the next seven chapters of this book. As far as possible the data are presented to reflect my observations and experiences but to allow readers to develop their own opinions and interpretations. Throughout the book there is widespread use of my daily diary and this material is presented as it was originally recorded. Chapter 2 provides details on how the research was conducted and an introduction to the two case plants—Valleyco and Nippon CTV. The chapter briefly reflects on the choice of research method and the experience of 'doing ethnography' before detailing the case plants. Valleyco, the European-owned automotive components supplier, has many traits of 'traditional' manufacturing management but was seeking to introduce cellular manufacturing, TQM, JIT inventory control, and team working during the time of the study. Nippon CTV, the Japanese transplant, makes colour televisions. This plant has many of the characteristics of lean production, HRM, and 'new' industrial relations and has been cited as an exemplar of 'world class manufacturing'. The chapter outlines the processes, organization, and context of each of the two plants and draws certain distinctions between the 'directed chaos' of Valleyco and the 'bounded JIT' of Nippon CTV.

Chapter 3 presents detailed research findings on the processes of management control at the Japanese transplant. The chapter includes data on the nature of behaviour monitoring and surveillance at the plant, the process of new recruit induction, the role played by team leaders and supervisors at the plant, and the role and style of production management. The findings demonstrate that the management control system at Nippon CTV is sophisticated and multifaceted and that the nature of the production technology, systems, and work organization are important in understanding the process of control. In this chapter we begin to discern the tensions between the rhetoric of 'best practice', for example with regard to team working, and the shop-floor reality of the experiences for the workers. The ethnographic research method provides insights into the *informal* nature of control.

Chapter 4 describes the management process at Valleyco. At this plant there are a number of key features which distinguish it from Nippon CTV and which inform the differing nature of workplace relations at the two plants. Primarily we see the enormous influence wielded by the car assemblers over suppliers such as Valleyco. We also see the reliance of management on informally negotiated solutions to problems due to the uncertainty inherent at the plant. More obviously than at Nippon CTV, where management has successfully marginalized the effects of uncertainty, the shop-floor relations are clearly and explicitly founded upon 'negotiated order' between management and labour. As we will see, the case of Valleyco exhibits numerous continuities with past research; for example workers in some areas of the plant are still paid on a piece-rate system and the worker 'misbehaviour' is resonant of the studies of Roy (1952) and others.

Following this explication of managerial processes of control, Chapter 5 focuses attention on the contested nature of shop-floor relations and on labour and management as social agents. In particular we will see that workers continue to combine aspects of 'co-operation' and 'resistance' as they seek to survive their working days. However, through contrasting the two sites, we can draw a number of important conclusions regarding the degree of choice available to workers and the extent to which informality of activity may be marginalized on the shop-floor. The chapter also demonstrates that while workers may continue to share collective goals, the nature of collective response is placed under severe pressure at Nippon CTV where workers face very strict coercive controls.

Chapter 6 deals directly with what motivates workers in contemporary manufacturing environments by reporting workers' views on *why* they do what they do. The findings presented here call into question the accuracy of research which has argued that HRM may win over workers' 'hearts and minds' and the argument that 'Japanese-style' workplaces may provide better employment relations and secure for management the heightened commitment and obliga-tion of workers. It is clear from the research presented here that the workers are experiencing a harsh and coercive managerial regime and that workers comply because they conceive that they 'have to'. The research shows that the workers at the two plants have not identified with, nor have they accepted, man-agerial goals. As we will see, workers regularly go to some lengths to demon-strate the distance that remains between themselves and 'their' organization.

Much of the rhetoric of contemporary management concerns the need for the involvement and active participation of employees. Chapter 7 discusses the impact of team working, quality circles, and problem-solving activities on the nature of shop-floor work. The findings provide strong evidence to question the intentions of management at the plants with regard to worker participation and also demonstrate that the workers themselves are not persuaded to contribute discretionary effort. The reasons for this are discussed further in Chapter 10.

Chapter 8 addresses the role of trade unions at the two plants. The 'Japanese' model and lean production have been used to argue that employees no longer need the protection of trade unions from their employer, since a new unitarism will characterize contemporary workplace relations. The evidence presented here does not support that position. The industrial relations structures at the two plants are very different, with Valleyco having multi-union collective bargain-ing and Nippon CTV a single union no-strike agreement, a company advisory board, and no collective bargaining. However, this chapter shows that there is considerable similarity between the two plants in that workers are still per-suaded of their need for strong and effective collective representation, but each of the unions is failing to have any effective impact on management decision making and on the running of the plants. The findings presented in this book also question the relevance of unitarist managerialist notions of HRM since the workers at these two plants remain sceptical of management's intentions and clearly favour an oppositional stance from their own representatives. The chapter therefore reflects on the implications of this for trade unions. In particular there is clear evidence that the 'inclusive' structures of HRM are designed to mar-ginalize and circumvent union representation and that union activity which is organized around individual workplaces within a multi-site, and in these cases multinational, corporation is unlikely to prove effective in the current economic climate.

The final two chapters first summarize the conclusions that may be drawn from the research and then seek to locate these findings within broader debates surrounding contemporary manufacturing and the 'Japanese' model. The find-ings indicate that management at Nippon CTV has successfully marginalized the impact of uncertainty on operations through the combination of tight process controls and internal reliability and flexibility within a stable and pre-dictable environment. In addition, management at Nippon CTV has combined quantitative and qualitative efficiencies and extended its control of the shop-floor. This has not been achieved through any heightened sense of commitment on behalf of the workforce, who remain opposed to many of management's goals and mistrustful of the rhetoric of team working and mutuality. Indeed, the heightened control at Nippon CTV appears to have come at the cost of the withdrawal of discretionary effort by workers. The outcome at Nippon CTV is a 'high surveillance—low trust' regime in which workers actively demonstrate their disaffection with management. As a result the dynamic of improvement central to the contemporary model of manufacturing best practice is missing. This raises serious questions over the transfer of 'Japanese' management techniques, the efficacy of lean production, and the appropriateness of the 'Japanese model' outside its indigenous institutional context. Finally there are some implications for state policy when I reflect on the outcomes of the UK government's actions in attracting foreign investment based on low technology, low value added, and low wage operations. Some comparisons are drawn between the type of investment and nature of operations in the Mexican *maquiladora* region and those attracted to the UK. In the final chapter I argue that the UK has effectively become the *maquiladora* of Europe and the implications of this are identified.

2

Researching the Shop-Floor: The Cases of Valleyco and Nippon CTV

'There's this world,' she banged the wall graphically, 'and there's this world,' she thumped her chest. 'If you want to make sense of either, you have to take notice of both.' . . .

My needlework teacher suffered from a problem of vision. She recognized things according to expectation and environment. If you were in a particular place, you expected to see particular things. Sheep and hills, sea and fish; if there was an elephant in the supermarket, she'd either not see it at all, or call it Mrs Jones and talk about fishcakes.

Jeanette Winterson, *Oranges are not the Only Fruit* (1991: 32, 43–4).

INTRODUCTION

At many points during research projects or programmes, individuals face choices about how to proceed and these choices are, in their very definition and in the selection of alternatives, reflections of the researcher. During the course of this chapter I outline and explain the choices which I recognized and acted upon. The research presented was gathered during periods of participant observation as an operator in two British factories. The chapter begins with a discussion of the ontological assumptions informing this decision to utilize ethnographic research in relation to the research questions, and an explanation of the appropriateness of this for the purposes of this study. Next I describe the process by which the project was put into operation and outline the practice of participant observation with reference to the research carried out. In the second part of this chapter I introduce the two case plants, and make particular reference to their environment, processes, and organization.

THE QUESTION OF UNDERSTANDING

According to Weber (1949), all forms of social science must achieve both an *understanding* and an *explanation* of the particular phenomena under investigation. Accordingly, sociology is defined as 'a science which attempts the interpretive understanding of social action in order to arrive at a causal explanation of its cause and effects' (Weber 1947: 90). In social settings such as workplaces, we are required to distinguish our research subjects from those of the natural sciences. In the social sciences, the challenge is to understand and interpret complex forms of social activity which are defined by the actors themselves in terms of their own subjective meanings. Freund argues that, 'Whatever the type of activity, it has consistency only to the extent that its individual or collective agent gives it meaning' (Freund 1979: 168). The argument therefore runs that human action possesses an internal logic (the subject's 'meaning') which must be understood in order to make that action intelligible; in the social sciences, the subject-matter has a subjective comprehension of its own activity (Gill and Johnson 1991).

Rejecting Positivism

In the natural sciences, the researcher is spared the complexity of 'under-standing' because the phenomena under investigation are passive objects without an internal logic of their own. The basis for *positivism* is the use of research methods which are 'borrowed' from the natural sciences. However, in seeking to explore the situation and experience of workers under the 'Japanese' model for example, the position is very different from that which pertains in the natural sciences. Within the 'observational field of the social scientist—social reality— has a specific meaning and relevance structure for the beings living, acting and thinking within it' (Schutz 1962: 59). This 'field', the research arena, comprises a setting in which the research subjects are social agents, actively engaged in the 'accomplishment' of their world (Mehan 1979). To follow this line, since the research subjects 'act toward things on the basis of the meanings the things have for them' (Blumer 1969: 2), the researcher must get close to the subjects and must be in a position to understand the meanings ascribed to actions by those subjects. The implications that this has for the research methodology to be employed are underscored by the nature of context in understanding social activity. This is especially critical for this research since the *situation* of the workplace relations is of key significance. Meaning may only be understood within the specificities of the context of the action and actors' behaviour must be understood in the light of their definition of the situation (Garfinkel 1967). Thus, in contradistinction to positivist approaches, this 'social action' approach is one of analysis of the 'subjective' rather than the 'objective'; the task of the social sciences is seen to be that of 'seeking to explain and understand behavior with reference to underlying motives and meaning systems' (Godard 1993: 288). For example, we may observe workers working in the manner directed by man-agement, but how should we understand their actions? Have these workers accepted and internalized the goals of management, or are they subjected to restrictive and coercive pressures to *conform behaviourally*?

Clearly, these questions speak very directly to the case of workers under contemporary manufacturing management techniques where certain authors have assumed common interests among managers and workers while others have reported harsh and repressive work situations. For the purposes of this research project, a research methodology which facilitates the exploration and under-standing of complex social relations and their context is key. The basis for the study involves 'being true to the nature of the phenomena under study' (Matza 1969: 5). Equally, a review of the literature regarding new management techniques and the 'Japanese' model indicates a pattern of research areas, not a set of hypotheses which lend themselves to a process of testing and validation or falsification. Under the process of *deduction*, theories are formulated before the research is undertaken and the empirical evidence is used either to reject the theory as 'false' or to validate the theory as 'true'. However, the nature of this study is not consistent with the positivist deduction of a priori hypotheses to be 'scientifically' tested and does not share the ontological assumption of a logical order of things, nor that this logical order may be studied in an 'objective' manner. The purpose of the research is not to impose a framework on the social relations but rather to explore and understand these dynamics within the context of capitalist development, the changing form of workplace relations, and the transfer of the 'Japanese' model. Consequently, the epistemology of logico-deductivism is inappropriate in this instance.

Ethnography and the Place of Theory

The social action approach, unlike that of positivism, sees 'reality' as socially constructed through ongoing processes of action and interaction and consequently as having no objective ontological status of its own beyond that of the human activity which produced it (Berger and Luckmann 1967; Godard 1993). This approach to understanding social settings leads to priority being given to 'ecological validity', the closeness of the data to the behaviour of the subject, and 'internal validity', the identification of the correct cause and effect (Wass and Wells 1994). This form of explanation relies on the identification and description of the actors' internal logics (Gill and Johnson 1991). In turn, there follows a series of epistemological assumptions regarding the research process and, consequently, methodology. Qualitative research methods which allow the researcher to get close to the subject, and which are incorporated into an inductivist approach that rejects prejudgements, are required.

My research has adopted such an approach, ethnography, which is defined as 'The direct observation of the activity of members of a particular social group, and the description and evaluation of such activity' (Abercrombie *et al.* 1988: 90). This was adjudged by the researcher as the rational research method for this particular study and I reject any notion that this may constitute an 'unscientific' approach. This choice of research method may be seen as my response to the self-interrogative: 'If I want to understand what it is like working under JIT and TQM shall I sit in my office and mail out questionnaires or shall I go and observe it, experience it, and ask people about it at first hand?' These direct observations primarily involved the researcher as a participant observer in the research setting and also included the shadowing of certain key personnel and the unstructured, informal interviewing of many different members of the two plant sites involved. These data were augmented by formal interviews with certain members of management and key union officials and supported with data from various written sources including company documents and reports by third parties.

This research is actually founded on a form of 'theoretical realism' rather than a truly naturalistic perspective. Following Bhaskar (1978) and Keat and Urry (1975), this position regards social action as occurring within relatively enduring social-structural conditions which do not determine those actions but do constitute a form of 'objective reality' within which those actions take place (Godard 1993). These economic and social-structural arrangements serve as what John Godard calls 'generative mechanisms' giving rise to 'empirical tendencies' rather than definite outcomes. For example, workplace relations under capitalism are *potentially* conflictual since they are fundamentally predicated upon conflicting interests. However, the challenge for researchers is then to explore how the subjectivity and choices of actors mediate and influence the observable outcomes. In this book, the inherent conflict within capitalist workplace relations constitutes the generative mechanism. The research itself is intended to develop a detailed or 'thick' description (Geertz 1973) of how this conflict is manifested in certain specific contexts. In other words, it is intended to provide evidence of a natural tendency which may be used to reflect the outcomes of social action within these contexts and which may help in understanding and interpreting the form and content of the contemporary manufacturing environment. In Elam's words, 'to translate the abstract notions of system, trajectory and paradigm into more concrete terms' (1990: 33).

While this position accepts the validity of theory as constituted by the generative mechanism, it does not follow the deductive process of theory validation or falsification. Thus, theories are not taken as determinant of empirically observable outcomes. Consequently, unlike the positivist outlook, such theories are not for the sake of prediction and control, but rather for understanding and explanation (Godard 1993). Within this perspective, moreover, theories are best understood as abstractions against which observed data may be measured with the understanding that the social world is too complex for these abstractions to provide a mirror of reality. This allows for research to analyse underlying causes and to seek explanations of observable phenomena but acknowledges the limits of theory and the importance of interpretation and debate.

This perspective is consistent with the goal of developing an enhanced understanding of the transfer of the 'Japanese' model and its implications for workplace relations in the West. The research methodology is deliberately based upon an epistemology which will avoid being 'mesmerized by idealized contrasts between production paradigms or broad brush conceptions of Japanization' (Elger and Smith 1994: 12); the detail is all. Of equal importance is the prospect of providing *explanation* of why things are how they are. In a strong exposition of the need for ethnographic research in the study of comparative workplace relations, Paul Edwards and his co-authors point out that, in many case studies, 'The problem is that explanations are left at best implicit' (Edwards *et al.*

1994: 12). This study will seek to develop a detailed description of the reality of workplace relations and to relate these findings to contemporary theory and other studies of 'empirical tendencies'.

DOING ETHNOGRAPHY

The actual practice of ethnography is dependent upon many constraints and external factors beyond the control of the researcher and these are often impossible to foresee. For this reason the 'how to do it' prescriptions in many research methodology books are not useful beyond a certain level. Still, it is important for researchers to be aware of as many of the potential pitfalls as possible. My experiences have underlined that the keys to successfully completing an ethnographic study are flexibility and pragmatism. As one ethnographer put it, 'behave like a gentleman, keep off the women, take quinine daily and play it by ear' (Evans-Pritchard, quoted in Bell and Encel 1978).

Since ethnography involves the immersion of the researcher into the social setting under study the whole process can be very complex and confusing. The researcher is exposed to a minefield of political activity, behaviours, and attitudes which may be very different from those which he or she may have previously encountered or which they may not even recognize. In such situations, the researcher must be sensitive to the dynamics of the social group and remain pragmatic about what is feasible. This is what Buchanan *et al.* (1988) recommend as an 'opportunistic' approach, since 'Fieldwork is permeated with the conflict between what is theoretically desirable on the one hand and what is practically possible on the other' (p. 53). Quite aside from the practical problems of ethnography, there are some issues with this research methodology regarding the impact of the researcher on the social setting and the related issue of bias.

Bias in Ethnography

My position as observer of, and participant in, the social settings of the research was known to the majority of those with whom I came in contact. Each time I was introduced to someone and spent any length of time in their company, the conversation would naturally turn to who I was, where I lived, how long I had worked for the company, and so on. At this point I would say that actually I was working and studying at university and that this company had allowed me to spend some time studying how they did things. I would stress in these first few sentences that I was not an employee of the company and that, while I was grateful to management for the opportunity to conduct research, I was not beholden to them in any way and that anything anyone said to me would be completely confidential. There is only so much one can expect to achieve through baldly stating these sentiments and the communication skills of the researcher are immensely important. I remember making my introductions while sitting on the insertion line at Nippon CTV and not being able to make eye contact with one of the workers and this was very difficult; the statement felt very thin without any body language and eye contact to emphasize that I was genuine.

In the early stages, patience and care are the watchwords and the longer the research proceeds the better the opportunity to form relationships in the field. In this case, the length of the research periods was dictated by external pressures—what the company would agree to and what time I could spare while working as a research assistant. For me, the most important element of gaining acceptance and beginning to be confident that people were acting and speaking as though I were not there, was the time spent just being there and being part of the normal day at work. For this reason, the opportunity to observe as a full or at least semi-participant was very significant. Sometimes my level of skill or competence would preclude this, but when I first entered the research sites it was very useful to appear as 'ordinary' as possible. Of course with regard to bias, as the research is conducted over a period of weeks and months, the chance of people acting 'abnormally' lessens:

> They [i.e., the people in the field of study] are enmeshed in social relationships important to them, at work, in community life, wherever. The events they participate in matter to them. The opinions and actions of the people they interact with must be taken into account, because they affect those events. All the constraints that affect them in their ordinary lives continue to operate while the observer observes. (Becker 1970: 46.)

In seeking to minimize the effect of my presence, I was often required to act and behave naïvely or like a chameleon and adopt different views and values at different times. This requires a 'feel' for the situation and during the research it was important to be as aware as possible regarding the positions and perspectives of those around me.

Since the researcher is a part of the social world that is being studied and has intrinsic values and beliefs from which they cannot wholly detach themselves, absolute neutrality or true objectivity is impossible to achieve. From conception through implementation to analysis and final interpretation, an individual's personal values and experiences will affect the research process. The challenge for the researcher is to be aware of these pressures and to ensure that they do not render the work unintelligible, unrepresentative, or irrelevant. As Godard (1993) puts it, the challenge raised by what he calls 'postmodernist' critiques of 'traditional' research is to 'make our stories as convincing and relevant as possible' but that 'rationalism and objectivity remain central to our work, if only as unattainable ideals' (p. 301). The way I see this challenge is thus: the researcher is responsible for persuading the reader that the work is worthy of their time and consideration, rather than rendered useless due to the biases inherent in collection, interpretation, and presentation of the data.

This study, while perhaps not quite taking a *tabula rasa* approach, reflects an exploratory and flexible approach which is consistent with the ontological and epistemological assumptions articulated earlier. As a guard against potential bias, I entered the field in order to identify important and significant events and behaviours *during* the research rather than running through a checklist generated from reading Roy, Lupton, Burawoy *et al.* This at least enabled me to select and specify the aspects of the workplace which appeared important in this time and context, rather than selectively to check those which others had settled on in a different setting. The inductive nature of the research demands that the researcher be able to adopt a flexible approach in order to be able to track key issues as they arise. Of course, gathering the data in such an unstructured way places a special onus on the initial collation and interpretation of that data and this will be discussed later.

Building Relationships

To have any chance of minimizing the impact of the researcher's presence in the social setting it is essential to form relationships with fellow members. Moreover, the experience of uprooting and putting oneself in an alien place is a very isolating and intimidating one. The researcher will need to make acquaintances and friends just in order to live their life while researching, never mind to actually assist in the research process. The first period of research for this study began at 8.00 a.m. on 2 January. The previous afternoon I had travelled back from north Wales after spending New Year with friends. When I eventually arrived at the local valley line train station it was dark and raining. The station had no telephone and was situated outside the town itself. After more than half an hour walking the streets in the pouring rain looking for a phone, I considered getting on the next train back home. The next morning, I went out on to the shop-floor and into the unknown, afraid that a wrong word or a misunderstanding might ruin the research at a stroke. There was real pressure and intensity during the fieldwork, particularly during the early stages when I was negotiating my informal access and acceptance into the group. I developed a nervous tic in my cheek during the first two weeks, something I have never experienced before or since.

The building and sustaining of friendly relations takes time, and the familiarity which that brings, in overcoming the natural suspicion that people have of outsiders. This was especially the case when I joined the shop-floor of the first factory which was sited in a small Welsh valley community. I stood out like a sore thumb, I was even noticed and looked at in the street. My actual participation in the tasks which faced the workers helped to break down the barriers and several people approached me over the weeks and told me that when they actually saw me sitting there alongside them day after day they began to have some respect for what I was doing. It was important to be able to develop some shared ground. My intention was to become known as a 'good bloke', someone who was cheerful and friendly, in order that people would feel comfortable in my presence. In practice, the relationships developed over long hours working on the shop-floor, chatting over lunch, moaning about the weather, and so on. In the close-knit valley community, I soon got involved in long conversations about families, mine and theirs, which was a most unusual topic of conversation in the social world from which I had come. In many ways, the common ground that we found in our family lives cemented relationships and founded them on something other than a student/subject basis. The research process is two-way: 'it is no more than common courtesy to reciprocate by satisfying the curiosity of my informant' (Wax 1960: 93). I believe that a sincere interest in the people surrounding the researcher is prerequisite for ethnography; such a research methodology requires a genuine commitment to the study and a willingness to engage oneself fully with the field of study.

In both of the factories I had and encouraged what might be called 'key informants'. In practice, their most important roles were to guide me through the norms of the shop-floor (and show me where the canteen and the toilets were) and to act as people who would vouch for me and introduce me to other workers. William Whyte (1948) describes a similar role for one of the group members in his study of a street-corner gang. This protection and backing from an individual was very important during the early stages at both research sites. At both plants, I was linked with an individual and from then wholly reliant on their initial good will. I was fortunate that Roy at Valleyco and Vanessa at Nippon CTV were supportive, popular at their respective plants, and willing to introduce me and vouch for me with their workmates.

As a final aspect of building and maintaining field relationships, I kept my presence as low key and 'neutral' as possible. While I entered the sites overtly, I avoided taking notes while on the shop-floor and I avoided bombarding people with questions. Many of the topics which I was interested in exploring came from initial conversations instigated by workers and were regularly discussed without my prompting. Of course, there were opportunities to lead conversations and to ask direct questions, but the length of time that I spent in and around the research setting meant that these could be explored over a period of time. Having plenty of time makes the questioning less intrusive. People are typically likely to speak and act more openly if they are not being constantly reminded that what they are saying and doing is being recorded. Invariably, I would write a very short prompt for myself or remember key instances when they happened and then snatch a few moments alone in the toilet or elsewhere to scribble some reminder on a scrap of paper. Once my presence in the field of research was secure and accepted then I was also able to conduct some shadowing of key personnel and some more formal interviews which I recorded openly at the time. Quite often during the shadowing or interviews, since the subjects had learned to accept and trust me, they would say, 'this isn't for your notes, but ...' or, 'don't write this down, but ...', and they seemed able and willing to distinguish me as a person that they knew as well as a researcher.

DEALING WITH THE DATA

The basic data in this ethnography are my diary notes. I would collect my various thoughts and scraps of paper every evening and prepare a handwritten account of each day. This was a very arduous task at the end of a day making windscreen wipers or circuit boards for televisions and there were occasions when I could barely find the energy for the job. I remember once or twice hardly being able to hold the pen because of the aching in my hands. As Donald Roy himself records in his Ph.D.:

Picture the participant observer, after a gruelling eight hours on the production line, slumped in a kitchen chair in his modest apartment, oil and metal chips dripping and dropping from his trouser cuffs into his shoes and over the linoleum, his face sagging into a plate of beans that he is too tired to eat, and with the immediate job before him of recording in his work diary the events and feelings of a day that he would like to forget. (Roy 1952: 49.)

Despite the difficulties, it is important to try and record the events of the day as soon as possible since there is a greater likelihood of ethnocentric bias creeping into the data the longer the records are left (Shweder and D'Andrade 1980). Since the intention of the research was to record all aspects of work and work-place relations and to allow important and interesting themes to emerge from the data, the diary notes are completely unstructured beyond chronology and wide ranging in their content. Occasionally during the research period, typically over a weekend, I was able to take time to review some of the material and identify any specific aspects which appeared to be significant and accordingly ensure that I was able to explore some of these issues. However, no systematic attempt was made to collate or structure the data generated from the research during the fieldwork itself.

At the end of the research period, I had generated hundreds of pages of handwritten notes describing and recording the day-to-day events on the shop-floor of the research settings. The challenge of collating and making some sort of coherent sense of these notes was a major one. I was determined that the 'findings' of the study be as accurate a representation of what I had seen and heard as possible. I believe this to be fundamental in trying to win the faith of the reader. Through the course of organizing and presenting the data from the study I have sought to remain true to the inductive process. In other words, I have tried wherever possible to ensure that the data inform what and how I write.

Once the field notes were completed, I read through the first set from Valleyco and began to pick out themes which emerged from those notes. At first this consisted of noting any type of event, interaction, or comment which occurred more than once. After generating a very long list of such instances, I then grouped these around a set of tentative themes which had begun to emerge. In the first round of reviewing the data, I identified about 150 key events or notes from my first month at Valleyco and labelled these under one or more of nine themes. I then grouped the second month's notes from Valleyco within these themes and added to or amended the themes to cope with additional instances. I repeated these iterative loops on a weekly basis for the Nippon CTV notes until I had centred on thirteen issues which came from the data.

The data were labelled according to these issues but multi-issue labels were made where necessary so that the issues were not treated as mutually exclusive and data were not forced in one direction or another. The thirteen labels were:

- QLTY—denoting issues of quality management
- SYS—the manufacturing system at the plants
- RELS—data regarding formal and informal relationships between actors
- UNTY—denoting issues of uncertainty and informality in the workplace
- CONT—issues of control and surveillance
- WORK—workers, their roles, and experiences
- COMM—communication issues and practices
- MGT—managers, their roles, and perspectives
- ACCOMM—issues of accommodation, indulgence, and resistance
- UNION—the role of unions in the workplace
- RES—issues pertaining to the research process
- COFACT—factual data on the companies involved
- JAP—data relating specifically to Japan and the Japanese

The most important of these themes may be considered as the fundamental aspects of workplace relations and are represented graphically in Figure 2. In this figure, issues regarding the manufacturing system and quality issues (particularly the formal procedures and rules), the informality and uncertainty within that system, and the role of organized labour are seen as the workplace backdrop for the interrelationships between management and labour. These relations are seen to be constituted around key aspects of control and surveillance, accommodation, indulgence and resistance, and communication.

Once all the individual pieces of data were labelled, I was able to group them around common themes. The presentation of the data has been carried out in a way which attempts to remain as transparent as possible, so that the reader may be able to find an empathy with the writer and the research setting and participants. Extracts from my diary notes are included in the book and are presented as they appeared in the diary. I have attempted to describe the situations, themes, and the events as clearly as possible.

The structure of the book basically follows from the inductive process described above. After the research settings and characters have been introduced, there are chapters detailing the control systems in place at each of the two plants, and then chapters describing what workers do, why they do it, their involvement in what they do, and the role of organized labour on the two shop-floors. These chapters allow the issues of control, accommodation, and resistance to be explored, include detail on the communication between management and labour and the role of trade unions at the plants, and discuss the procedures, rules and

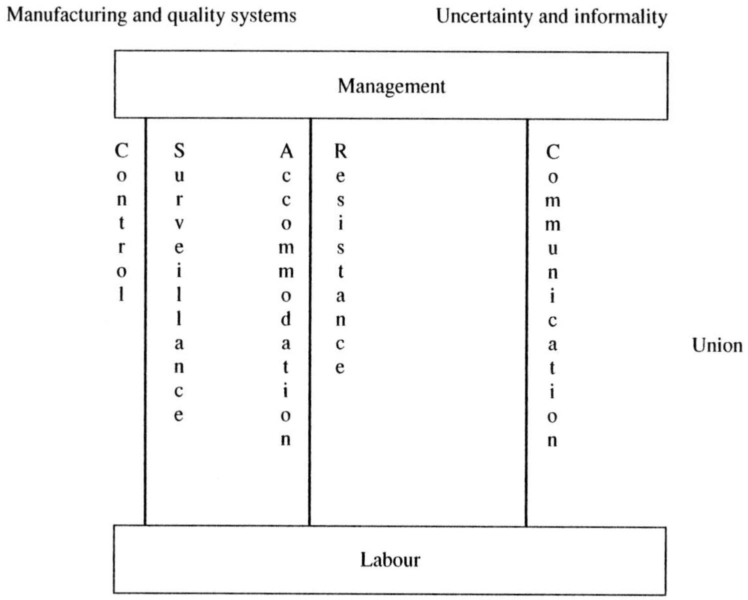

Manufacturing and quality systems   Uncertainty and informality

Management

Control | Surveillance | Accommodation | Resistance | Communication | Union

Labour

FIG. 2 Aspects of Workplace Relations

systems, and quality issues pertinent in understanding the two cases. The following sections of this chapter introduce the two plants. In keeping with the need to contemplate both the technical and social aspects of managing manufacturing, I will review (for each site in turn) the physical plant and equipment, the manufacturing processes employed at the plants, the organization's structure, and the wider company organization within which the plant is situated.

RESEARCH SITES

The research was conducted in two manufacturing facilities during 1991. The first period lasted for three months and was in a European-owned automotive component maker situated in a south Wales valley town. This plant was selected as one which would offer the opportunity to witness and study the adoption and adaptation of contemporary manufacturing management at an established 'brownfield' site in the UK. This plant had been undergoing some radical changes to its manufacturing practices and work organization which meant that the management claimed to be introducing just-in-time production and total quality management. The plant, Valleyco, had the structural features of organization I was looking for—group working, cellular manufacturing, reduced inventories, no end-of-line quality inspection—and was operating in the UK motor industry which had been undergoing significant restructuring following the competitive threat of the Japanese assemblers and the arrival of Honda, Nissan, and Toyota.

The access at Valleyco provided the opportunity to witness at first hand the introduction of new manufacturing practices into a brownfield UK plant. To allow for comparative analysis in the study, I also negotiated access with a Japanese 'transplant' in the south of England. This plant contrasted in a number of ways with Valleyco. I spent four weeks at Nippon CTV, a consumer electronics plant, with all but a few days spent working on and around a single line in the panel shop at the plant.

Valleyco

The Valleyco plant is sited on the outskirts of a small town, called here Cwmtown, in one of the south Wales valleys. People travel to work at the plant from further up the valley and other towns in the area. The valley communities are close knit with a strong sense of identity. The valleys of south Wales have suffered from a decline in traditional employment, particularly the coal mining industry (British Coal cut the number of working pits from thirty-five to four during the 1980s), and have had unemployment levels consistently above the UK average. The problem has been compounded because many of the jobs that have been lost were in the area of permanent skilled employment and the 'replacement' jobs have been unskilled contracts. During the 1980s, employment in the coal industry was cut from 35,000 to under 5,000, while 10,000 jobs were lost in the iron and steel industries, and employment in the manufacture of motor vehicle parts (Standard Industrial Classification 3530) fell from 18,200 to 7,400 (Welsh Office 1994). The Valleyco plant is in a valley which has been identified as one of the poorest and most deprived areas in Wales with rising unemployment (it was at 14 per cent during 1991), rising numbers of people registered as permanently sick, and a declining population (Morris and Wilkinson 1995). Figures from the 1991 Census show that a quarter of the population of the valley over the age of 16 are either unemployed or registered as permanently sick, a steep rise from the 17 per cent recorded in the 1981 Census (ibid). Male unemployment is approaching 20 per cent in the area (Welsh Office 1994).

At the time of the research, there were 225 employees at the plant, of whom about 180 were shop-floor workers. The majority of shop-floor workers were women, around 80 per cent of the total. In keeping with local trends over recent years, the plant has seen a reduction in workforce numbers and the length of service has dropped to about four years. However, there were a large number of mature and experienced women on the shop-floor who had worked at the plant for many years. Many workers had relatives working on the shop-floor and it seemed that most people knew each other.

The plant recognizes two trade unions representing shop-floor workers and between them the General, Municipal, Boilermakers' trade union (GMB) and the Amalgamated Engineering Union (AEU) (now the Amalgamated Engineering and Electrical Union, the AEEU) had about 160 members. The unions and management engage in annual, plant-based negotiations over pay and conditions.

All of Valleyco's products are for the motor industry and the plant had a turnover of around £12 million per annum during the research period. The major customers of the plant are Rover Group, Jaguar, Peugeot, and Nissan.

Plant, processes, and equipment   There has been a plant manufacturing components for the motor industry at the Valleyco site in Cwmtown for more than twenty-five years. During that time five different companies have owned and operated the plant and Valleyco took over in 1988. The main floor area of the plant covers about 8,000 square metres and was divided into five main areas when the research began—the moulding shop, the main assembly areas, the stores, the offices, and a fifth area which is sub-let to another company. The majority of direct workers work in the assembly area. In the moulding shop there were eighteen injection-moulding machines and two new blow moulders. Some of the injection-moulding machines are more than twenty years old and the joke on the shop-floor was that they were still insured against Viking raids. The blow-moulding machines were purchased after Valleyco took over at the site at a total cost of around £250,000. During the research period, the blow-moulding machines were moved out of the moulding shop and on to the main shop-floor area to improve materials flow. Figure 3 shows the layout of the shop-floor.

The moulding shop is noisier than the rest of the shop-floor and can get hot during the summer months. The operators are paid an additional bonus for working there because of the noise. There are two shifts of operators and setters working from 6.00 a.m. to 2.00 p.m. and from 2.00 p.m. to 10.00 p.m. The setters are responsible for setting the machines and loading the raw materials while there are half a dozen operators per shift who clean the mouldings of the 'flash' which is left around the edges with scalpels and break the mouldings away from the 'sprues'. These jobs are extremely simple, although it can often need great care and dexterity to be able to clear the flash without damaging the moulding. The setters' tasks are made more difficult because of the age of the machines that they use; 'We're still in the dark ages up here,' one of them told me. The tools often do not fit in the machines properly and the setters have to use blocks and clamps to set the tools in place. This means that the accurate and safe setting of machines can take up to three hours when it should be possible in minutes. The setters ritually cross themselves in mock prayer before running the machines.

The moulding shop was run on a weekly schedule and the mouldings typically went into the stores area before being called out on a 'pull' system by the assembly areas. Informally, the foremen in the moulding shop would set up for longer runs and work ahead of schedule where possible because of the long set-up times for the injection moulders. In practice, the foremen use 'the grapevine' and their own experience to amend the formal schedules. The moulding shop can produce around 500 different part numbers, including materials variations, and has about 300 tools. There were about eight 'regulars' on every schedule, while some mouldings may not be used more than once a year. There was a

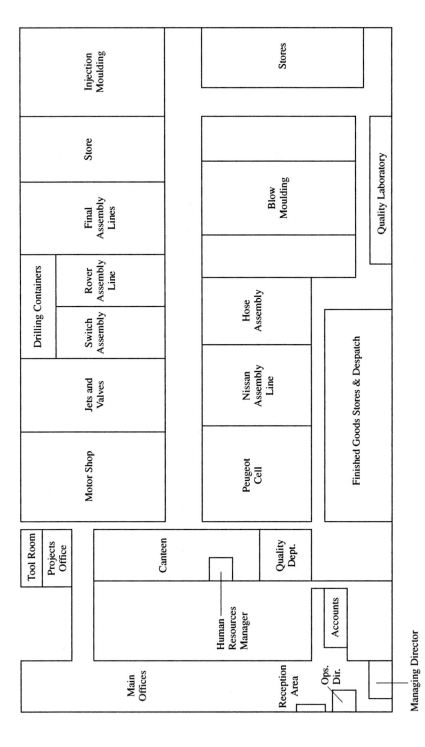

FIG. 3 Shop-Floor Layout of Valleyco

certain scepticism about the scheduling on the part of the moulding shop fore-men: 'They ask us where things are that they haven't ordered, and ask why we've made things that they did order. They even ask us for things we don't make!'

Quality is the responsibility of the operators in the moulding shop but there is a quality controller (QC) on each shift who takes a sample test of each new run and an hourly sample test. The QC is required to sign off each batch before it passes on into stores. In practice, there is too much work to properly test all the dimensions of the mouldings and the QCs rely on a visual check. One of the QCs said that he relies on the operators to check as they work and that, 'My job is to stop the rubbish, but if they say, "That's the best we can do," then I will pass them.' There are also statistical process control (SPC) charts to be com-pleted for the blow moulders and the QC commented, 'Of course, we haven't been doing it properly. But if you just show people you're doing something and filling in the sheets then they're satisfied.' He had been plotting the aver-age weights of the bottles but had not calculated any confidence limits for the tests: 'You just can't win with this job. They play hell if you stop production, but they play hell if you let through faulty goods. So you just do this and do that and think, "It's only another hour and I'm out of here".'

Apart from the moulding shop, the rest of the shop-floor works a single shift running from 8.00 a.m. to 4.30 p.m. on Monday to Thursday and from 8.00 a.m. to 3.30 p.m. on Friday. There are some automated machine presses and the motor shop has an automated line for assembling motors but the majority of work is manual and the processes are labour intensive. There were a wide variety of simple tasks across the shop-floor, including inserting bearings into jets, attach-ing hoses to bottles, and assembling windscreen wiper blades. Many of the products are so simple that they take one operator only a handful of seconds to complete the full set of tasks. Most of the work consists of individual, self-contained tasks although, on the final assembly lines, the hoses, jets, and motors are assembled with the containers and this involves three or four operators work-ing on the product consecutively. Their work is carried to the next operator in the line by a conveyor.

Apart from the mechanized assembly in the motor shop, all the work is operator paced rather than dictated by machines or moving assembly lines. The operators work on a weekly wage plus production bonus based on a simple piece-rate. Many of the components have standard times set at the rate of several hundred per hour (the piece-rate system is explained in detail in Chapter 4). At the time of the research, the basic pay for an operator was £102 for a 39-hour working week and the piece-rate system allowed for a maximum bonus of an additional £35 per week. The average gross weekly earnings for manual female workers in Wales during the research was £153.30 (Welsh Office 1994).

The plant was reorganized and given a new layout during my research period in an attempt to group operations around product and customer lines and to improve the flow of materials. During most of the time there were the following areas: jets and valves, hoses, drilling (of bottles), final assembly, the motor shop, the Nissan and Rover lines, and the Peugeot cell. The Peugeot cell was the first of the areas to be laid out and structured as an independent cell and was the model for a number of the changes introduced. This cell had two small lines of production with each operator passing their work-in-progress to the next 'customer' in the line. Each operator is responsible for checking the work of their cellmate. The work-in-progress is held in small trays or stands which physically prohibits the build-up of excessive inventory. The technology in the cell has been introduced from Continental Europe and includes some *poke-yoke*, or fool-proofing devices, which do not allow operators to assemble faulty products.

Before I arrived, the plant management had set out to reduce dramatically the amount of inventory out on the shop-floor and had introduced internal *kanban* between some areas of the plant, that is, a physical 'pull' system for scheduling production. For example, they used colour-coded trays to carry components and had a set number available for storing work-in-progress. Once the number of trays dropped below a certain level marked in red on the wall, this triggered the building of more components to replace those used. However, many of the finished products are very simple assemblies which involve the work of only one or two operators on a single line with no internal flow between areas. Production is based on a daily priority build list which is sent out every morning by the production control department. A planned production list is also circulated so that stores personnel can check that they have what will be needed. The charge-hand of each line then identifies their priority build products, orders the components that they need from stores, and assigns the job to an operator. The completed job is packed and left at the end of the line for collection and despatch.

In practice, production control at Valleyco is reliant on the informal relations between the charge-hands and the 'progress chasers', each of whom have responsibility to ensure the on-time dispatch of a particular set of products. The system at Valleyco has a number of characteristics which create uncertainty and unpredictability and the consequent need for informality in order to overcome these problems. The more significant of these factors at the plant are the poor quality of incoming materials, the unreliable functioning of the new motor assembly operations, and the unpredictable and varying schedules from customers. The plant has also had an ongoing problem with absenteeism. Occasionally, one, or a combination, of these factors conspires to disrupt the scheduled build patterns. The uncertainty caused by these events results in a form of *directed chaos*; it is directed in the sense that there is the completion of customer orders, but chaotic in that the various progress chasers frantically negotiate for the completion of their orders in competition with their colleagues, with the formal schedule counting for nothing. The uncertainty is 'directed' by the taking of arbitrary informal decisions over the reprioritization of batches, often founded on the personal relations between the progress chasers and the charge-hands.

The uncertainty and unpredictability of the manufacturing system at Valleyco causes the bureaucratic order to falter and the ensuing directed chaos is predicated on negotiation and informality. Working with reduced stock levels and tighter time horizons from order to shipment had significantly increased the importance of coping with the uncertainty, or 'directing the chaos', and the management called JIT, 'Japan induced terror'. As Geoff Evans, the operations director, put it in an initial interview, 'We do have a sort of JIT. Our customers are committed to JIT and so we have no choice but to adopt those principles of our customer base.' The plant had little alternative but to follow its customer base because of the regular audits conducted by its customers. Once the Valleyco production and scheduling procedures break down and cannot cope with the uncertainty, this places special emphasis on personal relationships, the swapping of favours, and the element of panic with which managers encourage workers to make extra efforts to meet customer demands.

The twin implications of directed chaos were emphasized during two conversations that I had with managers during a social event one evening. The first told me that they had set up a 'task force' with the business unit managers in order to improve the efficacy of the company's bureaucratic procedures. He told me that the intention was: 'When someone says, "I can't do that because . . ." then they [the unit managers] can say, "Do this about it . . .". In other words, it's to cover all possibilities and make sure there are no excuses or problems. If they can't do the job then that's it.' The second told me that the single most important thing he had learned while working as a shop-floor manager (he was then working as engineering project manager) was that it was 'helping people that was important' and that, 'It's the personalities that are important in getting your job done'.

Quality in most areas of the shop-floor is the responsibility of the operators and testing is often a discrete task in the production of goods. For example, once a batch of jets has been completed, the whole batch is water tested against leaks by the operators. In many areas of the shop-floor, this was problematic since management were still seeking to use a piece-rate system for quality inspection. The plant had had a group of quality inspectors who patrolled the shop-floor but most of these were laid off before I joined. Individual operator responsibility for quality was best established in the Peugeot cell where each operator marks their work with a colour-coded paint to indicate who has personal responsibility. The plant is responsible for the delivery of goods of an acceptable quality to its customers and occasionally there was reworking of goods sent back by a customer. The quality performance and quality control systems of the plant were regularly audited by the plant's major customers during visits to the plant. While I was at Valleyco they received an 'A2' rating from Rover and a 'B' rating from Jaguar. These were 'acceptable' ratings as far as the customers were concerned. The importance of the customer in the operation of the plant was evident and regularly reinforced (see Chapter 4).

The importance of quality was something that the management had sought to impress on the shop-floor in recent months. The Peugeot and Nissan lines had seen ample evidence from the customers themselves that good quality was vital and the majority of shop-floor workers seemed to have taken these messages on board. Certainly a number told me that things were different from how they had been in previous years, when almost anything would be passed as acceptable quality.

Work organization and plant structure   Before my arrival, the plant management had announced a restructuring of the organization in line with the reorganization of the plant layout. The plan was to move to a system of 'business units' which were consistent with the introduction of cellular manufacture on the shop-floor. These changes were being made during the research. The intention was to organize each unit as a mini-business, or profit centre, with a unit manager taking responsibility for all aspects of operation pertaining to that unit. At the time of the research, most of the shop-floor was laid out in lines for the different products of different customers.

The first of the units operational was the Peugeot cell and this was in place before I joined the shop-floor. This cell has a single unit manager and he is supported by members of the quality, engineering, and production control departments who are assigned responsibility specifically for the Peugeot lines. The Peugeot cell consists of two separate lines, one producing the wiper blades and one producing the motor linkages. Each of these has a charge-hand who is responsible for co-ordinating the activities of the three or four operators on each line. Due to the devolution of responsibility to the unit manager, the charge-hands do not have as much responsibility or autonomy in the Peugeot cell as elsewhere on the shop-floor since the manager is much more closely involved on the shop-floor himself.

During the research period, the majority of the other lines were run by charge-hands under the control of a single manager. Since he has a much wider span of control than the Peugeot cell manager, the charge-hands are given much more space and responsibility to act for themselves. The number of operators in each production area varies but one or two charge-hands co-ordinate more than twenty workers. The moulding shop is also formally the responsibility of this manager, but in practice the two shift foremen run those operations themselves. There are clear demarcations between different job classes at the plant, with labourers, setters, and quality controllers all paid on different grades and generally wearing overalls of a different colour. There is also a clear gender division, with virtually all the shop-floor operators being women while virtually all the 'indirect' workers are men. All the assembly area charge-hands are women but the more senior managers are all men, except for the human resources manager who was promoted during the research.

During my first meeting with the operations director he told me, 'I can't speak highly enough of the workforce,' and added that labour productivity and particularly employee relations had 'helped tremendously' with regard to the plant's overall performance. He also claimed that workers had 'an increased involvement in what they do. It's morally soul-destroying if the workers have no input into their work.'

Valleyco world-wide   Valleyco is part of a major European auto components maker with an annual turnover of several billion US dollars. The main headquarters of the plant are situated on the Continent and at the time of writing the company has eighty manufacturing facilities in fifteen countries. In total, the organization employs more than 25,000 people. Valleyco in Cwmtown is part of one of the organization's nine product divisions. During the research, there were manufacturing operations in France and Spain making products similar to those made in Wales.

The head of Valleyco's division is based in Europe and the company maintains close control over its foreign-based plants. The plant conducts a limited amount of design and development work on-site and also has some quality testing responsibilities for the products which it manufactures, but the main research, design, and development work takes place on the Continent. For example, the products made in the Peugeot cell were developed in France and the cellular layout and process technology were both piloted on the continent before being introduced at Cwmtown.

The head office monitors performance at individual plants through its corporate function heads to whom each plant's functional managers report directly. For example, the quality manager at Valleyco reports directly to the divisional quality manager in France. At a corporate level, the organization has set goals to be 'the leader in "total quality"'' and the company's 'quality philosophy' is 'total quality is the key to success' and 'do it right first time to be the best' (Valleyco corporate literature 1991). The latest corporate material identifies 'total quality' as one of the five core strategies required to succeed in the company's 'one objective: customer satisfaction'. The literature states: 'The objective of the quality improvement process is to develop a common total quality culture among all Valleyco employees to ensure total external and internal customers' satisfaction.'

Nippon CTV

The Nippon CTV factory is situated on the outskirts of a mid-size city in the south of England, called here Torport. The workforce come from the city, the surrounding area, and from the next county across the river. In some ways like the south Wales valleys, Torport has seen traditional industry decline dramatically and consequently skilled permanent employment is at a premium. Employment in the key local industry dropped from over 15,000 (a quarter of all those employed in manufacturing in the area) to 5,400 during the 1980s (Gripaios *et al.* 1992). The personnel manager described the area as one of 'not high employment'. The two local counties had unemployment of around 10 per cent during the research period (compared to the national average of 7.9 per cent and 6.1 per cent regionally during the same period) and average yearly household incomes are below the UK average (Gripaios and Wiseman 1994). While there are some similarities in economic situation, the people from Torport are different in position and outlook from those of Cwmtown. The city and the plant are both much bigger and there is not the closeness of personal relations and family ties which characterize the valley community.

The factory employs around 1,000 people and is a major employer for the area. The numbers employed on the site have been increasing throughout the past decade as operations are expanded. The average age of employees on the shop-floor is lower than at Valleyco, and the recruitment of new workers has meant there is a mix with the experienced, long-service employees who have been at the plant for five years or more. On the shop-floor as a whole the proportion of women is less than that at Valleyco, but in the panel shop where I was working more than 90 per cent of operators are female.

The plant management has a single union arrangement with the Electrical, Electronic, Telecommunications and Plumbing Union (now the Amalgamated Engineering and Electrical Union) which includes a no-strike agreement. However, the union is not formally involved in negotiations with management which has set up a company advisory board as the primary mechanism for communication. Union membership at the plant stands at between 50 and 60 per cent of those eligible.

Plant, processes, and equipment   There has been a plant on the Nippon CTV site for nearly fifty years. The Japanese first became involved in the late 1970s when they entered a joint venture agreement with the then owners of the plant, SouthWestern Electronic. About fifteen years ago, the joint venture was closed and Nippon CTV took over full ownership and reopened on the site. At the time of closure, the joint venture employed over 2,500 people in four factories. Nippon CTV opened a single factory and selected 300 employees who were willing to accept a new 'flexible' way of working. The plant is housed in two buildings with a total floor area of 26,100 square metres (see Figure 4).

Unlike Valleyco, Nippon CTV produces a finished product ready for market and its 'customer' is its sales and distribution arm, Nippon CTV (UK), and other group sales companies in Europe. There are three main production areas at Nippon CTV and these follow the flow of production. The plant buys in printed circuit boards (PCBs) from Japan and the first stage conducted in-house is the automated insertion of small components. This involves operators loading strings or 'bandoliers' of components into computer-controlled insertion machines and ensuring that these machines are running correctly. The machines themselves have red, amber, and green lights which flash to indicate whether the machine needs operator attention. The automatic insertion area (the 'machine shop') runs on two shifts from 6.00 a.m. to 2.00 p.m. and from 2.00 p.m. to 10.00 p.m. There are thirty-two machines in the machine shop for 'sequencing' and axial and radial insertion.

Once the machine shop has inserted the small components, the PCBs are pushed on trolleys to the 'panel shop' where the rest of the components are manually inserted. The panel shop consists of eight assembly lines and a ninth area which makes up panels for service and repair work. The panel shop is a very large, open, and well-lit area and each of the eight assembly lines consists of both pre- and after-bath sides. On the pre-bath side of a main panel line, a

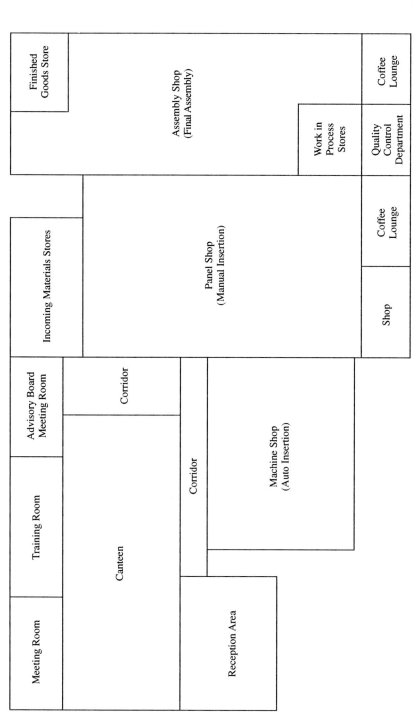

FIG. 4 Shop-Floor Layout of Nippon CTV

group of up to twenty-five operators sit inserting components into the PCBs as they move down the automatic conveyor belt. The components—resistors, capacitors, wires, and the like—are held in containers within easy reach of the operator. Each operator will insert about ten components in a job cycle of around thirty seconds. Above the head of every inserter is their work manual, a photocopy of the panel with the insertions that they must make highlighted in colour. Before the panels go into the solder bath to affix the components, they are inspected to ensure there are no components 'missing' or 'reversed' and that there are no 'wrong values', that is, that the correct component is in place.

Once the panels have been through the solder bath, they are removed from the conveyor line and inspected to ensure that the solder has taken properly and that there are no 'dry joints' or 'short circuits'. If there are defects, then these are reworked on the line by the inspectors. The solder is then clipped before the panels are tested in an automatic testing machine. Then the panels are carried by a conveyor to the 'modifications' ('mods') area where operators will add any components that are needed to the back of the boards before they pass to the tuning and testing area. Once the various panel tests are completed the panels are put on trolleys and taken out to the final assembly area. Apart from the five main panel lines, there are three small panel lines which produce text and audio-visual panels for insertion into the main panels. These lines are basically the same as the main lines, but smaller and with fewer operators.

The final assembly lines area is next-door to the panel shop and there are five main assembly lines, each one supplied by one of the main panel assembly lines. The panels are held in an area at the head of the final assembly shop and brought in when they are needed. At the head of the assembly lines, groups of operators assemble the cabinets and connect the boards to the chassis of the set. Then the tube is connected and assembled into the cabinet. The panels and cabinets move along lines with boards on rollers which are paced by the operators rather than automatically, which is the case in the panel shop. However, there is space for only three or four sets between each work station and any build-up of boards is immediately visible and obvious to the team leaders who patrol the final assembly lines. Once the assembly is completed, the televisions are turned on and transferred to an overhead area for a two-hour 'soak test'. The sets are then tuned and tested for colour, definition, sound performance, and so on. At the end of each line there is a packing area and an automated transfer-out into the finished goods store. The panel shop and final assembly areas are much more labour intensive than the machine shop and most of the capital equipment in use there is for transferring or testing the products.

These panel shop and finals lines are very closely linked in production and work on a single shift of 8.00 a.m. to 5.00 p.m. from Monday to Thursday and from 8.00 a.m. to 12.15 p.m. on Fridays during the 'low season' from January to July and from 8.00 a.m. to 5.15 p.m. from Monday to Friday with one half-day per month for the period of August to December, their busy or 'high' season.

The pay is annualized and based on an average 39-hour working week over the course of the twelve months. The average annual pay for a Grade Two operator was £7,883 at the time of the research.

The company keeps a planned stock of one and a half days or less of completed panels between the panel shop and finals, and in practice the stock often runs below that level. Management restricts the number of trolleys available. This means that there is a definite number of panels that may be stored. The production control manager co-ordinates the schedule on a monthly basis and then breaks this down to a daily plan on a line by line basis. Unlike Valleyco, Nippon CTV do not have to deal with schedule uncertainty from its customers daily, nor even weekly, because the information from the sales organizations is set firm a month in advance. This is a major benefit to Nippon CTV because its internal schedules therefore do not vary significantly from the plan and there is none of the uncertainty and informal negotiation of production common under Valleyco's directed chaos. There are no progress chasers and the individual team leaders are responsible for ensuring their lines keep to the schedule. The emphasis is on problem prevention, through right-first-time production and regular preventative maintenance checks, rather than on coping with problems once they arise. The production director told me, 'We have to get our procedures right to eliminate uncertainty as far as possible.' The system at Nippon CTV does not rely on personal relationships or informality to the same extent as that at Valleyco.

In the panel shop, the main panel lines typically work on batches of between 400 and 600 at a time, although they may run batches as small as 200 panels. Daily production is around 700 to 800 per day, depending upon the standard time of the panel and the manning levels, and this means there is usually a change-over each day. The line feeder leaves a number of gaps in the conveyor line to allow the inserters to prepare for a batch change. The components required for each different batch are collected from the stores area by 'b' (for batch) station workers. The 'b' station workers collect the components which have been picked by stores workers according to the master production schedule. The stores workers try to work a day ahead of the schedule. The 'b' station worker then lays up the components, gathering together the components for each individual operator, and checking that the correct values and numbers are prepared. The pickers from stores weigh out the components, but the 'b' station workers count out 100 of each and put these in a bag separately. It takes one worker around five hours to prepare the components for a main panel batch of 500 and over a day for a main panel batch of 1,000. Once the batch is laid up on trolleys these are collected by the off-line workers supporting insertion.

As a batch approaches the end of its run, the line feeder leaves a gap of four cradles (about two minutes) before the final 120 panels. During this gap, the inserters count to make sure they have twenty of each component left before they open the bag of the final 100 pieces. If they are short then they call to their off-line support workers and they will collect the additional pieces required. Before the inserters start on their final 100 panels the line feeder leaves a gap of two panels so that the inserters can empty their bags of components into the trays at their work stations. Apart from the gaps left for batch change-overs, the only gaps in the line are left for operators to be able to visit the toilet. Inserters are given three-minute 'toilet breaks' on four separate occasions during the day, twice in the morning and twice in the afternoon. These are the only occasions when workers leave the line while it is in motion.

Nippon CTV stresses the importance of quality in the work of each employee. There are banners and posters throughout the plant indicating that quality is vitally important and the quality record of every line and individual worker is publicly displayed. Every individual operator is personally responsible for the quality of their work. The off-line workers and team leader will check with the in-line inspectors every hour to see if certain mistakes and defects are recurring. If they are then they will immediately inform the worker responsible that they are making this mistake. All errors are traced to the people responsible, and inspectors are also monitored, with those who miss defects also warned. The quality control department maintains computerized daily records from the sheets that are completed at different points in the production process. The following morning every quality sheet is reviewed, managers looking for any mistake that happens more than once. These are traced to the individuals responsible, who are given feedback, and further action may be taken. This action may involve a red card being posted beside the worker's station with a special reminder not to make this particular mistake or it may involve 'counselling' regarding their performance and/or a warning as to their future performance.

Work organization and plant structure   The basic unit of organization for the production areas at the plant is the team. There is a team structure throughout each of the machine shop, panel shop, and final assembly areas of the plant although the number of operators per team varies according to individual line requirements. For the panel shop, there is one team leader for each assembly line, while the final assembly lines have two team leaders per line. The spans of control are wider than at Valleyco and the main panel lines and final assembly lines have around forty team members. The team leaders very rarely work on the line and are supported by a number of additional off-line workers, called 'senior members'. Unlike the operators, labourers, setters, fitters, and maintenance personnel at Valleyco, between whom divisions exist, the ordinary team members, 'b' station workers, and maintenance people at Nippon CTV are all on a similar grade, with the senior members and team leaders on correspondingly higher grades.

The main final assembly lines have a team leader to oversee the assembly of the main and small panels into the chassis and the construction of the cabinets, and another who is responsible for the testing and tuning of the finished product. Each of these has the support of one senior member. The team leaders on the finals lines have particular responsibility for maintaining the output speed of their lines because there is no automated conveyor line. The scheduled and actual output of each finals line is recorded and displayed on teletext televisions throughout the plant and updated by the team leader each hour.

On the P3 main panel assembly line where I worked, the team leader had responsibility for four senior members and forty members in her team. On P3, there are two senior members on the insertion side of the line, and two on the after-bath side. These senior members have additional responsibilities for monitoring quality, overseeing the supply of components, and covering for absences or when operators cannot keep up with the line. The team leaders take significant responsibility for their line, including the output and quality performance, certain personnel and supervisory issues, and discipline. Unlike at Valleyco, there are no production controllers on the shop-floor and the team leaders are solely responsible for the output of their line. The P3 team leader also has two 'technical assistants' who are responsible for monitoring quality and the rework of more complex quality problems.

In each of the three areas of the plant, the teams are overseen by a superintendent and a shop manager. The finals manager is also the senior production manager and he works very closely with the other production managers in the panel shop and machine shop. In the panel shop, the manager works with her superintendent in co-ordinating the team leaders' activities. The three production managers report to the production director who takes overall responsibility for the output, quality, and efficiency performance of the plant. The stores, materials handling, and 'b' station activities are co-ordinated by a separate set of team leaders.

The plant management has what are described as 'elastic boundaries' and the managers do not have job descriptions. Rather, all members of the organization are required to do whatever is necessary to ensure production is maintained at the desired quality and efficiency levels. Primacy is given to production, with support from stores and materials, technical services and maintenance, and engineering. The head of each of these functional groupings reports directly to the most senior of the six Japanese nationals at the plant who is the assistant managing director. The main board consists of this Japanese manager and the British managing director plus the directors of production, personnel, materials, and finance.

Nippon CTV world-wide   The UK operations of Nippon CTV are part of the corporation's activities in twenty-three countries. Overall, the corporation has sales of more than $US30 billion in consumer products, information systems, and heavy electrical apparatus. Nippon Denki Corporation (NDC), a pseudonym, is Japan's oldest electrical and electronics manufacturing organization and comprises twenty-seven different manufacturing companies.

The headquarters and major operations and research centres of NDC are in the Tokyo and Yokohama areas of Japan. The corporation spends huge amounts on research and development, in excess of $US2 billion during the year of the research period. The company first became involved in the design and manufacture of colour televisions in the 1950s and opened Japan's first plant specializing in the mass production of colour televisions in 1965. This plant is the model for the Nippon CTV Torport plant, which makes many of the same models, and the process technology and final assembly operations in the UK are based very closely on those successfully employed in Japan. The panel shop operations in Japan are undertaken by a small subcontractor. The standard times for each model of television and panel assembly are all set in Japan. The corporation has a number of Japanese nationals working at the Torport plant in the UK and the key figure is the assistant managing director of the plant. He and the managing director report to the divisional general manager in Tokyo.

The NDC company union in Japan has 63,000 members and was established during the years immediately after the Second World War. In the first few years the union fragmented and one of the two entities took a strong line. During the early 1950s the company re-established control during a 'red purge' (as described in company union literature) and installed right-wing leaders at the head of the reunited single company union. The union claims 'an excellent environment promoted by mutual dialogue' based on the 'basic concept of the Union-Management Consultation System'.

SUMMARY

This chapter began by explaining the research method and the practice of ethnography. It went on to introduce the two plants which were studied and began to identify certain key aspects to those plants' production processes and work organization. It also noted certain external factors regarding the local situations of the plants. From this introduction it is clear that there are number of ways in which the two plants differ, and these points must be borne in mind during our interpretation of the chapters that follow.

The research makes it clear that the production processes in operation at Valleyco are not as stable and controlled as those at Nippon CTV. In contrast Nippon CTV has sought to decouple itself from market uncertainty through vertical integration with a wholly owned retail subsidiary, a form of 'bounded JIT'. This is an interesting feature with regard to the introduction of 'Japanese' manufacturing techniques into western sites, where market uncertainty or instability may be more pronounced than in Japan. The description of how informality underpins the work systems under conditions of uncertainty at Valleyco is very significant when we interpret the position and experiences of workers at the plant which are discussed later. It is important to note that this situation was only accurately distinguished through research on the shop-floor; descriptions by managers and workers provided only partial, and in some cases misleading, information.

The plants also have a number of formal points of contrast, *inter alia* nationality of ownership, industry sector, process and product technology, formal industrial relations situation, which allow for comparison. These points of comparison form the backdrop to the following chapters which discuss, in turn, the control systems at Valleyco and Nippon CTV, the role of workers and the nature of the workplace relations, the motivations for workers' actions, and their involvement in the systems and processes in place. The role of organized labour is examined in a separate chapter (Chapter 8).

3

The Process of Management Control
at Nippon CTV

'Sometimes I don't feel like a manager. I feel like a social worker, a solicitor, a policeman.'
Marcia, panel shop manager, Nippon CTV.

'It's hard for me because I have to be a mother figure to the girls as well as a leader.'
Angie, P3 team leader, Nippon CTV.

INTRODUCTION

In order to understand the ways in which management seeks to exert control over workers our point of departure must be the technical/bureaucratic, or rational, elements of the system to be found in the workplace that were introduced in Chapter 2. By the term rational, I am referring to the systematic *structures* of both the manufacturing technology and the management practices. In other words, the *formal* systems of pay, supervision, work organization, and so on are seen here as part of the rational/technical element of control although they refer directly to people issues. These form the structural backdrop to the social, political, and emotional forces which shape the *process* of management control. The formal systems may be seen as indicative of the espoused theory within the organization; this is important, but not definitive, in contextualizing our interpretation of the *theory in use* and how this comes about in practice.

As has been well rehearsed, the typical basic employment contract is 'incomplete and inexplicit' in nature (Goldthorpe 1974: 428), and the 'silences and voids . . . have to be filled daily by interactive trial and error' (Storey 1981: 21), even in the most formal and bureaucratic of organizations. The fascination of the workplace relationship lies in the unintended consequences of bureaucracy, the refusal of social settings to be wholly predictable, the very nature of interaction which configures that relationship despite the best efforts of those seeking to control it.

As was pointed out in Chapter 2, the two plants possess different forms of manufacturing technology and very different management systems for controlling labour. These technical and rational differences do not completely explain the varying workplace relations that were witnessed, but they are central in building a picture of the plants. Certain aspects of these differences are fundamental factors as we seek to interpret and understand the social interactions and experiences within the two plants. While apparently quite different, the managerial systems of control at Valleyco and Nippon CTV are both based on a combination of technical, bureaucratic, and direct supervisory control. This chapter begins with a brief review of the key comparisons between the two plants which were introduced in the previous chapter. The remainder of the chapter deals with the process of control at Nippon CTV. The following chapter provides details of the control process at Valleyco.

ASPECTS OF CONTROL

Process and Product Technology

Both Valleyco and Nippon CTV are basically mass assemblers of standardized products. The majority of workers in both plants are semi-skilled and employed to carry out tasks which have a cycle time of under one minute. Particularly at Valleyco, some workers can expect to repeat their designated task several times in a single minute. However, a colour television set is a considerably more complex product than those produced at Valleyco and, at Nippon CTV, a single finished product will have involved direct production effort from more than fifty different operators at the plant. In contrast, at Valleyco, many of the items that are shipped have been worked on directly by only one or two people in the plant.

Valleyco has a much more widely differentiated portfolio of (very simple) products, including windscreen wipers, pumps, jet nozzles, and bottles whereas Nippon CTV produces colour televisions of different specifications. At Valleyco, work is differentiated across the various product lines (and latterly, business units), while at Nippon CTV there are different tasks involved in making the same product—machine insertion, manual insertion, and final assembly. The labour process at Valleyco is more varied across different areas of the plant. At Nippon CTV, the vast majority of shop-floor workers sit alongside production lines, either at a moving conveyor belt (in the panel shop) or at a free moving roller line (in final assembly).

At Valleyco, there is less emphasis on co-ordinating groups of workers, since the work tasks are so fragmented. Therefore the majority of work takes place at individual, stationary work stations. The few work areas where there are lines of flow typically involve only three or four workers and do not include a moving assembly line, nor even an automated transfer line in most cases. Apart from one or two stations in the pumps area at Valleyco none of the jobs is 'machine paced' whereas the pace of work is defined by the moving conveyor belt in Nippon CTV's panel shop insertion lines.

Work Organization and Supervision

Both plants have small groups of workers within simple hierarchical supervisory structures. However, at Nippon CTV this is formally recognized as a *team*, whereas at Valleyco this work organization is regarded as a grouping around an area or product and the language of team working has not been adopted. The front-line supervisor at Valleyco is the charge-hand, and this is the first level in the hierarchy above the operator positions. There is one charge-hand for each work area and these people are responsible for overseeing production and lineside supplies, including some day-to-day scheduling, determining operators' jobs, and monitoring worker behaviour. Charge-hands will sometimes work on direct tasks and are almost always working in their area of responsibility. The span of control may be as low as three operators under a charge-hand and up to about thirty. Above the charge-hand there is a management position. Charge-hands wear overalls and have a desk beside their line, their superiors wear suits and ties and have offices. During the period of the research there was a reorganization at Valleyco and the shop-floor was divided into two business units, each with a number of charge-hands and a business unit manager. All the production charge-hands are women, the two managers are men.

At Nippon CTV the formal system is very similar, although the *language* of HRM 'best practice' has been incorporated. The team at Nippon CTV is led, and supervised, by a team leader. However, there is a formal position in the hierarchy between team leader and team member, that of senior member. The first formal line of supervision is the team leader; the senior member is basically an experienced member who works off-line in a support capacity to the line. The team leader is a very significant figure in the daily running of the plant because of the wide spans of control, particularly in the panel shop. Each team has between forty and forty-five members, normally with four senior members, led by a team leader. The team leader is responsible for some scheduling decisions, work allocation, overseeing supplies to lineside, and for the discipline and control of their members. More than the formal roles, it is the spans of control which clearly differentiate the two plants. At the Nippon CTV panel shop there is a panel shop manager, a superintendent, and nine team leaders with charge of 360–380 operators. At Valleyco, under the business unit system, there are two managers and seven charge-hands for fewer than 150 operators.

The basis for managing the effort bargain at Valleyco is a piece-rate system. With one or two exceptions, this is an individual piece-rate system based solely on the time : output ratio for individually timed jobs. At Nippon CTV, every worker is paid on a straight time-rate with a seniority component. At Valleyco, the output bonuses available potentially make up a significant proportion of the total weekly wage. 'Making the number' is an important factor in the labour process of the operators at Valleyco whereas at Nippon CTV the pace of work is basically dictated by the linespeed. The speed is set according to a series of industrial engineering standards, although, as we will see, this is not an absolute given.

At both Valleyco and Nippon CTV there are aspects to the surveillance of behaviour which help supervision. At Valleyco, the relatively narrow spans of control and the fact that the charge-hands work in and around the work area aid their effective monitoring of worker behaviour and performance. However, the surveillance system at Nippon CTV is rather more advanced and integrated within the manufacturing system. As at Valleyco the first line of supervision works in and around, although not often on, the line and their ability to monitor behaviour is aided by the simple line and flow layout. The removal of all but a minimal buffer, held on trolleys away from the line, also helps the visibility of the work process.

THE SYSTEMS IN PRACTICE—NIPPON CTV

As we have discussed in Chapter 2, the manufacturing system at Nippon CTV was far more predictable and under control than that at Valleyco. As a consequence the control systems at Nippon CTV were also more stable and predictable. In Chapter 5 we will detail the dynamics of resistance and counter-control which were distinguishable at each site. This section will describe the workings of the management control procedures at Nippon CTV.

At Nippon CTV, every step is taken to avoid uncertainty and unexpected occurrences and wherever possible rules and procedures are detailed to direct action at each juncture. In the manufacturing areas, the key principles which guide these are that lines should achieve their efficiency targets while producing at acceptable quality levels. The efficiency levels are calculated through the use of standard timings for each panel and each set. These detail, down to a tenth of a second, the time required for every single individual task necessary to complete that item. For example, time to a tenth of a second is recorded for tying wires at the back of the set (see Figure 5). In the panel shop, every operator has a set number of pieces which they are responsible for inserting correctly into each panel. Each component has a specific time for insertion, most commonly 2.7 seconds. Every individual operator's tasks are laid down in a 'manual' which is displayed above the worker's head.

All aspects of the production of an individual panel are laid out in minute detail. For a specific panel, the manuals indicate how many inserters are required, how many pieces each will be responsible for inserting, and the speed at which the line should be set. All this information has been incorporated into the monthly schedules which are sent down on to the shop-floor. Therefore, by appearance, the production and control systems are in accord with traditional scientific management procedures.

Equally, by appearance, the area for negotiation and concern for management lies more squarely with the need for maintaining high quality performance. With the productivity of workers apparently tied to the speed of the conveyor belt, the grey area in performance remains with the level of quality produced by the line. There are quality checkers at the end of the insertion line, both before and after the solder bath, and at the end of the panel line before the panels pass into final assembly. Very detailed and precise quality records are maintained at

Standard Times for Pre-Bath Activities

PANEL SHOP STANDARD TIME								
P.B.		**TYPE**						
INSERTION PROCESS ITEM	**LOC**	**LEGS**	**CUT**	**STD TIME**	**QTY.**	**AUTO INS**	**HAND INS**	**TOT STD TIME**
LOAD/UNLOAD				11.0	0			
RESISTORS	R	2	0	2.7	0	0	0	0.0
CAPACITORS	C	2	0	2.7	0	0	0	0.0
DIODES	D	2	0	2.7	0	0	0	0.0
COILS/CHOKES	L	2	0	2.7	0	0	0	0.0
LINKS	JP	2	0	2.7	0	0	0	0.0
IMPEDANCES	Z	2	0	2.7	0	0	0	0.0
CRYSTALS	X	2	0	2.7	0	0	0	0.0
RESISTORS	R	3	0	2.9	0	0	0	0.0
TRANSISTORS	Q	3	0	2.9	0	0	0	0.0
IMPEDANCES	Z	3	0	2.9	0	0	0	0.0
RESISTOR/K901	R	M	0	3.4	0	0	0	0.0
DIODES/DE40	D	M	0	3.4	0	0	0	0.0
COILS	L	M	0	2.9	0	0	0	0.0
DELAY LINES		M	0	2.9	0	0	0	0.0
IMPEDANCES	Z	M	0	2.9	0	0	0	0.0
VARIABLE RESISTORS	R	M	0	2.9	0	0	0	0.0
TRANSFORMER	T	M	0	2.9	0	0	0	0.0
SWITCHES	S	M	0	2.9	0	0	0	0.0
INTEGRATED CIRCUITS	Q	M	0	3.4	0	0	0	0.0
ADDIT. TIME FOR I. C.		M	0	3.4	0	0	0	0.0
FLY BACK TRANSFORMER	T	M	0	5.5	0	0	0	0.0
ASSEMBLE HEAT SINK			0	8.1	0	0	0	0.0
HEAT SINK ASSY		M	0	3.4	0	0	0	0.0
ADDIT. TIME FOR H/S		M	0	3.4	0	0	0	0.0
KNOT MINI CONN			0	10.4	0	0	0	0.0
TAPE MINI CONN			0	22.0	0	0	0	0.0
LEAD WIRES/MINI CONN	J/M	2	0	4.9	0	0	0	0.0
LEAD WIRES/MINI CONN	J/M	1	0	3.0	0	0	0	0.0
P/F FOR MINI CONN		1	0	3.0	0	0	0	0.0
PLUGS	P	M	0	2.9	0	0	0	0.0
SOCKETS		M	0	2.9	0	0	0	0.0
SHIELD CASE/PV01	B	M	0	3.4	0	0	0	0.0
ADDIT. TIME FOR S/C		M	0	3.4	0	0	0	0.0
PHONO JACK	S	M	0	3.4	0	0	0	0.0
SINGLE PIN TERMINAL	P	1	0	2.4	0	0	0	0.0
SPACER		M	0	2.4	0	0	0	0.0
BRACKET		M	0	3.5	0	0	0	0.0
FUSE HOLDER	F	2	0	2.9	0	0	0	0.0
PICK UP PANEL			0	2.9	0	0	0	0.0
INSERT PANEL			0	3.1	0	0	0	0.0
LEAD ARRANGEMENT				2.0	0	0	0	0.0
RING ANODE LEAD				6.2	0	0	0	0.0
TWIST & BEND				0.8	0	0	0	0.0
PLUS FIXED TIME				2.0	0	0	0	0.0
AFFIX TAPE				4.3	0	0	0	0.0
AFFIX FBT JIG				5.9	0	0	0	0.0
AFFIX CRT JIG/WEIGHT				2.9	0	0	0	0.0
BEFORE BATH INSP				0.1	0	0	0	0.0
INSERTION TOTAL SEC.					0	0	0	0.0
MODEL CHANGE		2.5%						0.000

Standard Times for After-Bath Activities

MODEL			
BATCH NO			
AFTERBATH PROCESS ITEM	**STD TIME**	**QTY**	**TOT STD TIME**
COMPONENT INSPECTION	0.1	0	0.0
LEAD DRESSING	2.0	0	0.0
WIRE CLIP FITTING	3.2	0	0.0
CABLE TIE	6.4	0	0.0
INSPECT & TOUCH UP			
METHOD 1	0.2	0	0.0
PLUS FIXED TIME	42.5	0	0.0
METHOD 2	0.11	0	0.0
RESOLDER	1.0	0	0.0
REMOVE SOLDER	1.5	0	0.0
COMP. CUTTING	0.4	0	0.0
PLUS FIXED TIME	1.2	0	0.0
INSERT SOCKET	1.0	0	0.0
SOLDER SOCKET	2.9	0	0.0
HEAT SINK ASSEMBLY	17.4	0	0.0
SHIELD PLATE/COVER	4.2	0	0.0
CLOSE CRT BASE CAP	3.6	0	0.0
INSERT MINI CONN	3.1	0	0.0
SOLDERING	2.5	0	0.0
COPPERSIDE COMP. FIX	10.9	0	0.0
INSERT & SOLDER	6.4	0	0.0
SOLDER SHIELD CASE	2.5	0	0.0
W/W & SOLDER BY HAND	7.0	0	0.0
W/W BY AID GUN	3.9	0	0.0
TILT COMPONENT	1.2	0	0.0
APPLY ADHESIVE	3.0	0	0.0
AFFIX TAPE	4.3	0	0.0
AFFIX LABEL	4.3	0	0.0
REMOVE TAPE	2.4	0	0.0
DIVIDE PANEL	3.0	0	0.0
MARKING/STAMPING	3.0	0	0.0
PACKING	4.9	0	0.0
AFTER-BATH			0.0
PANEL TOTAL SEC			0
PANEL TOTAL HOURS			0.000
/0.85 R.A			0.000
TEST APC	0.011	0	0.000
	0.011	0	0.000
	0.011	0	0.000
	0.011	0	0.000
	0.011	0	0.000
	0.011	0	0.000
TOTAL TEST			0.000
PARTS FEED PCB	2.0	0	0.0
COMPS	0.3	0	0.0
SUB ASSY	0.5	0	0.0
PARTS FEED TOTAL			0.000
TOTAL STD TIME			0.000

FIG. 5 Standard Timings Sheet from Nippon CTV

various points through the production process and these records provide the information necessary to enable management to pinpoint culpability to individual workers.

Inducting the Workers

From the outset of their employment at Nippon CTV (indeed during the recruitment process itself), workers are left under no illusions regarding what is expected of them, what is acceptable, and what is not. All new recruits are put through a two-day induction programme during which they are given lectures on the importance of adherence to rules governing absence, quality of work, and so on. During my period at Nippon CTV, I joined a group of fifteen new recruits who were being employed on temporary contracts to cover the high season until the end of December. Most of these workers were destined for the final assembly areas but all new shop-floor members are given the same induction programme. There were eight women ranging in age from 17 to around 50, and seven men with ages from 17 to 43. Two of those being inducted had come straight from school and several had been unemployed until they received the offer of this job. The following are excerpts from the diary notes that I recorded during this induction period:

> The induction programme itself began at 8.30 a.m. and the first person to talk to the new recruits was Claire, the personnel officer. She introduced herself and then said, 'This will be a bit boring but I have to do it. We have to make sure you know the rules and things, so that you can't say you didn't know if you don't do something right . . . I'm only here for the money and I expect you're the same. I want to enjoy myself as well, but the money is the main thing.' She was rather cynical and sceptical, not the enthusiasm that I had expected at all. She was not very slick and far from enthusiastic about Nippon CTV. In many instances she refers to Nippon CTV as 'they'. Occasionally she does appear to remember the patter—'I want to show you what you're a part of here,' but, typically, she is rather frank. 'As I told you at the interview [clearly the induction starts then] Nippon CTV is harsh and strict but that's the rules.' The requirements for employment are initially laid out during the recruitment interview with people's reactions being monitored at that time.
>
> 'The rules', she stresses, 'come about because of problems; they are not just made up for no reason.' The examples she gives are that there is no chewing gum allowed on the shop-floor because some of it has found its way on to circuit boards and that we are not allowed to wear short shorts or skirts. She did not embellish on the reasons for this. She was keen to emphasize that management did not just sit upstairs and make up rules for no reason. With regard to the rules for new workers, she concentrated particularly on attendance and avoiding being late. She emphasized the rules at all points, 'If you're away three times in three months then it

may well be that we'll be letting you go. That may not seem much and at other places they may not mind but here that is a lot. And Nippon CTV won't accept it.' She tells people that if they do feel unwell, then at least come in and go to the doctor here. If you are then sent home then that is OK but you must avoid what she calls the 'Red S'. 'The Red S is terrible to Nippon CTV. They'll go mad if they see that.' The final piece of advice on this subject is, 'Don't be ill, it's easier that way'. The 'Red S' is the mark for unexplained [i.e., unscheduled] or unacceptable sickness and absenteeism.

Claire described the morning team meeting and indicated that this makes lateness very visible: 'You'll be seen if you keep turning up late.' This is certainly true and it is very interesting that management chooses to stress this at the very beginning of the induction programme. Claire also mentioned the warning procedures which 'can be very short' including verbal counselling, then a verbal warning from the team leader, then a final written warning. The exact sequence and timing of the warnings can differ depending on individual circumstances. She also mentioned grievances: 'If you don't like what's happening to you or the way things are being done [by the team leader] then you must tell someone.' It is interesting that this seemed to be the level of the grievances that was formally anticipated by management. Anything above or beyond a disagreement with a team leader would be treated as abnormal.

Claire mentions that people should phone in if they are ill and also that *all calls are logged*. 'If you do something wrong you'll be warned. It's the same up in the office, if someone doesn't log a call they'll be warned.' The office staff have to endure the same form of monitoring as a control mechanism it seems. Claire mentions this logging of calls to emphasize that people cannot claim to have called in sick if they have not done so. She rounds off our thorough briefing on the need to avoid getting ill by saying, 'People do get ill, though Nippon CTV doesn't believe it'.

Following this lecture the recruits were shown a video about the company and 'where you fit in'. Claire returned after the video: 'Oh yes and I forgot to mention about the union.' There was a very short speech about the EETPU: 'They can represent your best interests as an individual if you have a grievance or whatever. They don't get involved in what we call collective bargaining issues such as pay or hours, that doesn't involve them, but they can represent you so it may be useful if you decide to join. But you don't have to if you don't want to.' The position and role of organized labour are discussed in more detail in Chapter 8.

This part of induction was held in a meeting room, a well-decorated room used for the training course for senior members. Later (following a tour of the plant) we moved to the training room which is just off the shop-floor itself and is much scruffier. The new recruits are seated around three sides of a rectangle with Claire at the head, alongside the TV and video. There is a little nervous chatter but not much is said. Most are dressed casually, in jeans or ski-pants, a couple of the older women have smarter skirts, blouses, and higher heels. The quietness and concentration soon wear thin during the day. Boredom and familiarity breed more and more chatting with the shared experience the chief topic. The range of comments from the new recruits at this stage runs from 'It's well run' to 'I'm bored shitless'.

The induction programme was co-ordinated by Viv, the training and induction officer, and she then collected the new staff for a tour of the shop-floor facilities. She did not take them 'upstairs' to see the office areas. During the plant tour, the new recruits were introduced to the notion of individual accountability which is prevalent throughout Nippon CTV. It was stressed that, 'Each individual has responsibility for what they produce' while they were shown the quality test laboratories where TVs are tested for 300 hours of continuous use (some have been on for ten years). Tests are also made on functioning at extremes of temperature (–10°C to 40°C) and at 95 per cent humidity. Being shown these quality test facilities emphasized, for the recruits, the importance attached to quality.

We now land at the training room which is a little cramped for the 16 of us. There are narrow rows of fairly uncomfortable seats in front of the overhead projector, a white board, and TVs and videos. Viv now talks to us, mentioning that she has worked at this site for 39 years: 'There is more discipline with the Japanese, but things are much better run.'

Viv says that Nippon CTV is looking for 'the right sort of member' and hence she will 'assess you all' during these two days. She mentions that some people do not cope well with this work environment and she gives the examples of school leavers and building site workers. During the two days she did seem particularly concerned about the school leavers and how they would adapt. It is made clear that this search for the right sort of members may lead to an early parting of the ways—'We may decide you're not right for Nippon CTV. Or you may decide that Nippon CTV is not right for you.' This was 'If you can't stand the heat, get out of the kitchen'-style advice.

After lunch we were addressed by Bobby Best, one of the quality engineers. This lasted for over an hour, including a video which provided an illustration of a company that had failed to act properly with respect to quality. His presentation was quite long and clearly thought through beforehand. He used an overhead projector and asked people what they thought quality was. He had a list such as 'reliability' on a projection sheet but he drew people to this definition—'Customer satisfaction each and every time'. He quickly drew the line that quality involved everybody with each aspect of what they did. He used his own presentation and the fact that he had been a little late and unprepared as an example of 'bad quality'. Indeed, at times he spoke like he had swallowed a TQC manual. However, his emphasis lay at the bottom line, 'It's all about money'.

He talked of the make-up of the quality problems that Nippon CTV has and mentioned the fact that bought-in materials problems account for only ten per cent of the rejects found in the manufacturing area. In other words, the people and processes of Nippon CTV were responsible for nine-tenths of the problems. And it is 'everybody's business'. As he described it, 'The motivation for all of this is money. And that's why you're here after all, for the money.' This is all about making money was his message, but it was important for 'us' (him and the recruits) that the money should be made here, not Eastern Europe or Spain. Straightaway, the connection between quality and the operators' jobs was being explicitly and bluntly made: 'If we keep making Mr Nippon CTV money then we'll all keep our jobs. And the way to do that is to keep quality up.'

Best's talk about quality included a very brief history of total quality assurance; how it had begun in the US in World War II and from there how it had been transported across to Japan by Juran and other experts: 'Japanese goods used to be cheap rubbish'. A video about making garden gnomes with flashing lights followed with a series of little lessons to be learned including the value of market research. The presentation also included a description of the quality department in the plant with its role to inspect suppliers' operations (and award certifications of quality) which then allowed Nippon CTV to do away with any goods inward inspections. This was something stressed by Best particularly since it enabled him to draw a comparison with other places his audience may have been employed. In addition, the role of the quality engineers included the inspection and monitoring of the internal manufacturing processes of the plant and the attempt to achieve quality 'by design' and the inspection of finished goods before their arrival with the customer. He stressed how strict its final goods inspectors would be and how that was of the utmost importance since the processes were geared to customer satisfaction.

He considered in slightly more detail his own role with regard to the internal part of production, the examination of process faults and planning. He stressed the importance of the manuals and that these should be followed at all times, 'If you don't have a manual you can refuse to work'. The talk had begun with the use of rough examples to consider the savings that are possible. Starting from the 90 per cent of rejects that come from internal factors and the figure of £4 for an average rework, he came up with a figure of over £250,000 saving possible because the technical assistants who fixed the rejects would no longer be needed and hence their wages would be saved. This, of course, makes the explicit connection with worker performance, quality, and their own jobs.

After the quality talk, Viv ran through the hierarchical structure out on the shop-floor starting with Desmond, the production director. 'Below Desmond is Mark, the senior production manager and below Mark there is Marcia, who is the panel shop manager and the manager of the machine shop [Mike]. Below these people there are three superintendents, one each for the machine shop, panel shop, and finals. Below the superintendents come the team leaders.' Throughout the day, the role of the team leaders was stressed as the link for the shop-floor. Viv made it clear that any problems should be talked over with each individual's team leader in the first instance. She did also make herself available as a go-between if the new recruit felt more comfortable talking to her.

At the end of the day, Viv asked everyone in turn what they had learned. My favourite response was from a character called Ernie, who had been an apprentice carpenter on the docks at one time and was here now after his own business (a boat building enterprise) had failed. He said, 'I've learned not to be late . . . I've learned not to be sick,' with a rather rueful smile. Others mentioned the safety videos and the colour codings. Of all those present, only one actually talked about the quality training and presentation.

At the very end, the importance of communication particularly regarding problems was stressed. The new members were urged to 'Show willing and communicate' if they encountered problems. Viv seemed to anticipate that any such problems would involve a person having to do a job they didn't enjoy and her advice was as follows—'It's no good thinking, if I'm bad at this they'll move me. We won't, you have to show that you're willing to try. It's no good just giving up and waiting to be moved.'

This marked the end of the first day of the induction programme. The second part of the programme concentrated mostly on some more training on the colour coding of electrical components and on soldering iron skills. Before that we were introduced to Don Pendleton, the chief shop steward, and he gave us a brief discussion of the role of the union at Nippon CTV.

Don starts by saying, 'No doubt all of you or most of you know what unions are about and have been in one yourselves, so I won't bore you with what unions are all about.' He tells us that there are 'well over 1,000 people' employed here and that union density is over 70 per cent. He tells us that the EETPU is the only union recognized at Nippon CTV 'and that can be a good thing. We don't have any arguments between unions here. Like at Ford there's ten or 12 of them and they can never decide among themselves and what to even take to management.' Don is eager to paint his union in a good light: 'It's a good union, well advanced compared to others in my opinion.' He tells us that the union has an agreement with the company that there will be no strikes: 'We don't believe in strikes, we believe that you came here to work and to earn your money.' Despite what Claire told us, Don claimed credit for the union because of a nine per cent pay rise this year. 'The pay is not bad here but they expect you to work for it. It's really hectic here.'

Don is a very matter-of-fact fellow with a rather careworn attitude. He seems rather pessimistic about what action the union may be able to undertake and is very pragmatic regarding the role of the union. However, he did talk quite enthusiastically about some of the company's practices. Don explained that there are shop stewards in each of the work areas and encouraged people to see them if there are any problems. He stresses that the union may be very useful in representing individual grievances and it has an arrangement with a local lawyer to provide legal aid (first half-hour consultation free).

Don advised, 'They're tight on time here, if you decide to have a day off here, you won't last two minutes.' He was asked about the EETPU not being in the TUC by one of the new recruits and responded, 'Well, that's because we signed a no-strike deal. And if you look at what has happened in the last few years, there have been very few successful strikes. We believe that the best way is if there any problems, you carry on working and earning your money while we work to solve the problem. With these new laws and regulations, you can barely go on strike with-out breaking them. We don't think they [strikes] work. Look at the miners, those poor lads not earning for over a year and nothing to show for it. But don't think the union is a "yes man". You look at those rises, they're better than many you'll find round here.'

The process by which pay is set at the company is discussed fully in Chapter 8. Don concluded his presentation with some comments on overtime: 'They like you to work overtime here. It says in your contract that you'll be expected to work a reasonable amount of overtime. Of course, there might be problems because what you think is reasonable and what they think is reasonable may not be the same . . .'. He left, saying, 'We really do want to help you.' The presentation plus the questions lasted fifteen minutes.

We then proceeded with the colour-coding tests and then Viv tried to set everyone at ease before they actually went out onto the shop-floor. She stressed, 'The main thing is that you all participate in it. The main thing is attitude.' She told them not to worry, 'We're only human aren't we? Anyone can make mistakes.' This is a favourite phrase of Viv's and she tells the recruits that they must talk to someone if they have any problems, either her or the team leader. 'If you can't do something or that, don't just leave it because that will be bad. If you talk to people then we'll see what can be done. If you just leave, then you'll never get back in.'

Leading a Team

As is emphasized during the induction period, the team leader is the central link in the workers' relationship with Nippon CTV. All aspects of the management of the workers on the shop-floor are the initial responsibility of the team leader, including handling grievances and dealing with disciplining members. The team leader is responsible for monitoring the behaviour and performance of each of their team's members, including their attendance and time-keeping and their quality of work performance. The team leader's responsibilities are wide ranging but the processes for dealing with employees are laid out in company policy. Any employee who may need disciplining or warning, say for 'poor' attendance or quality of work, will be 'counselled' regarding the need for improvement in the coffee lounge directly off from the shop-floor beside the panel shop. This counselling is a one-to-one session between the team leader and the member in question. The team leader represents the primary form of direct supervision in place at Nippon CTV. The team leaders have each individual member's records at their desk beside the line and these are updated for attendance, disciplinary record, and so on, on a daily basis by the team leaders. All members are also formally appraised by their team leader on an annual basis.

Since the linespeed largely determines output, the primary focus of attention for the team leader regarding *work performance*, as opposed to attendance or time-keeping, is the individual quality performance of each operator. The detailed quality control mechanisms allow for very specific quality information to be recorded, including the identification of individual responsibility for errors:

> The numbers of mistakes per day are totalled, and displayed on a monthly basis. The display includes a colour-coded chart above each individual operator's head. There are red, yellow, and green charts with the words 'danger', 'warning' and 'good' respectively marked on them. The allowed number is 20 errors for a month [from a monthly average of over 200,000 insertions], if this is exceeded then the operator is 'taken into the coffee lounge' and 'counselled'. In other words, they are asked about why they have made so many mistakes and told that an improvement will be expected or else they may receive a written warning. Apparently, this counselling will include an intrusion into the personal details of a worker's home life to find out if there are any worries there that are causing problems. Of course, quite how this comes across depends a great deal on the personalities of the team leader and worker. Still, it should be noted that this was anticipated by the workforce and is regular practice regardless of the relationship of the two. In the case of P3, the team leader was unpopular and this did not stem purely from the fact that she had a position of authority relative to the shop-floor. Very few of the P3 workers would have talked to her as a friend and so much questioning was clearly seen as prying.

Janie, the girl I sat next to today, had had 40 plus rejects in April and had been counselled, 'I just got told that that wasn't good enough and I would have to improve'. At no stage did I ever feel that operators would respond to exhortations to improvement because that would be a benefit to Nippon CTV. Janie had to improve or else face disciplinary action and ultimately the sack. She had reduced the number of recorded rejects to 21 in May and did not receive a second counselling session. Instead, Angie, the team leader, leaned over her shoulder today while I was in easy earshot and said, 'That was better last month Janie, let's make sure you keep up the improvement. Try and get below 20 this month, alright', and then Angie was off as Janie nodded and then turned and said to no-one in particular, 'Silly cow, I hate her!'

The counselling sessions are conducted in private, but the actual process is very visible. Indeed, 'visual controls' such as individual performance charts for attendance and quality, and line charts on daily production and quality performance, are displayed throughout the panel shop, including the coffee lounge. On more than one occasion I witnessed members being taken into the coffee lounge, and on one occasion my notes indicate that the employee left in tears. While the 'soft' HRM rhetoric of joint communication and aid may be employed, the practice of counselling is definitely perceived as part of the disciplinary process by both the members and the team leaders. On particular days where performance had dropped, there was considerable conjecture over whether individuals would be 'taken into the coffee lounge'.

Along with Katie, there is Natasha at the end of the line inspecting quality. Natasha is allowed 25 errors per month as a quality inspector [note that inspectors are monitored as well]. She told me, 'I've been in the coffee lounge a couple of times. She just tells you that you must improve. It's like a slap on the wrist.' Today, there was some anxiety as to who would be counselled. The rest of the line were looking around seeing who was going to the coffee lounge next. Natasha said to Katie, 'It won't be me will it?' and Katie then responded, 'It's OK there were ones worse than us'. They were evidently worried and keen that they not be counselled. It's clearly seen as an unpleasant disciplinary measure.

The way in which team leaders must communicate with members is also laid down in company policy. They are instructed to be supportive, but clearly directive in what improvement should be shown. They are told not to be openly critical, but to explain what is acceptable and what is not:

The sheets for the quality performance of the operators for the first three days of the week came around today. Most were OK, but at least one girl I noticed had all red. I was told that she has been taken for counselling and given a week to improve. This information spreads informally up and down the line very quickly. Angie, the team leader said to me, 'Did you notice me talking to these girls? I didn't shout at them. You just have to talk to them and tell them they have to improve.' This particular girl had been here for about three months and is at the end of her probation. [The use of probationary periods allows 'unreliable' workers to be identified and they will not be allowed to take up their contracts.]

Elsie told me that Sharon (an insertion senior member) had been a team leader and, she continued, 'She used to shout at the girls. That was no good, we don't have that here.' The use of direct orders by team leaders is kept to a minimum, largely because the production system itself remains smooth and stable with each individual aware of the requirements made upon them. However, the team leader has direct authority. The only time I witnessed this openly questioned, the team leader immediately asserted her authority:

> During the morning the line stopped unexpectedly. We had run out of trolleys upon which to place the completed circuit boards. Everyone took out their brushes and began sweeping and cleaning the line. I heard one of the girls say to Angie the team leader, 'Clean up? Why?' Angie's response was, 'Cos I said so'. The girl then backed down and responded, 'No, why are we stopped?' She was given a direct order from the team leader at this point.

The team leaders themselves are under immense pressure to meet schedules and attain the prescribed efficiency targets. It is these dynamics which keep the team leaders obsessed with productivity and quality. They alone are held responsible for the performance of their line and the members and even the senior members are not inclined to do more than is necessary.

> I heard some complaints at the charts kept, 'That's what the Japanese want. It doesn't make sense, but they want it.' This was referring to the performance of the line and the quality measurements and attendance sheets, etc. This comment came from Sara, a senior member and she also complained about the manuals that determined the linespeed and the specific job requirements. 'It's sick,' she stated emphatically. She was basically not in agreement with some of the practices. Sara, as a senior member, has clearly not incorporated all of the company philosophy in the same way that was apparent with Angie the team leader for example. She was prepared to speak out against the system and to be more informal in the way in which she presented herself to me and described the job requirements.

The pressure is maintained on the team leaders through the visibility of the performance of their line and through intense competition between the team leaders themselves. The visibility of line performance and the detailed information system means that the senior production management have comparative performance measures readily available on a daily, and even hourly basis. The team leader on my line, Angie, was extremely unpopular with her some of her team's members:

> Gail was scathing of Angie, 'Some of the team leaders are nice, but she's not. She's too bossy. She's got ideas above her station. She's forgotten what it's like to be on the line. She'll get on but she doesn't care who she steps on along the way.' P3 is apparently 'the élite line' according to Angie who

takes great pride in the line and it seems she applies some rules other team leaders are more relaxed about. While I was there, Bertha told Gail that another panel shop line was operating with more operators in certain jobs than the P3 line had. 'Why do we have to do it with fewer workers? What's different about us?' Bertha is the senior member for this part of the line. Angie also sticks closely to the rules. 'You might not always get taken into the coffee lounge on other lines but on this line you will. She sticks rigidly to all those rules.'

Apparently, P3 had been the top performing line and consequently Angie had been the 'star' but recently this had not been the case and another team leader, who had taken over a difficult line, had taken over her mantle.

While the informal competition between winners and losers was not explicitly acknowledged while I was at the plant, it was certainly possible to identify whose lines were doing well (the stars, the favourites, the winners) and whose were struggling ('poor Wendy') and this is also informed by relative experience and improvements in the performance of lines over time. Not just by what was actually said, I began to be able to judge how the different team leaders were perceived by their peers and management. There is a lot of personality involved in being a team leader and a lot of responsibility falls squarely on the shoulders of that one individual.

The whole role that Angie plays is highly stressed and it is extremely difficult to balance her different pressures. She has clearly made herself unpopular with at least some of her line members. Sharon told me, 'She was the star over Carrie.' But that things had changed and now, 'She's going so hard for efficiency'. The implications of what Sharon is saying are that Angie's star is on the wane, that Angie herself has recognized this and is becoming increasingly desperate to try and hold on to her reputation and status, and that this is leading her to become ever more cavalier and ruthlessly self-motivated toward the line's performance. The underlying agenda here is Sharon's demotion. Sharon had been a team leader herself but was demoted to a senior member, 'Look at me, I helped people and now . . . I'm either doing her job or she's treating you like a bimbo.' It's apparent that when Angie feels the pressure, and becomes stressed, she is less polite and fully communicative with her members than she might be. Having seen the pressure she is under this is understandable, if ultimately unacceptable and counterproductive. This has led to a distancing of Angie from her line members who maintain their own good spirits with humour wherever possible, often at her expense. The good humour does not always hold and Angie is clearly a focal point for a lot of dissatisfaction that members on the line feel.

The very fact that Angie is so visible herself creates an added tension for her. To meet the efficiency figures she must constantly look to increase the linespeed and keep people operating as fast as they are able. Consequently she is regularly scrutinizing the line, looking for opportunities to increase the speed of the line so that she can keep on schedule and make her targets.

> Angie is not popular, as she walked up and down the line today, somebody muttered, 'Look at her stood there'. This was soon followed with, 'This job is fucking crap!' During the normal period of the day, Angie will constantly walk up and down the line looking to see whether she can increase the speed or not. This very visible level of control certainly helps to make Angie unpopular with the people on the line.

While the quality performance is the primary aspect of individual work performance of concern to the team leaders, at a line level the productivity performance is also under the auspices of the team leader. The standard timings (which are set in Japan) are not strictly adhered to because some are not achievable while others offer the opportunity to run the line faster than the standard time and hence count toward achieving the efficiency target set for each line. The target for P3 is 104 per cent efficiency and this can only be achieved through running the line an average of 4 per cent faster than expected under the standard timings or through using an average of 4 per cent fewer people than allocated.

> There are seven people absent from the P3 line today and this means Angie must juggle her resources. She increases the number of components each member must insert and then cuts the linespeed accordingly. She tells me that the standard is always 2.7 seconds per piece. However, in practice this counts for very little. Angie will gently tweak up the linespeed until members begin to have *real difficulty keeping up to speed* and there are a few calls of 'Left set' [the standard form of words used to provide notification that an operator has left a set unfinished because of lack of time]. Rather than automatically knock the speed back down a little Angie will then try and overcome these problems initially by giving certain of the more experienced and particularly adept members extra pieces from those that are struggling. As Angie puts it: 'I watch the line to see if the girls are coping or coasting.' She does literally stand and watch, looking to see if people are pressed, seeing if there is a lot of talking. She told me that she uses the level of conversation as an indicator: 'If they have time to be chatting then they could be going faster.' The line has, in fact, been slowed because of the absences but Angie says earnestly: 'We've got to keep running. P3 is behind on its schedule.'

The Management

With the detail of running each individual line delegated to the team leaders, the roles of the two more senior members of the panel shop management lie in co-ordinating activities across the lines and in ensuring the target setting has the desired effect on the performance of the team leaders. Marcia, the panel shop manager, is the link between the panel shop and the rest of the plant and she acts as the key decision maker and guide for the team leaders and as a referee when there are disputes between the team leaders, for example over the allocation of scarce resources (normally labour). In carrying out her function, Marcia draws on a broader overview of the activities of the panel shop than any of the individual team leaders. Each team leader has intimate knowledge of their own line's position against schedule but tends to be ignorant of the other lines. Marcia takes decisions which mirror her perception of the overall situation.

Each morning Marcia meets with the other production managers—Desmond (the production director), Mark (the senior production manager), Mike (the automatic insertion or 'machine shop' manager), Ichihiro (the Japanese assistant managing director) and Colin (the scheduling manager). During this meeting the position of each area of the plant is overviewed and any outstanding issues are discussed. Marcia keeps her own book of information on the current position both in final assembly and on each of her lines in the panel shop. These are extracts from my diary from one such meeting, which began at 8.20 a.m.:

Desmond invites feedback on the current problems: 'Let's hear about the disasters.' The machine shop manager reports that he has been 'on stop' for about three hours, but that the 'floats' between him and the panel shop are okay. Desmond quips, 'He is a smoothy, he must have too many working for him.' Someone pipes up, 'He'll have to train them to fall backwards when they die [of exhaustion].' There is no sign of my presence having any effect on the conversation and the banter. Next, there is some feedback on production levels from the scheduling manager and the Japanese assistant director.

There is a report on a member in stores who has been rude to female members. Bart is the assistant/deputy shop steward, he has been moved out of stores and put on a 'safety patrol'. Desmond said: 'I think that is time well spent.' Next there is a report on absenteeism. There are 31 out from the panel shop and 20 plus out of finals. I later find out that four of the 31 have been 'written off' so only 27 are now down as being absent.

There are some problems with P7 running close on its float with finals. The finals line is changing at 12.15 p.m., P7 has not started up yet. If there are problems with tests then they may hold up F1. Marcia reports: 'We have [test] gear problems.' Mark is straight on to the phone warning that P7 may hold up F1 and if that is the case then they should start making up arrears, etc.

Next there is a detailed report, area by area. Marcia reports first, listing lines that were off and schedule positions. Desmond responds to the absence levels, 'This is a bad business; they jump on the band wagon.' There was a discussion of absence, which is Desmond's particular bugbear: 'We need to come down hard on them or they take you for a ride.' Desmond has the report cards for those back after an absence. He picks out one, 'She has put down "exhaustion". This is very suspicious. We should dock her pay.' This is not very well supported and they decide on counselling. Apparently the member had asked for the day off and had been refused. Desmond is not happy.

Desmond notes the stoppages line by line and the reasons for them— P7 stopped for 45 minutes because of a stores hold up; P9 stopped for 20 minutes because of a stores hold up. Desmond responds: 'There are problems with our friends in stores. I think they all come from Liverpool!' Mark reports that finals is plus 83 (ahead of schedule), 'I don't believe it,' laughs Desmond. Mark reports on the levels of overtime on finals (which has been necessary to keep up on the schedules). There have been problems with stores there as well but finals can go and get their parts themselves.

Next the scheduling manager reports on progress. 'We are nearly ready for July [next month]. We should be ready tomorrow, including the material calling schedule. This has been spaced back two days from the main schedule.' Marcia feels that two days are not enough in some cases. Moreover, there is no space to put that material anywhere. Marcia says there are problems in 'binning' up batches for lines. Some are needed before the evening of day one to have time to bin up on day two. She complains that the informal relationship between 'b' station and stores that kept things running may have broken down. 'Fred used to talk to Steve, but I am not sure if he talks to Mike in the same way.' The schedule manager comments, 'communication is the key'. This all progresses without comment from the Japanese.

Next there is a document entitled, 'Procurement bill status report, 20 June' for review. There are problems with some material needed for the autumn. Q501 is described as 'threatening'. The schedule manager notes that 'There is no promise of supply on source of Q501'. Desmond responds, 'Do we go incomplete?' It is a 64 leg [i.e. metal pins that have to be fitted into holes on the circuit board] component so this is not popular. Marcia adds, 'It is only because I am behind I have not stopped [through] needing that already.'

The meeting is completed by 9.15 a.m. The relevant information is then relayed to various other managers at a further meeting back down on the shop-floor.

Each team leader has to complete an 'Ins and Outs' book for each day's production in which they list the inputs and outputs for that day. Angie arrives every morning at around 7.15 a.m. to complete her paperwork from the previous day. The whole system runs on a collection of bureaucratic rules regarding which different inputs are to be booked against which outputs. Despite the procedures, these often prove to be areas for negotiation and Marcia is the arbiter of what team leaders may or may not avoid booking against their line. What follows are further notes from a day shadowing Marcia. These events all took place within a 45-minute period during the morning:

Our conversation is interrupted by Angie who has to report that 200 panels have had the wrong AV panels inserted. Angie has called some people over from the offending line and sat them next to the side of P3 to rework these defects. Angie is assured that these will not be included in her numbers. There was a clearly discernible fear here in reporting back to Marcia. Competitive tension between the team leaders is also more and more clearly identifiable.

Mark pops into the coffee lounge, he has spotted that P3 has stopped. Everyone has responsibility for everything it seems. Next, Marcia is disturbed by a man (from quality) about a problem with 'dressing the leads' on a new panel. There is a complaint from the team leader about a change on the drawing, the tie 'wasn't to be done here on the first mass drawings'. There is a problem because the ties now need to be made nearer the power panels. There is a problem out in the finals during assembly and testing if the ties are where they were supposed to be according to the original drawing. The team leader is not at all happy, 'I brought that up on my problem sheet but . . . he would not come down and I have now done 500 and I have got to rework them. They are in TVs out there.' The incontrovertible rule is to work to the drawings.

Marcia tells me that there have been problems with the quality of drawings that people are required to work to. She says, 'I cannot give a member a written warning for poor quality if I can't see myself if it is wrong.' This has caused some personnel problems. According to Marcia, there have been people leaving and even sackings. One member 'wanted to move jobs but was told "no" and now she is not here, she is leaving'. Apparently this member was put on to the absent list then 'written off'. Marcia can be like a mother figure and she advises the team leader, 'Be careful dealing with Jim or he will freeze the whole batch [that is, refuse to pass the batch and insist that all units are inspected again for quality]. Get your point across but he can be a bugger'. There was a clear situation here where quality control is playing a policing role.

The procedure of booking 'Ins and Outs' also applies at the level of the panel shop itself and Marcia and Joan are responsible for preparing these details. As with each individual line's inputs and outputs, there are sometimes situations where certain elements are contested.

Next, Marcia has to deal with a problem regarding the booking of rework on some defects against the panel shop. [In other words, finals have claimed that the labour time that they put into reworking some defects should be booked against the panel shop efficiency levels.] Marcia is not happy, 'I supplied lots of the labour, I am not being booked for that. This will get their [finals] efficiency up by me owing them stock.' There is a debate over who did what rework. Marcia gave 11 members [to finals] during overtime to do the P1 rework required. Apparently they did not do that work, they did something else instead. There is confusion about who did exactly what during the overtime. 'I am not getting stung for that,' retorts Marcia. The efficiency recorder, a woman in the QC office in finals, tells her it will be booked against panel shop's efficiency for the rework. This appears to satisfy Marcia, at least partly. 'Make sure you only use what [the amount of labour time] is needed,' she warns.

Thus, in a similar way to that in which each team leader is responsible for their line's performance, Marcia takes responsibility for the panel shop and the bureaucratic and output controls are very similar in each case. The situation for each line is closely monitored through quality records and through efficiencies and position against schedule. The quality department generates very detailed information on the quality performance of each line for each panel they have made (see also Chapter 2):

We go back to the coffee lounge where the printouts from the quality department are waiting. There are three thick files of computer printouts which contain a record of all rejects from each line on the panel shop. This information is broken down by: category of fault (not connecteds, short circuits, faulty components, wrong values, dry joints), by process, by batch, and by line. 'We don't worry so much about individual faults but if it happens more than once we want to know why.' Yesterday's quality report is available by this morning. The report further notes if the component was auto insert, hand insert, or after bath. There is a daily report on 'lost time for breakdown and materials'. There is also a weekly report on quality by each department and a weekly report on business planning.

Marcia informs me that the team leaders consider the printouts on quality every day against set targets regarding the ratio of quality leakage to finals divided by the quality [of components going] into the panel line. Each line is set a particular target that is generated from their past record, so for example P3 has a 3 per cent leakage target while P4's is 0.5 per cent because P4 is a small panel line. For the main panel lines leakage is targeted at 3 per cent except for P1 which deals with the hardest panels. However Marcia says, 'They [P1] have made the best improvement over the last two months. There was a change of team leader [Carrie for Sharon] in mid-February and the improvement began in March.' Marcia let this sentence hang in the air.

Whilst the panel shop's monthly schedule is broken down daily by batch, Marcia engages in a day-to-day juggling of the schedule as she takes decisions dictated not only by the schedule but also the position regarding different lines, floats, and the situation in finals and with stores. Marcia has been having some problems with test gear. She ascribes these to the individuals doing those jobs, i.e., the test gear staff not her production members. There is considerable informality around the schedule regarding production and much of what happens appears to be controlled by Marcia herself, in consultation with her team leaders.

The improvements to 100 per cent efficiency are possible through using less labour than is set in the standard time while still meeting schedules or by producing above the schedule rate. 'So if the standard time is 50 you do it with 48 [people]. You must watch quality.' Marcia explained a further case of these targets and the monitoring of line performance, 'This gives information on my team leaders, about who makes those targets and how they do it.' She continued, 'You can't just let them sit back, you will have to set challenges.' This area, too, has a certain degree of informality and specific control measures are centred very closely to the line itself. Standard times are set in Japan 'but we do things quite a lot different here, for example, safety rules are different'. Marcia was referring here to the make-up of sets for the European markets, etc., and this manifests itself mostly in the need for certain amendments—'mods' to be made at certain junctures. If these are not in the manual then they have no standard time, for example, taping wires, etc. This relies on the awareness of the team leaders to take advantage of the holes in the bureaucratic procedures, 'If they [the team leaders] are not astute then they will suffer'. However, the alternative is that they will need to cover extra difficulties. For example, the need for a person on taping may require someone extra than is accounted for in the standard time. Alternatively, 'Sometimes we may have made improvements, say scrapping screws. We don't get on to the phone and tell the Japanese.' In this way some of the improvements made by the team leaders can be stored secretly to help attain target efficiency levels.

This is a very important dynamic in understanding the actual processes on the shop-floor. Marcia, the production manager, withholds information regarding improvements from more senior management in order that her team leaders will be able to continue to meet their efficiency targets and, consequently, the panel shop meets its targets. This is not consistent with the continuous improvement objectives of the organization. In an interview, Desmond Sweeting (the production director) claimed that improvements discovered at the plant would be fed back to Japan in order that the standard times in the manuals may be updated and improved. In practice, this information is held within the panel shop by the team leaders and middle managers in order that they may meet the very demanding targets set. This provides further evidence to question the appropriateness of a unitarist perspective in interpreting contemporary manufacturing since in this instance managers themselves are actively subverting the organization's formal rules and procedures and prioritizing their own self-interest over company objectives.

In the same way that the inputs and outputs control system is replicated for different levels in the organization, so the competition and tension that characterize the relationships between team leaders are also evident between Marcia and the manager responsible for final assembly, Mark. The cause of the tension is similar—the need to record inputs and outputs in order to demonstrate that the target performance levels have been reached. This was illustrated during my time with Marcia:

> An interesting incident now occurs which highlighted some of the tension between the panel shop and final assembly. There have been problems with P7 line both yesterday and today. Yesterday the line was down for one and half hours because of a power outage. Today it has been stopped for one and half hours waiting for materials from stores. Consequently, F4 final assembly line has used up its float, and today it has been down for two hours awaiting panels from P7. Marcia tells me that Mark wants overtime tonight to get back to schedule 'but there is no way'. There is no time to organize the overtime and there is no opportunity for instant overtime [in the panel shop]. Apparently 'b' station has had to use several members on one batch for a rush job and have neglected the other batches. They have therefore fallen behind and the problems have begun. Marcia is very unhappy. The schedule has been upset and she also states that warnings to Mark about problems with supplies from stores and the difficulties her lines are in have been ignored. 'They don't care unless finals are stopped. I have been on about this for weeks now and it all blows up in my face.' There is a most definite 'blame' attached to failings and it would appear that the tensions are most likely to surface when problems arise and this blame must be apportioned. This is compounded by the internal budgeting of time and resources between lines and departments. The problems today have been increased because F1 had to stop at one stage because the warehouse was full and there was nowhere for the finished units to be put. Finals have now run out of cabinets for one model and there are no panels from panel shop for the next batch. So there is nothing for those on overtime in finals to do.

With the system stripped to the minimum, in terms of manning, inventory, storage space, etc., uncertainty and unanticipated events almost immediately generate problems. In accord with the bureaucratic monitoring procedures every problem must be recorded and booked against efficiencies. Hence this creates questions over responsibility since every individual team leader and manager has personal targets for which they are held accountable.

SUMMARY

This chapter has described the various aspects of the control systems at Nippon CTV and begun to indicate the process by which these are implemented on the shop-floor. As we have seen in this chapter, the control systems at Nippon CTV combine direct, bureaucratic, technical, and performance-based controls. The technical design of the system, including the use of a moving line and the removal of internal buffers of time or stock, is a key part of the process of management control. The controls are underpinned by an information system which gathers detailed information on quality, inputs, outputs, and so on. This chapter describes occasions when there has been informality regarding decisions, most notably regarding the speed of the line. The extent to which this informality affects the situation of workers is considered in detail in Chapter 5. Chapter 4 describes the process of management control at Valleyco.

4

The Process of Management Control at Valleyco

The objective of the quality improvement process is to develop a common total quality culture among all Valleyco employees to ensure total external and internal customers' satisfaction. In project management, emphasis is given to prevention at each phase by using controlling management tools and procedures and the systematic application of audits followed by corrective actions.

Valleyco company literature.

INTRODUCTION

This chapter discusses the process of management control at the Valleyco plant. Unlike Nippon CTV, the processes at which are described in the preceding chapter, the plant does not have a single formal production and control system to cover all operations. The operations and the way in which they are controlled vary across the plant at Valleyco. As was pointed out in Chapter 2, the plant management have been reorganizing and restructuring their operations since Valleyco took over two years prior to the research. During the research period, the plant had four identifiably different shop-floor structures for control, primarily through the transition toward a business unit system and the regrouping of work around individual customers.

In the moulding shop at Valleyco, during the research, there was a supervisor for each shift who was responsible for maintaining production, ordering raw materials, scheduling (in liaison with the production control department), and people management issues. Also, in the moulding shop when there were two shifts, there was a charge-hand responsible for operator activities in the mornings. The operators worked for a group bonus which was set and which did not reflect actual production because there were not job timings available for each machine. In contrast, on most of the assembly lines, the system was based on an individual piece-rate with a charge-hand responsible for production, negotiating scheduling with production control, and, at least notionally, for people issues. These lines were based around products and grouped accordingly, for example, the jet line, the pump line (or motor shop), container assembly, and so on. All of these lines were the responsibility of a single manager, Lee Eggar, under the business unit system.

The other lines were centred on individual customer assemblers—Rover, Nissan, and Peugeot. The Peugeot area was the first of the production cells to begin operation. There were two lines, each with a charge-hand, managed by the business unit manager, Mark Smith. This area was the sole responsibility of the manager, he had no production controller, and he spent much of his time in and around the lines. Consequently, the charge-hands were far less significant than in the other assembly areas where the manager very rarely took an active role. In the Peugeot unit, the operators worked for a group bonus based on daily production figures. The Rover and Nissan lines were the next to be incorporated into the business unit scheme but even at this time they were slightly different from the other assembly lines. These lines were run by charge-hands and the operators worked for individual bonuses as on the other lines but, especially on the Nissan line, the awareness of the importance of quality was heightened, quality testing was more prevalent, and the significance of the customer's role in influencing and controlling activities at Valleyco was most evident.

In this chapter I detail the process of management control and these systems in practice with particular reference to the Peugeot unit and Nissan line, in contrast to the rest of the shop-floor, since this represents the clearest distinction between the 'old' and the 'new' management practices at the plant. Once I had begun my research at Valleyco, the extent of variation in practices became clear and it was evident that the organization was in a period of transition. In this instance, the observations drawn from Valleyco provide an insight into the processes of change involved in attempting the implementation of the 'Japanese' model in a western plant. As will become clear through the course of this chapter, there are far more problems in detailing the management control systems at Valleyco without beginning to discuss aspects of the workplace relations which are primarily the foci of subsequent chapters. This chapter leads us to the need to consider accommodation, resistance, informality, and worker involvement in more detail if we are to capture the situation and dynamics of Valleyco's shop-floor relations accurately.

THE SYSTEMS IN PRACTICE—VALLEYCO

Valleyco gives a far more transparent example of 'negotiated order' (Strauss *et al.* 1971) or 'structured antagonism' (Edwards 1986) than Nippon CTV and the endemic conflict of workplace relations is evident daily. Unlike at Nippon CTV, the chaos of the shop-floor was also immediately apparent and, while Valleyco has certain bureaucratic procedures designed to control shop-floor activity, these are nowhere near as wide ranging nor as effectual as at Nippon CTV. As a consequence, informality, personal relations, and negotiation play a far bigger role in the day-to-day workings of the Valleyco plant and hence there is far greater uncertainty and variation in actual practices. As discussed above, this is compounded by the different structures and systems being run concurrently on the shop-floor. In addition, Valleyco is far less successfully protected from uncertainty and difficulties which stem from the organization's environment, primarily the actions of the plant's customers. In other words, in relation to Nippon CTV, Valleyco has proven less successful thus far in securing a stable and predictable external environment or a reliable and flexible internal environment.

DAILY WORK SHEET

DEPT. NO. _____   SECTION _____   DAY _____

CLOCK NO.	NAME		DATE				WORK STUDY ONLY		
		TIME						TRAINING	PREV
PART NO.	OP NO. or DESCRIPTION	ON	OFF	QTY	SMV	EXCESS		ALLOW	PERF

LOST TIME CODE	DOWN TIME	REASON FOR LOST TIME

CLOCKED HOURS

APPROVED BY:

H.E.(W.S) CWMTOWN   vws 05

FIG. 6 Valleyco Daily Work Sheet

The primary strategy of management for the control of labour is an individual (or group) piece-rate system. As this implies, the primary concern of management control is productivity. While quality is officially seen by management as important, there is little evidence that this view is consistently brought to bear on the actions of individual workers outside those lines dedicated to a specific customer, most notably the Nissan line. As was described in Chapter 2, Valleyco's management struggles to maintain its production control and scheduling systems, in which event, schedules, quality, and inventory controls become open for negotiation in a form of directed chaos as the plant management attempts to keep to its customers' mutable requirements. Indeed, as we will see, the role of the customer car assemblers is especially significant in the operations of the plant.

'Making the Number'

For most areas of the plant, each operator has a time-sheet on which each job, the time taken, and the quantity produced are entered for the day (see Figure 6). Each job is weighed out on a small pair of scales, usually by the charge-hand, to give the exact quantity required for that order. This sheet, along with a single minute value (SMV) number for each of the jobs carried out, is then sent to the offices each day.

The standard timings are set by a job timer who decides on the appropriate SMV after timing an operator on the job; each of the jobs has an SMV which is multiplied by 60 to give the target number specified per hour in order to meet the 100 per cent level performance index (PI). If operators work at less than 75 per cent of the target number then they get no bonus at all to add to their basic weekly wage. The company expects operators to work at 100 PI and if they manage that over the full eight hours in the day, there is a £4.30 bonus. The maximum bonus is for 120 PI and operators do not get paid for anything over that performance level. The earnings are averaged over a full eight-hour day, and individual jobs can be worked at over 120 PI without being knocked down but that does not apply to the overall daily performance. However, as Jenny on the jets line pointed out, 'You mustn't work too fast on the easy jobs, or the office will notice the timings are too easy and get them upped.' The operators therefore keep their performance around 120 PI on those jobs. Indeed, examples of 'systematic soldiering'—the term F. W. Taylor used for the deliberate withholding of effort (see Rose 1975: chapter 2)—are widespread.

> I talked to Jenny about the bonus systems. The earnings are averaged over the whole day. This includes the 20-minute morning break which must be included as part of the day. Each break is marked by a stampede down to the canteen. Today Jenny had a PI of exactly 120, the maximum. She had achieved this by about 3.45 p.m. and then stopped for the day, there was no point in continuing. 'I know exactly the numbers I need for each

job, and I just aim to do that and no more.' The success of Jenny (one of the faster workers) in achieving her bonus is primarily dependent upon the job she has to do. If she is on one job all day then she may well reach the 120 PI. If she has to continually change jobs, this obviously slows her down. Today, she and Tony had been on the same job, doing it jointly, and therefore both earning 120 PI, 'Tony keeps me going at it', she said. Jenny reckons she can manage 120 PI two or three times per week on average. The numbers are taken in each day and a full sheet with each day of the week is passed out on Thursdays with the payslip. Last week, Jenny managed 120 PI twice and also had 113, 90, and 83 PI.

The bonus earnings are very important when you consider that the basic pay is £102 per week (£112 per week in the moulding shop because of the noise and where there is a group bonus). A performance index of 120 earns a bonus of £7.70 per day, 100 PI earns a bonus of £4.30 per day, and 75 PI earns nothing. As mentioned in Chapter 2, these wages represent below average pay for women in manual work in Wales. The daily sheets show the PI for each day, the actual PI score even if it is above 120 or below 75. These performances are very much determined by different abilities, and some of the operators clearly struggle to earn anything worth while:

> During the afternoon I worked for three and a half hours, putting two eyes into a jet. I worked as quickly as I could but the job was rather fiddly and became extremely tedious. I managed almost exactly 200 jets per hour for each hour. To earn 100 PI bonus I would have needed 340. I would have earned no bonus.

Throughout the entire period that I was at Valleyco it was extremely rare for me to come close to the numbers required to achieve a reasonable bonus. Equally, there were a number of others whom I noticed were either unable or unwilling to work fast enough to earn a bonus. In addition, some timings are much more difficult than others.

> Bethan's line [jets] is certainly busier than some at the moment. She had at least three operators report to her this morning at the beginning of the shift because, 'There was nothing for me to do on my line—containers. If there's something there tomorrow I'll be back up there, otherwise down here again.' Bethan regularly gets these 'spare' workers. Moving to jets is not popular though because the bonus is very hard to get there—'I don't like it on jets, the timings are too hard.' Apparently, the operators stay on a particular line unless there is nothing to do, and so many of the jets operators always have a struggle to earn a good bonus. 'Now you can see what these girls are up against,' Bethan said to me when I was told some of the (staggering) performance levels required to earn bonus pay.
>
> I began today on the valve line, which Bethan is also in charge of. I worked on a valve that needed a spring and washer fitted between the

two outer halves of the case. The two halves are securely snapped together using a hand-operated press. The job is quite fiddly but I soon got used to it and I felt I was working fairly successfully. One of the other operators came up and said, 'I hope you're not going to ruin our numbers'. In other words she hoped that I was not working too fast and possibly causing the job to be retimed. She was joking. The target for 100% performance is about 425 per hour. At best I was managing 225 per hour. How anyone could obtain 100 PI is completely beyond me. On this particular job, it also appeared beyond the other operators. Apparently, someone had done it all day last week and had the equivalent of an hour and a half's work! 'These numbers are ridiculous. We ought to get these jobs [the hand-operated press jobs] retimed. We need to ask Bethan, but she can be a bit fiery.' Kay, an operator at the plant for 19 years, said, 'I don't know how these girls have stood it for so long [she only joined the valve line last year]. Mind you, they're thick. I have to work out their bonus for them every night.' She added that whoever had been timed on this job must have 'had propellers on their behind!' I was told, in response to questions about me working too fast, that if I went above the numbers they would 'smash my face in'. They were joking, but still the message to keep within the right levels was successfully communicated. May, an operator who has worked here for about three years and is in her fifties told me, 'I'm only here for the money. I'm not a career woman!'

The job timings are taken by a timer from industrial engineering, who selects the people he wants to time himself. A union steward is not present at the timings, which are taken fairly regularly since there are often new jobs to be timed and occasionally there are new timings taken on old jobs.

There was a timer on the [jets] line this morning. He was there to time two jobs that are not on the new timings list. He was there for only a few minutes and the results came back this afternoon. Bethan told me that there are some operators that the timers refuse to time, 'May is too fussy and Sherry is not good enough'. (Sherry appeared to have a PI of 70 yesterday which means no bonus.) Bethan told me that the timings would probably be 'better' if the timer used a good operator, in other words, they would not be so high. She said that if a poor operator did the timing then it (the SMV) would be raised, whereas they (the timers) may trust more readily the timings taken from a skilful operator. When the timings came back, Bethan appeared to be trying to persuade the operators that they were reasonable, 'I know Tony will be able to do that easily. That will be a good one for you, Tony.' Tony is the most experienced (and the fastest) operator on the line. 'He is the one who does my difficult jobs for me,' said Bethan. The rest are less likely to manage the new rates. Jenny had not tried that job, but felt that it would be OK once she had some practice and got used to it.

Naturally, the operators themselves try to ensure that the timings are not too hard and the bluff and double-bluff between the timers and the operators make a mockery of the notion of 'scientific management'. Indeed, this informal battle between the timers and operators is a cause of some of the uncertainty in the production system at Valleyco.

> Justine can do 120 PI on the jobs she is likely to have to do . . . Whilst I was talking to Justine, Heather came up and told her that the timer would be coming over to time her on the new jig for Jaguar. This new jig was for a completely new part of the new Jaguar model . . . Heather told me much the same as Bethan had, the timers like to take good, experienced operators. I met Laura, a younger operator who apparently becomes very nervous when she is timed and goes 'too fast'. She is called a 'flyer' by the other operators. Heather said, 'We have to try and calm Laura down when the timer comes up here.' Justine certainly gave the impression that she would not be going too fast, and she had never even seen the job before that morning and so was unlikely to be at top speed.

It is interesting to note that both Bethan and Heather, the charge-hands, were concerned to ensure that the timings were not too high for their operators. If the timings are too difficult then the operators will not be able to earn bonus and hence will be unhappy and unwilling to take on the job. They would also then be likely to work much below their normal speed since anything below 75 PI earns no bonus. The role of the charge-hands as the link between the shop-floor and management is a complex and contradictory one and will be further discussed in the next section.

> Kay, the most experienced operator on the line, was scathing in her criticisms of the timings on the valve parts. 'There's no point in trying [for bonus] on some of these jobs. If you know you'll only get a 90 if you go hammer and tongs then why not take it easy and get your 75 [the minimum PI, carrying no bonus]? It's only worth a pound or two anyway.' May was working on another hand-operated press. She complained that recently, though not today, the two halves of the casing had not fitted properly and so the job had become awkward and this had slowed her progress. 'But they don't change the timings do they? They never say it's not your fault you can't meet the numbers.'

It is impossible to describe the piece-rate system at Valleyco without immediately discussing the way in which operators seek to overcome the constraints through systematic soldiering, misleading the timers, and securing some counter-control on their work speed during the day. The operators themselves seem to decide early each day whether they will 'make the number' and how hard they will try on a particular job. The intense effort tends to come in the mornings and many operators ease off in the afternoon:

While Katherine was chattering away to me, the others on the line also appeared more relaxed and talkative in the afternoon, less concentrated on their bonus. As Jenny told me, 'You can't keep it up all day anyway. You're bound to get tired.' We're on second break (10.15–10.35 a.m.) and second lunch (12.40–1.10 p.m.) this week. But there are no afternoon breaks and it would be a long afternoon if you're in on first lunch (12.00–12.30 p.m.). As yesterday, the operators packed their things away and tidied up at about 4.15 p.m. They waited for the buzzer from about 4.20 p.m.

The operators were supposed to finish at 4.25 p.m. and clean up their work spaces before clocking off from 4.30 p.m. but, despite being on a piece-rate the shop-floor came to a halt by 4.20 p.m. at the latest on most days. On one occasion I had about 100 casings (about 30 seconds' work) to finish off when the 4.25 p.m. buzzer went and I decided to finish them. Although I still completed the job well before 4.30 p.m. I drew several comments, 'He's a conscientious bugger, isn't he?' and, 'What are you after, overtime?' from workers as they started to queue for the clock.

In contrast to the main assembly areas at Valleyco, the Peugeot cell works to a group bonus while the Nissan line appeared to have easier individual job timings than many of the lines. I first noticed this because I was actually able to achieve a 100 PI here, making up bottles. The Nissan line is different in a number of respects from the majority of the assembly lines. For example, the line has 'process control sheets' displayed above each work station detailing the job procedures, and including a diagram of the component. The operators on the Nissan line are formally the responsibility of Heather, the hoses charge-hand, but in practice they are largely left to their own devices:

I chatted to Gladys and Irene later in the day and they told me that they work as a team, Irene assembling and Gladys testing the jets. They do this of their own volition because, 'Some people are better at some jobs than others. It is not that you just try harder, it's that you're better at it. Take me and Irene, I'm good at the testing and can do the number on that and Irene does the assembling and can do the number on that. If I did the assembling and she did the testing we would not get our numbers out so we work together and pool the numbers each day.' It appeared that Gladys and Irene are on the maximum bonus each day. They are left to get on with it by Heather and so by working out the best way for them to earn their bonus they also turn out the higher number of products for Valleyco. The motivation for this is purely and simply money. I found that doing the same job all day is extremely frustrating and boring; the time passes slowly and your body aches from being in the same position consistently repeating a handful of actions. But virtually all the operators I have spoken to prefer to do the same job all day as long as they can get their number done.

I also witnessed the benefits of worker self-co-ordination in the moulding shop where one of the two shifts had organized themselves into a team and helped each other during their working day. Instead of each operator staying at their designated machine, they circulated around the injection moulders as a group. This meant that they had the opportunity to talk but also that they could concentrate their efforts on the more difficult jobs. They consistently out-performed the other shift on output. Both in the moulding shop and on the Nissan line the charge-hands were perfectly happy to let the workers organize themselves since the outcome was improved production numbers. On the Peugeot line the group members are forced to work together because of the flow layout of the cell and since the pay basis is a group bonus system.

> I talked with Joy about the payment system on this line (Peugeot). Unlike elsewhere in the plant these operators are paid according to a group bonus, depending on what is actually packed and has an IDN (an identification number as a completed box) each day. The operators must still fill in an individual daily performance sheet but pay is group-related. Joy preferred the old system of an individual bonus for performance and her reasoning clearly illustrated at least implicit peer pressure, notwithstanding the fact that the final assemblers (her 'customers' in the line) were apparently sympathetic. She told me, 'I like the individual bonus, that way I can go at my own pace. So, you know, if I don't feel well then I can go a bit slower. But with this you have to keep going for the others. It's not as though it's just down to you.' Something else Joy said also showed the way the group system creates problems among work mates, 'They're good workers on here and we do earn a good bonus, but see Joan and Nia smoke and I don't. You can't expect them to give up their fag time but . . . you know what I mean?' She had not actually said it, but she obviously felt put out by the fact that some of her work mates had a few minutes off every now and again. Joy told me that she and her colleagues earn 'good bonus', there is still a maximum set. I asked Joy about the consequences of one person being absent and she said that this did affect the bonus earned.

The Peugeot cell is run independently of the rest of the shop-floor at Valleyco and, consequently, absence affects more than the bonus that workers can earn since 'spare' labour is not introduced from elsewhere in the plant. This was graphically demonstrated during the first day that I spent with the Peugeot cell:

> Because one of the four operators was away, Joy was kept very busy trying to feed both final assembly operations. Normally when someone is absent the right-hand drive line is stopped but Mark wanted to finish an order and so was running both for a short while. This meant Joy was forced to work extra fast because she alone was feeding the two operators with the sub-assemblies. Even Nia, one of the final assembly operators, said,

'Look at poor Joy rushing. She's getting all het up trying to keep us both going.' To compound Joy's problems one of the tools she was using did not work properly. In the end, she became so worked up she had to 'go to the loo to calm down', she told me. The installation of a 'customer ethos' between workers, allied to a system which does not allow for any work-in-progress buffers, has led to work intensification for part of the line. The very fact that Joy today saw herself as feeding those two final assemblers, and therefore needing to work even harder, demonstrates that the operators feel responsible for the next worker in the line's supply.

Unlike Nippon CTV, Valleyco does not have an effective quality control system for most of the shop-floor and its piece-rate system of controlling labour actually produces pressures which lead to quality problems. The operators themselves are concerned about their numbers, but not about the quality of their output because they are paid on the number produced before testing has identified any rejects.

While I was using the jig, Derek came over to fix a bent pin and kept going on about how it was always the operators' fault when the tools got broken and how stupid some of them were. He also talked about one operator, 'She's a flyer, she is. All she's worried about is turning out her number. Say she does 600 an hour, only 400 will be any good, the rest will be rubbish.'

In fact, unlike Nippon CTV where quality is made everyone's concern and everyone is individually monitored on their performance, Valleyco has not established the importance of quality among many shop-floor workers. It was unusual to find anyone beyond the quality department who would take proactive responsibility for quality improvement, and this was compounded by the company's own procedures, as my personal observations bear out:

This morning I water tested jets, checking that there was no leak and that the stream was directed properly. In a three-hour stint I failed 73 out of 500 because of leaks. The leaks were largely caused by the quality of the moulded component that had come from the moulding shop. However, all I had to do as the operator on tests was put the defects in a separate bag. This job is timed and so my concern was to test as many as I could, not to try and sort out the problem or even communicate it to anyone.

When I began my period of research at Valleyco there were a number of 'viewers', or quality inspectors, on the shop-floor (they were subsequently made redundant). On one morning I was able to join Ann, a viewer:

While I was watching Ann she tested 20 valves for leaks, about half failed and she felt this was due to a slightly low pressure setting on the mechanical press used to seal the two halves of the valves. She went off to find Derek, the setter. She also told Katherine, the operator, but work continued. Derek did not turn up for at least half an hour and so the faulty production had continued during that time since Katherine needed the numbers for her bonus.

Elsewhere in the plant, the operators themselves were critical of the quality control department. Paula and Vera complained that they had received little or no help from the QC department in trying to deal with the numerous problems which have beset the motor shop. They claimed that they have been told that they must identify defects produced by the machines and the reasons for the failures, and only then would the QC department become involved.

> Meanwhile the machines continued to run until the operators do the quality checking. Vera said, 'They [the QC department] should take samples during the day, we're only the operators, it's not our job.' The motor shop has obviously had plenty of problems because there are a few jokes along the lines of, 'We'll call you when the lines running, but you'll have to be quick!' The operator I spoke to has obviously completely lost faith and confidence in the management. She feels she has contributed to any success the firm has enjoyed and yet has received no recognition or encouragement, 'If they hadn't had conscientious workers on this line they would have been in all sorts of trouble . . . but now I can hardly be bothered to come to work the way they treat us.'

At least in part, the lack of concern over quality is a historical legacy from when quality was seen as even less of a concern. An operator told me that quality had been worse and she recalled a charge-hand who had worked on the final cleaning and inspection function at the end of her line.

> As Vera described it, anything would be passed. 'At the end of the day she'd be sat there not bothering to clean them [the products] and then testing them. They all went out to the customers. The light would be flashing [to indicate a "fail"] but they still got into the box.'

The areas where there is a heightened awareness of the importance of quality are the Peugeot and, particularly, the Nissan lines. When I was first introduced to the Nissan line workers they immediately made it clear that quality was a priority. This was the first line that had even discussed the need for quality with me. On the first day on the Nissan line, after I overheard Gladys ask Heather, 'He's not from the time study department or anything is he?', the operators made it clear that if I had any problems or questions then I should ask. 'We'd rather you asked than let any defects through,' they said, and added, 'Don't worry about speed, just concentrate on getting it right.' This presumably also explains why I found the standard times easier on the Nissan lines since management would not want the operators to rush jobs to earn bonus at the expense of quality. The role of Nissan itself has been highly significant in securing this attitude of quality first:

Irene told me her motto was, 'If in doubt chuck it out' and this is clearly an attempt to ensure Nissan takes delivery of no rejects. 'There's been no complaints about our work so far,' Gladys told me, and apparently they were taken into the office to be given a 'pat on the back' by Nissan recently. When Gladys found out there was to be another visit (by Nissan) tomorrow, she joked, 'Back to congratulate us again, I expect'.

It seems that Nissan have regular visits to the plant, they were here the week before last because of the problems with the pumps from the motor shop. The visits have been by both Japanese and British employees at Nissan. Gladys said that there had been several visits by Nissan and that the Japanese are 'very particular'. The aim of the visits is to 'check that we're doing things just so'. Gladys said that on one visit while she was water testing some jets she thought she saw a very short Japanese man out of the corner of her eye when in fact it was a Nissan manager on his knees checking that the sprays of water were going through the holes properly.

A similar situation existed on the Peugeot lines where the operators were also very aware of the importance of quality and that this was *their* responsibility. On the Peugeot line there were examples of the individual monitoring and accountability practices so prevalent at Nippon CTV:

> Nia told me that each operator has their own colour paint with which they mark the products that they have assembled. She marks each motor and linkage assembly with a red paint pot. I pointed out a yellow mark on one of the sub-assemblies that she had just used and she said, 'That's from France. If there was any problem with that they would write to France telling them what colour was marked on it.' She told me that there had been no problems so far with the work they have produced here.

The importance of the customers of Valleyco in determining what happens in the plant is something to which we will return in a later section of this chapter.

The Charge-hands

The position in the hierarchy of the charge-hands at Valleyco is basically the same as that of the team leaders at Nippon CTV and their roles are formally similar. There are seven in the plant and I was told on a number of occasions by different charge-hands that their responsibilities have been increasing in recent years. The charge-hands are responsible for the direct supervision of the operators and thus for deploying the workers on different jobs and overseeing the piece-rates. Since some workers do not earn any bonus on their jobs the charge-hand will directly instruct workers on occasions, although this is rare. As we have seen above, the operators are given a fairly clear run at working around the piece-rate system where they so choose. However, the charge-hands do occasionally exert their authority:

Whilst Bethan was showing me the valve section, one of the girls who had transferred down from a different line asked her if she could get a tissue from her coat which I thought seemed rather strange. This was later explained by Bethan; apparently, the same girl had worked with her on Friday and had gone to the toilet twice inside an hour, once being away for 15 minutes. 'Well, I'm not having that. My girls don't do it. I gave her a right going over,' Bethan added. Later, still discussing the same topic she said to a colleague, 'If she's on this line, then she has to work. That's the way it is.'

In part this depends on the relationship that the charge-hand has with her operators. Bethan seems stricter than some and I noticed that when she had to go to the office, this often triggered an impromptu coffee break among the line and I also noticed that a number of the line tell Bethan if they are going to the toilet. Conversely, the valve line is physically removed from the jets while Bethan spends the bulk of her time by the jets line and I was informed by May on valves, 'We can get away with quite a lot here, because Bethan's up with the jets. So we can have a chat and a coffee when we like. Bethan's OK, you have to humour her sometimes. Kay has a fag break every now and again and I go with her. I don't smoke anymore, I just go for a skive, you know.' In fact, while the charge-hand will tend to keep an eye on where the operators are and ensure they are at their work stations they make no attempt to influence the speed at which they work under normal circumstances.

The responsibility for output is not tightly controlled at Valleyco in the way that it is for the team leaders at Nippon CTV. Whereas Nippon CTV has monthly schedules, the Valleyco charge-hands are sent a daily production priority list, from which they select and prioritize the jobs for their line(s). There is no formal schedule to which the charge-hands must adhere, and as we saw in Chapter 2, the scheduling is prone to breakdown, at which point informal relations may come into effect. Consequently, the output and performance controls that are employed at Nippon CTV to control and direct the team leaders are not there to affect the charge-hands at Valleyco. The system simply is not in place.

The charge-hands tend to perceive themselves as part of the shop-floor and do not generally associate themselves with management. This situation is created in part by the fact that the charge-hands fulfil their duties by ensuring that the operators can meet their numbers. In other words, the task of the charge-hand is to ensure that there are the necessary supplies available, to distribute the jobs required, and to oversee the production process itself. Since the primary concern of many shop-floor operators is 'making the number' and the charge-hands facilitate this, they are seen as being 'on the same side'. This is a different situation to the one at Nippon CTV, where close monitoring and bureaucratic output controls demand that the team leaders must work to secure efficiencies against the wishes of the operators. As with the team leaders and members at Nippon

CTV, the relationships between individual charge-hands and workers at Valleyco are partially dependent on individual attitudes and personalities.

> I discussed with Heather the changes she has seen as a charge-hand over the last few years. She confirmed what Paula had said about increasing responsibilities for charge-hands and that they had ended up taking over many of the responsibilities of the old supervisor position that has been done away with. I asked her how her job compares to the supervisor position that still exists in the moulding shop and Heather said, 'Oh they're "The working class can kiss my arse" [types], we're not like that'. Heather told me that she believed in seniority and agreed with the last in first out system that operates for shop-floor workers. 'I wouldn't become staff even if they asked me. There they can get rid of anyone. At least here I'm safe.'

With regard to wider responsibilities, the position of the charge-hands appears to be approaching something broadly similar to that of Nippon CTV's team leaders and, typically, the charge-hands spend little time actually working on production. I spoke with Paula, the charge-hand on the motor line, at some length regarding the changes in her job:

> She is unhappy about the increase in her responsibilities—'We never used to have to do all this paperwork'—that has come without any increase in pay. She now has to deal with the operators' time-sheets, and holiday and sick leave sheets, and their attendance. 'Now I have to go to the office with their problems, before it used to go to my manager.' She also has to deal with the daily production list, although at present, this has no relevance for Paula, 'I don't look at it, there's nothing on it for me. I just make what I can.' The charge-hand responsibilities for production have also chopped around, 'Oh, they're always changing that'.

However, the increase in number and range of tasks has not been met with increased authority and, when I examined further Paula's change in responsibilities as charge-hand, she said that while she had more paperwork and takes more of a role in, for example, what used to be personnel functions, she still needs Lee, her manager, to sign any forms. The leading hands are not trusted to sign the sick notes, etc. Paula started off as a charge-hand when she began work here eighteen years ago but, she says, 'I gave it up because it was too much hassle'. She has been a charge-hand on and off ever since. The job brings a better basic wage and there is a fixed bonus. However, the charge-hands have worked out that their wages are only £2 more per week than those of an operator earning 120 PI bonus every day.

Since there is no effective formal line performance measurement by which charge-hands may be monitored they come under pressure on an *ad hoc* and informal basis. This leads to further instances where personalities and inter-relationships inform what goes on. Paula has a strained relationship with the operations director:

She is particularly fed up with Geoff Evans's sarcastic attitude. 'I'll say anything to him and I'll take it but if he gets sarcastic with me and says, "Well, if you can't cope I'll find someone who can," again then I'll bloody tell him to go and do just that. I'm not taking all that for £2 a week extra.'

And the difficulty the charge-hands have in acting as the 'middle person' between the shop-floor and management was clear when a refusal to work was orchestrated by the unions on the grounds of the low temperature on the shop-floor (see Chapter 8). The charge-hands, who are union members, joined the sit-in and Paula commented about Geoff Evans:

'I bet he has us [the charge-hands] in for a bollocking for being in here. He'll say we're supposed to be part of management. I'll bloody give him part of management. Maybe once we're paid management wages . . .'

There is distrust between the shop-floor and the management at Valleyco and this is felt most keenly by the charge-hands who are the 'go-betweens'. This is compounded by the tight and close nature of the local community where 'everyone knows everyone'. Paula warned me at one stage that one of the operators on her line was living with a mate of Geoff Evans, 'So watch what you say to her'. Paula said that once this woman had told her something that Geoff had mentioned to her about the line and Paula said she responded, 'I don't care what Geoff Evans says, I run this fucking line'. Paula also told me about how she clocks on and off for a blind woman who works at Valleyco. She said that if anyone called her into the office then they would give her 'a bollocking' for doing two cards without even bothering to find out the truth. This rather sums up the feelings the shop-floor has towards its management. Though there is no formal record kept, Paula keeps a personal daily record rather similar to the 'Ins and Outs' books at Nippon CTV. She records what is produced every day and she also keeps a record of any problems she has, such as a machine break-down or parts shortage. She does this so that she can counter management criticism and blame. She said that she keeps the record 'or else they'll turn around and complain [about me]. I like to have a record to protect myself.'

The personal antagonism between Paula and some of her managers aside, other charge-hands also feel the lack of trust between the managers and themselves and are correspondingly defensive and secretive. For example, when I was working on a hose line I was asked by Heather to cut some pipe that Derek had already done. Although this was a genuine error of no great consequence, Heather decided to 'hide' the box of pipe I had just completed until it was needed so management did not see it, and she commented, 'The last time this happened and we hid a box under the table, it was there for weeks'.

The distrust and uncertainty felt by the charge-hands is compounded by the inconsistent approach of management and the difficulty they are having in maintaining system discipline and control. The informal approach of, for example, the production controllers undermines the charge-hands as they seek to find order and it also negates any effort toward instilling a 'quality ethos'.

> Bethan complained to me that some of the parts she had completed on an order for Unipart [for retail as replacement parts] had been taken by production control for a rush job. 'They're always doing that. Making up rush jobs from anywhere. Course, that leaves me short again now. That's not the way things should be done. They get it right for a bit and then things soon get lax.' Such shortfalls are apparently 'always made up from Unipart orders' and when I gave Bethan some jets that the viewer had said were not OK she said, 'Oh, I expect they'll send them to Unipart. They send any old stuff to them. It's no good, is it? I get my spares from them.'

As discussed in Chapter 2, the role of personal relationships was highly significant in maintaining the system, which is heavily reliant on informal actions. Bethan mentioned a production controller, Bryn Jones, saying of him, 'He's from the old school and he does things the old way. It's not right but there you are. He'll come up and say, "Look Bethan, I've made a mess of this, can you sort me out with this?" Still, he's OK and he'll rob himself to help out others as well.' The daily production priorities sheet means very little in practice.

> Later in the afternoon, Bryn Jones came up looking for something, he had obviously dropped behind on. 'Well, what a time to tell me he needs that,' said Bethan. This juggling of orders is commonplace. As Bethan pointed out, it's the major customers—Rover, Land Rover, Volvo—that get priority and the others will be put back to make sure that major customers get what they want, 'You can understand it but it's not right really'.

Rush jobs, or 'panics', mean that the charge-hands need to encourage individual workers to produce at a particularly high speed. In these circumstances, Bethan would turn to her more experienced workers. On a number of occasions Bethan and Tony worked together to provide the output for a rush job when a production controller came begging. In fact, rushing to meet panic jobs during periods of directed chaos often meant that workers were encouraged to work faster than the standard times, with the charge-hands using customer demands to legitimate this break from the procedures.

Who's in Charge?

In principle, the production control department is responsible for co-ordinating the schedules and each day a production priority list is passed out to the plant. This list includes the part number, customer, and quantity. The production controllers are also responsible for ensuring the necessary components are available for each job. Production control prints out a job sheet for each job required and this has the components needed and the numbers of each required. These cards then go to the stores where the necessary parts are located and brought lineside along with the job sheet. There is no due date on the job sheets and the charge-hands select the jobs from their daily priority list.

In practice, there is considerable variation from the expected schedule sent by production control. When the charge-hands receive the priority list they will match the list with the job sheets that they already have. They will also match the component requirements with what they have lineside. Commonly, the charge-hands will not have job sheets for the jobs on the priority list or, if they do, they will not have the components required. So, for example, at one stage Paula did not have the components available to make the R6 pump that was required. Therefore, she built up a stock of two pumps for Nissan since that was what she could actually produce.

> When the parts are ready (from stores), they and the job sheet are passed on to Bethan. There was no due date on these cards and Bethan does what she is asked for. However, today was a good day because Bethan had cleared all the jobs that appeared on this list, although she still has plenty of job cards in her box. Quite often the jobs on the priority list have not been sent to Bethan at all. She then informs Lee and he will check the stores are not still waiting for parts or 'someone in production control will be getting a rocket'.

A day spent with the production control department demonstrated why there are such unreliable schedules out on the shop-floor. The customers send production schedules on a regular basis which estimate demand for the forthcoming periods. However, the Valleyco controllers are in regular contact with the customers and are constantly being updated on changes to the assemblers' own schedules and they, in turn, are negotiating what Valleyco can actually get away with sending at any given time. This process relies to a considerable degree on the personal relationship between the two individuals involved. One production controller told me:

> 'Now, I know Paul at Rover and I can say to him, "Look, it says on your order that you've only got two days of so and so . . . How many have you really got?" Then if he's actually got some spare I can get him to accept delivery a bit later than the order says.'

A combination of the assemblers being unable to set stable schedules, the daily negotiation of what must actually be delivered, supply problems, and internal constraints on what can be achieved make the schedules unreliable even on a day-to-day basis. Hence the charge-hands make what they can and the production controllers need to chase what they actually require. The disruption is compounded by last-minute rush orders from customers:

> Production on Bethan's line and I assume others, has been hindered by a degree of confusion in the stores department. The department is being moved because another company is taking control of part of the plant.

Apparently, there are over 100 job cards in the store waiting for parts to be found and distributed to the lines. Bethan had a very quiet morning, 'I've got no bits', and there was no production priority list passed around at all today. However, at about 2.30 p.m. 'all hell broke loose' and the jets line suddenly had two rush orders from Rover that were urgently needed. The orders were met, in a flurry of activity, and I asked Bethan why the rush had come so suddenly. She said that the problem was 'more than likely here'. She did not even have a job card for one of the two orders.

The uncertainty places a clear emphasis on informal relations to actually get the job done. The combined effects of uncertainty and the need for informality to overcome it emerged strongly in the conversations I had with managers (as noted in Chapter 2):

I played ten pin bowling with some of the office staff tonight. I had a couple of chats. In one, I spoke to the commercial manager who told me that a task force had been set up for the business unit managers. The aim was, 'When someone says, "I can't do this because . . .", they can say, "Do this about it". In other words, it's to cover all possibilities and make sure there are no excuses or problems. If they can't do the job then that's it.' And in the second conversation that I had, the engineering project manager told me that what he had learned in working with the shop-floor was that it was 'helping people' that was important. 'It's the personalities that are important in getting your job done.'

The exceptions to this directed chaos, informality, and muddling through are the Nissan and Peugeot lines. While with the production control department, I learned that Nissan has far more reliable schedules, does not entertain nego-tiated settlements on what should be delivered, and does not accept unreli-able delivery patterns. Nissan has imposed a discipline on the scheduling and delivery arrangements and has removed the uncertainty from the scheduling system by insisting that Valleyco deliver to a warehouse near to the Nissan assembly plant in Sunderland. In this way, Nissan has worked contrary to the principles of 'waste elimination' but has secured a more stable and predictable external environment—in effect creating a 'bounded organization' rather in the manner of Nippon CTV's 'internal JIT'. The scheduling for Peugeot has been devolved to the level of the business unit manager and he does not have to work with a production controller. This situation is simplified because the Peugeot cell deals with only two main suppliers, both of which are owned by Valleyco, and a single customer plant. The two lines make six products—two right-hand drive and two left-hand drive linkages and two wiper arms. As with Nissan, Peugeot insists that Valleyco deliver to an intermediary store.

The introduction of the Peugeot cell as a single business unit has devolved and focused responsibility and this has assisted the lines in avoiding some of the chaos which characterizes the operation of the others. Mark Smith, the Peugeot business unit manager, reports directly to Geoff Evans and he has complete responsibility for production, scheduling, and day-to-day personnel issues in running the cell. Mark determines the weekly production target for the cell based on the information which Peugeot faxes through on the preceding Friday. From this he determines targets for each day. These targets are communicated to the operators and charge-hands, and Mark maintains a record of the target and actual production levels on a daily basis. During the research period, the volumes ordered by Peugeot had been dropping and the operators were able to meet the targets, although, as reported earlier, absences could put considerable strain on the remaining workers. Mark told me that workers are not working so fast now but that they are paying a price because their bonus is down. He also told me that Geoff Evans had asked whether the performance levels could be increased so that it would be harder to earn bonus.

The reduction in volumes had allowed Mark to take advantage of the slack and regain control of the production system. Demand for the linkages dropped from a norm of 2,500 units per week during most of the previous twelve months, to only 1,600 units or fewer per week during the time of the study. This reduction in the necessary pace of production had allowed Mark to plan his inventory levels. The higher and fluctuating demand had led to the need for Valleyco to hold stocks in order to meet customer requirements. His intention was to turn his stock around every week, and the cell is designed so that all inventory may be held at the work stations. The lines are very compact and everything is very quickly and easily visible. There are very limited spaces available for holding work-in-progress and any build-up resulting from one worker working faster or slower than another is immediately apparent. Indeed, there are many similarities between this production cell and Nippon CTV regarding the visibility of the processes and the opportunity for management surveillance of individual workers. There are no such similarities with Nippon CTV on the rest of the shop-floor at Valleyco. While there is no moving assembly line, the group pay system, the design of the technology, and the visibility of workers effectively ties their activities together:

> Mark told me that individual bonus systems led to individual workers going faster than others and hence a build-up of stock, 'This [group pay] system means that the operators focus on end products rather than their individual tasks.' Mark knows exactly the individual requirements of each of his operators to meet the daily production targets. He told me, 'Now, she's 100 per cent final assembly [indicating Nia], while then on this job there's only 7.3 hours work per day and then she'll fill in her time elsewhere. While Joy has 60 per cent of her time here and then may be 20 per cent here and 15 per cent there to make up the day and ensure the 280 units target production for the day.' This in-depth knowledge of the daily requirements from each of his operators means any problems are easily visible and are identifiable with a particular individual.

Unlike those in the other areas of the plant, the charge-hands have seen a reduction in their responsibilities as Mark has taken over virtually all supervisory and managerial responsibilities and they basically work as operators and they are included in the group bonus system.

Throughout the plant, the influence that the customers have over what takes place on the shop-floor is enormous. For example, Nissan determines all aspects of the way jobs should be done, although this is prone to modification by the individual operators. Valleyco must adhere to Nissan's demands if it wants the business and the workers themselves have recognized the need in meeting Nissan's demands:

> When she learned that Nissan were coming, the operator started to mark each successfully tested pump as she did it rather than at the end of each tray, 'It's the way they [Nissan] want it done. I don't know why, I suppose they think we might pass some faulty ones. It's our job if we make a mistake.'

Nissan has established the importance of quality by acting swiftly and thoroughly when problems arise:

> In the afternoon, I was given the job of testing some motors for pumps and the reason was intriguing. Apparently, the Nissan visit on Monday was prompted because they had been supplied with a faulty pump by Valleyco. Paula told me that there was only one out of 700 that had been 'dead' but Nissan had still found it and took remarkable action. Not only did they send a visitation down to Valleyco from Sunderland, 'The office knew they were coming on Thursday but nobody ever told us', they also demanded that all the pumps made and in stock were re-tested, hence my job. What is more, two Valleyco workers, a setter and an operator, had gone up to Nissan today to test all the pumps that were actually at the Sunderland plant—an overnight stay being required . . . There is certainly no doubting the power and influence Nissan wield over Valleyco.

The problem was exacerbated because these were the pumps that Paula had made ahead of schedule since she could not produce for Rover. There were therefore boxes and boxes of these pumps as work-in-progress stock that needed to be tested. This is precisely the reason that organizations have sought to reduce the level of internal inventories and it demonstrates the problems of attempting to introduce JIT manufacturing into western brownfield sites that have unreliable suppliers and unreliable equipment.

When Nissan introduced the new Primera model at the plant in Sunderland, the company had brought a car down to Valleyco to show the employees on the Nissan line. Gladys talked about how nice it was before saying, 'I don't like foreign cars, mind'. Nissan's influence over its area of production is pervasive and constantly in the minds of the workers who would see the customer as 'being in charge' rather than their own management:

While I was testing jets, Irene was inserting the eyeballs and adding a gasket. She was using a jig to insert the eyeballs and I asked why she did not have a jig that automatically set the eyeballs in the position required by Nissan. Apparently, Nissan insisted that the job was done in this way because it ensures that each individual jet receives operator attention and thus each is tested and adjusted to specification manually. I asked Gladys about this, 'Well, I suppose it stops us just chucking them into the box without testing them. Not that we would. That's all we could think of. Still, it's their money isn't it? So if that's what Nissan wants, that's what they get. At least it gives us a job.' This is probably true. If the jig was set to accurately aim the eyeballs in the jet, even if 100% water test was used, then almost half the time would be saved.

The clearest possible demonstration of the power and influence of Nissan came on a particular day early in February. The preceding day, Nissan representatives had visited the plant and this had included a brief look around the shop-floor. However, everyone had been well aware that the visit was to take place and consequently all the extra tidying and amending of charts and labels that normally attends a customer visit had been carried out. The previous afternoon Irene and Gladys had stopped work early and tidied their work area while singing, 'We're cleaning the line because Nissan are coming', to the tune of, 'We're all going to the zoo tomorrow', and, 'We are Japanese if you please', to the tune of, 'We are Siamese'. In fact, though the visit was on everyone's lips until 2.30 p.m. when the two representatives from Nissan finally arrived on the shop-floor, it lasted for only five minutes and Gladys for one was rather let down after all the anticipation. However, the next day:

At some time early in the morning, maybe at around 9.00 a.m., I noticed Geoff Evans come past me to see Heather [the Nissan line charge-hand]. Nissan were here again! As far as the shop-floor was concerned this was a complete surprise, although I later heard that Nissan were expected back for a meeting but not back on to the shop-floor. It appeared then, that the two Nissan employees returned and asked to go back on to the shop-floor as well as having the prearranged meetings. I said to Irene that this was a surprise after they had been on to the shop-floor yesterday, and she said that it was, and that Geoff Evans had come out of the office 'flapping' saying, 'Oh my God, Nissan are here!' This news led to Heather and the others rushing around tidying up, boxing up finished goods, unboxing and putting raw materials into containers and adding *kanban* cards to the work-in-progress bins. Bearing in mind that there was a visit yesterday, there appeared to be plenty of extra work to do just a few hours later. Whilst she was hurrying around, Heather came over to me to tell me what I was making, 'These are filler necks for the basic model in case any silly cow asks you'. And I said, 'So this is where the worrying starts,' and Heather replied, 'That's how we stay in business, by worrying'.

Soon after we got back from break the Nissan people, Gavin Millward (a sales manager), Lee Eggar, and another Valleyco manager arrived on the line. The man was today wearing a blue Nissan padded jacket and had a stop watch! He started to time Gladys as she was carrying out the water testing. He told Gladys they were looking for ways of speeding up the process. He may also have timed Irene who was sat next to her, Irene did not know if he had or not. When I saw the stop watch I became quite nervous at the thought that they may come over to me. I rushed through the rest of the filler necks before they finished with Gladys! In all, the Nissan employees stayed on the line for about an hour and a half. The line only has about seven or eight work stations, and five operators including me, so they gave the place a good going over. Gladys had clearly been surprised to be asked if, 'I could take just a few timings', and said that she had just gone her 'normal' speed. However, she was certainly keen that the Nissan people will not think her a slow worker and I expect that she actually went faster than her average speed over a day, which is still around the maximum bonus level. When Gladys finished one testing job they (the Nissan people) asked her to go on to another one and as she stood up Lee whispered to her out of the corner of his mouth, 'Slow down'. Irene said that she had heard Lee say, 'Of course, she couldn't keep this speed up all day' to the Nissan timer. Gladys did the other test at a reduced speed, although she said that the pressure I had used to assemble the jets she was testing meant that the right jet went into the hole without needing adjusting, 'So how could I make that slower!' This was the first time Nissan had timed any jobs apparently. They also timed Helen on some containers, and Gladys said, 'Look at her going like hell'. So Lee had not got a whispered message to her!

Once Nissan had left I went over to Gladys and Irene to find out what the visit was all about and why they had been timed. They did not know and Gladys in particular was obviously upset and annoyed that the management had not told her what they had wanted, 'I just went my normal speed, if they had wanted anything different they should have come and told us'. The lack of information and surprise nature of the visit had left the operators confused as to the reasons behind it and worried about the implications of the visit. There have been rumours that Valleyco might lose the Nissan business, especially since the problems that they have had on the motor shop line recently. There was speculation as to what the visit may mean. Valleyco have been having trouble with the bought-in jet heads, from a plastics supplier in Birmingham. One of the eye cavities has been too large. Gladys told me that this problem has led to arrears building up with the jet. She said that 900 per day are due and they have been 'scraping together 500 to send off'. This is while 'Nissan rant and rave down the phone'. The problem is with the moulding tool which is Valleyco's. These problems have led the operators to believe that the Valleyco management has been blaming the paucity of supply on what they called 'operator trouble' rather than telling Nissan the truth. I should add that they have no proof of this, but I was told, 'If anything ever goes wrong, it's always "operator trouble"'. Hence, when Nissan arrived today the girls thought that they maybe were checking on their performance, so it was not surprising that Gladys was eager to work fast and 'show that I'm a good worker . . . the problems aren't our fault. At least they know we can do the job.' Still, Gladys was not very happy about the whole episode—'Can you be sacked for working too fast?' she asked Irene and me.

Heather was not clear regarding the reason behind the timings but she went to see Lee. He told her to come back later and this meant that the confusion and speculation continued until the afternoon. Eventually, Heather came back to report that the visit had gone 'brilliant' and that the timings were with regard to 'costing'. She also said that Lee 'hadn't been able to get away and tell the operators not to go too fast'.

This particular visit by Nissan was unusual in that it was a surprise and that timings were taken; knowledge of operator timings means Nissan knows what price it should be charged for this product because it is involved with the suppliers of the raw materials. All of Valleyco's main customers regularly visit the shop-floor and check the practices employed, further establishing their authority and the need for quality in the minds of both the operators and the management. Valleyco is systematically audited and graded, typically annually, by its customers, with the threat that unsatisfactory performance will result in the business being sourced elsewhere. This is unlikely to prove merely an idle threat since the car components industry has been through considerable restructuring during the 1990s as the car assemblers reduce their supply base (Turnbull *et al.* 1993).

The plant management is also under considerable pressure from the French owners and the threat of closure still hangs over the site. The plant is regularly visited by Valleyco's senior management:

Today, Charles Jacques, the head of this Valleyco division in Europe, visited the plant. I did not notice him, but apparently he did stroll around the plant. Derek knew he was coming. 'I thought something was up because Geoff Evans was in at 6.30 in the morning and you don't often see that.' Apparently, according to Sue [with whom I lodged during the research], Jacques visits once per month and today listened to presentations from each department (hence the anxiety I saw with some members of the office staff yesterday). Normally, Jacques just talks to the heads of each department. Sue said to me, 'The French don't just leave us to get on with it. They want to know what we're up to.'

SUMMARY

This chapter describes the process of management control at the Valleyco plant. We have seen that, in contrast to the situation at Nippon CTV, the Valleyco plant management has various different practices for different areas of the shop-floor. The focal point for management at Valleyco is productivity, and quality control is haphazard. At Nippon CTV, productivity performance is relatively assured and management's attention is focused on quality control and improvement. Also, when compared with the process of management control at Nippon CTV, the situation at Valleyco is far more prone to informal decision making and the significance of inter-personal relations is also amplified. Another distinction between the two cases is the degree to which external influences, particularly the customers, impact upon the internal situation at Valleyco.

While Nippon CTV has decoupled its manufacturing operations from numerous external sources of uncertainty, Valleyco's failure to secure such stability has placed additional emphasis on internal flexibility and informality. In the case of the Nissan line at the plant, there is some evidence of increased stability and also a demonstration of the effect that major customers may have on an organization's internal management practices and structure. This may be considered evidence of coercive pressure toward isomorphism and the adoption of the lean production model (see DiMaggio and Powell 1983). However, the problems in implementing just-in-time production in a western context are very clear in the Valleyco case.

The following chapters explore the dynamics of the shop-floor in more detail, particularly with regard to the role played by workers, the extent of their involvement, and the reasons behind their actions.

5

What Do Workers Do? Patterns of Negotiated Order

'No one's going to come and help you out on this side. I've stuck it out and I feel literally exhausted. I mean this isn't hard manual work but it's the tension that gets to you. Nobody likes a pile of work sat beside them. It's the rushing. The work's piling up and you get worked up, don't you? You get tensed. It can be exhausting sometimes.'

Lesley, P3 line worker, Nippon CTV.

INTRODUCTION

The preceding two chapters describe the process of control in each of the two case plants. As we have seen, the management control strategies of Valleyco and Nippon CTV are both founded on output or technological controls which are underpinned by forms of bureaucracy. Still, the two cases differ in a number of ways and in practice the process of control varies between the two plants and even between areas within a single plant. Following on from the descriptions of the management control strategies in place, this chapter documents what workers do, particularly in relation to those control strategies. This chapter provides evidence that workers combine aspects of what we may call co-operation and resistance in their everyday working lives. Workers also face differing degrees of choice; opportunities for resistance may be severely restricted and the scope for choice very narrowly defined. This chapter reveals that individual workers engage in very different behaviours within a similar context, emphasizing the importance of subjectivity in discussing worker action.

WORKING AT NIPPON CTV

Stuffing Boards

The day begins with a buzzer just before 8.00 a.m. which signals the morning meeting. In the panel shop, the workers from the line assemble at the 'bottom' end beside the solder bath and the team leader reads from a photocopied sheet that has been distributed by the office staff via Marcia or Joan (see Figure 7 for an example). Each morning, Angie tells P3 the output performance of their own line. This is accompanied by a comment on the line's performance, 'So, well done. That was very good, keep it up.' As a proxy measure for this line's quality, the quality performance of the final line which is supplied by P3 is also announced on a daily basis, 'That was very good so let's keep up the good

F1: 8.3% 470; F2: 82.6% 920; F3: 89.9% 590; F4: 93.9% 590;
F5: 89.0% 520

B. Overtime tonight 4 hrs complete p8, p9, T/A. test only
    p3, p7, f5 4 hrs complete. B/station.
    2 hrs f1.
B. Overtime tomorrow 4 hrs p8, p9, p3, p7, test T/A. B/station
    4 hrs f5.
B. All areas close down arrear batches A.S.A.P.
    Also P/shop must close down this month's batches before they are finished in finals.
B. The managers 9.30 meeting will take place back in the P/shop coffee lounge from
    today.
F. 2812 DBT pre-prod to be completed today.
P. Pre-prod 21 RDNT panels to be made in panel shop today
B. T/A training today 4.00 with C. Kelly. p / T.A + 2 from finals
P. All areas make sure all coffee room tables are cleaned after each break time.
    8.00/ 10.45/ 1.30/ 3.45 each day.
B. A ladies watch has been handed in. Also a small leather wallett. If lost
    contact M. Gates.
B. Read out briefing note.

F1 + 86 ; F2 +108; F3+127; F4 +99; F5 −334

FIG. 7 The Team Leader's Morning Briefing Sheet, Nippon CTV
Note: This was handwritten on a page of a diary.

work on that as well'. At the end of each meeting, which is scheduled for five
minutes but normally lasts nearer two, the team leader asks, 'Anybody got any
questions?' or, 'Any problems?'

Sometimes the performance has not been to Angie's satisfaction,

> We had completed more than 840 boards yesterday and this was above
> schedule. However, quality was not so good and Angie warned us in a
> stern voice. She broke the faults down by section of the line and read out
> that there had been 48 faults attributable to insertion, 'I've had a word
> with a few people on the line and they know things have got to improve.
> Everyone must make an extra effort, this isn't good enough.' Everybody
> just stood there. Angie rounded off the meeting by asking, 'Any problems?'
> There was none.

In fact, throughout the research period there were only two occasions when
workers had a question. Both times, this was to ask when some replacement air-
powered solder clippers would be available; these make the clipping of excess
solder from the back of the boards much easier than with the manual clippers.
Workers often pay scant attention to the content of the morning meeting, chatting while Angie is reading from her sheet or timing their arrival at the end of
the line to coincide with the end of the meeting. Indeed, one member seemed
to time her return from the toilet perfectly in conjunction with, 'Any problems?'
each morning. Feedback is never made at an individual level in these meetings. The workers' attitude to these meetings is an example of the way in which
they distance themselves from the company's activities. This will be discussed
further in Chapter 6.

Just before 8.05 a.m. the buzzer goes again and all the members take their places at lineside. The line then begins to move. On the insertion side of the line, each individual operator has a series of small components to be inserted while the board moves across their position on the line. The workers have to sit very close together and there is very little room to work up the line or to catch up once the board has moved past the member. As mentioned in Chapter 2, each individual piece has a standard time for insertion, normally 2.7 seconds, and the standard linespeed and labour level typically give each worker ten or eleven pieces and a cycle time of just under thirty seconds. The line hypnotizes you after a while and when it stops it seems as if it is going backwards. I became almost entranced by it on occasions. Sometimes if you are walking past, or if you stare at it, the line seems not to be moving. It can make you feel seasick. Most of the inserters have personal stereos and they have conversations as they work. The team leader uses the level of chatter on the line to decide if she can increase the linespeed. If an individual inserter has trouble keeping up with the line then she may leave a board. She then calls, 'Left set' and one of the two off-line workers will finish what has been missed further down the line. If a member is having difficulty she will call, 'Help's wanted' to attract the attention of an off-liner.

The workers will sit at their place on the line until breaks at 9.00 a.m. and then around 11.00 a.m., when there are gaps of about three minutes each left in the line so that workers may, one by one, take a toilet break. Nippon CTV inserted a radio cord on the line in an attempt to restrict the time that the operators can listen to the radio to one hour in the morning and one hour in the afternoon. However, there have been faults with the cord and most operators bring their own personal stereos:

> Almost all appear to listen to Radio One and 'Our Tune' [an agony aunt confessional part of a morning show] is greeted with great excitement. Those not actually listening to the radio are all told when it is starting and then turn their radios on for it. The line goes almost completely quiet. Because I don't have a radio, Vanessa gives me a running commentary on what is happening. Throughout the monologue from Simon Bates [the presenter], the silence is broken only by, 'Oh no, don't go back to him,' and 'That's my girl, dump the bastard'-type advice from the line. When the monologue is over, the events of the day's story are discussed, often in some detail . . . Mary, the line feeder, is meant to leave six gaps for the operators to go to the toilet at about 9 and then at 11 each morning. However, since 'Our Tune' starts at about 11 every morning, she waits until it has been on before leaving the gaps.

The women at the head of the P3 line seem to get on well and throughout the line sub-groups tend to form. The formation of these groups is helped by the fact that the majority of workers do not move from 'their' position on the line. It is necessary to show the ability to work on different jobs in different parts of the factory when moving to a Grade Two position but once they have done that, members typically return to their original work station. Workers must move if so instructed by their team leader but most work in the same position each day and it is unusual for someone to move to a different section of the line. In fact, most operators are very loath to move around and the request to move is often seen as a form of punishment. The opportunity to form relationships with fellow workers is very important in order to alleviate the tedium of the line and also to help individual workers achieve the performance targets and avoid disciplinary measures.

> As we worked during the afternoon, Janie began to make the odd mistake that was spotted further down the line. These were pieces that she had not inserted and that had been noticed because her fellow workers were inserting another component near to the space. This happened at least half a dozen times during the afternoon. The joke on the line was, 'Wait until after four o'clock, that's when the mistakes really start,' and sure enough it was true.

This worker camaraderie was vital for Janie who had had a very high number of rejects two months previously (see Chapter 3). On this particular day, Janie was recorded as having had two rejects but that number would have at least quadrupled without the help of her workmates in identifying and correcting her mistakes. The reject charts above the heads of the workers keep the pressure very visibly on the workers to perform to management's requirements and also symbolically illustrate the importance of quality. Janie was one of the operators who had earned the acceptance of the more experienced workers and hence she was helped. Other workers did not receive the same support and were openly criticized by their workmates if they did not feel that the member in question had 'been trying'. The inter-personal relations between workers and the ensuing peer pressure will be discussed in the following chapter.

The complex and contradictory nature of workplace relations is amply illustrated in this vignette for, while the informal activity of the line has assisted a fellow operator in avoiding possible sanction, the end result for Nippon CTV's management was better quality. Indeed, it may be that this informal action actually perpetuates the system because it keeps the reject records down. Without the informal action helping individuals to avoid rejects, the reject records would be such that (as required by the formal procedures), Nippon CTV's team leaders would have to counsel and threaten half the line with dismissal each month—clearly an impossible scenario.

The members at the end of the line also play an important dual role in maintaining high quality while restricting the number of rejects that are actually booked against individuals. When I first joined P3, Elsie worked at the end of the line just before inspection and she played a very significant role in the way the line ran in practice. She would call up the line, warning that there were mistakes—'R306 reversed', 'Push T134 further in'—and insert missing components before they reached inspection. Elsie was responsible for inserting the audio-visual (AV) and text panels that come from one of the supplier panel lines.

Vanessa told me that Elsie had not 'been on [small component] insertion but she could see it was hard sometimes. The thing I hate is the people who have never even done insertion sat at the end of the line booking every little mistake. They couldn't even do this job themselves.' Part of Elsie's responsibility was to check the components which lie under the panels she inserts and she would also check other parts of the board if she had time.

However, Elsie would also get very frustrated and become abusive to the operators—'Tell that stupid bitch that I'm not putting R301 in anymore, please' —if the same mistakes kept recurring, and she would not keep correcting the same mistake. This was very much a personal point of view from Elsie, 'I don't think it's fair to book the girls for all these things [bent pins and not connecteds]. Some of them are so loose anyway. When I was on inspection, I didn't book them for things like that. I just put them in myself. I had terrible rows with Angie about it. The silly old bitch.' The team leader, Angie, had moved Elsie from the inspection position. There is some leeway for the inspectors regarding whether they actually book all of the mistakes that they notice. However, they are themselves under pressure since any defects which they do not detect are booked against them by the after-bath inspectors (see Chapter 3) and because the team leaders and quality department have an anticipated number of rejects that they expect to see from each of the various panels. They will be suspicious if the number is low.

> The quality checker told me that there are 'expectations' of the number of defects that will be found from each panel. So inspectors are expected to book a certain number. 'If we don't book them, we'll get told off for helping the girls up the line by Angie.'

Occasionally, workers find that they are in positions on the line that they do not like or cannot do. In most cases workers are left to sort themselves out on a 'sink or swim' basis. It is very rare for workers to be able to engineer a move for themselves. This often means workers need to rely on their fellow team members for help. A young worker on the after-bath side of the line was in this situation:

> Trini has been at the plant for nearly one year but she started on insertion. She could not do that too well and after about two months at Nippon CTV she was told to change to this (clipping and inspection) job and that she 'had two and a half days to get it' or she would be out. Gail (an experienced worker) had trained her up and she had 'got it' in that time, 'I'd have told them that she had got it even if she hadn't. I wouldn't push anyone out on to the dole,' said Gail. It was clear that Gail had taken Trini under her wing and ensured that she would be able to carry out the job to an acceptable level.

The paucity of true flexibility is evident from the problems which arise on the insertion side of the line when members are borrowed from other lines and cannot match the linespeed. Often the stand-ins are not able to keep up with the line in the way that those who regularly work on insertion can. This means that these operators are constantly calling out for help or leaving sets and the team leader will then take one or two components from them and pass these to more experienced and competent workers. Angie knows which of her regular inserters can comfortably cope with an extra piece and she relies on the co-operation of these members to be able to balance the line and juggle the workload to keep the line moving at as high a speed as possible. Angie has a lot of tacit knowledge about what her line can achieve on each panel.

> Each operator will have about ten pieces. Vanessa had ten today but was given an extra piece because one of the newer girls could not keep up with the linespeed. This happened regularly while I was on the line, the more experienced, 'better' workers would be 'awarded' additional pieces.

It is very difficult for the workers on insertion to gain any respite from the pressure and rhythm of work incorporated into the conveyer belt. It is not possible to work up or down the line by more than a few centimetres, nor is there any opportunity for a break of more than a split second or else the board will be beyond the reach of the inserter. There are two ways in which the operators do enact some form of regulation of effort. Operators can save a few seconds to survive the system when they are under pressure by throwing the components on to the board without actually inserting them. These will be recorded by the inspectors as 'not connected' rather than as 'missing'. Under the rules of the quality control system, an operator is allowed ten 'not connecteds' before a defect is recorded against their name. However, this practice is likely to be noticed either by the end of line inspectors or by the off-liners.

> Today there was an inserter who had been borrowed from P7 on our line covering an absentee. She was clearly having problems . . . To the explicit and verbal frustration of the off-line senior member, she had been continually calling, 'Help's wanted' or, 'Left set' to attract the attention of the off-liners. Her problem centred around the fact that she was bending the legs in the 'heat sink' and she had apparently announced to Sara (the senior member), 'I can't do this' and had then proceeded to 'just chuck them on to the side of the board'. I know this because Sara was then stood at the top of the line telling everyone within earshot all about it. Sara was clearly pissed off, 'She's just not trying'. This drew the response from the operators on the line, 'Well, we all have to do it so she should too'.
> A little later the stand-in fell behind and called Sara for help. Sara came back up to the top end of the line and said, 'She was calling for help and she was only down to here,' indicating a line perpendicular to her right arm. 'I told her she was going to have to be further down than that before I was going to help her, it's pathetic.' In other words, Sara had told her that she must be stretching further down toward the next inserter before calling for help. This had received general consent from Sara's audience at the top of the line. Sara told Angie about the problems and she just shrugged and pulled a face, but I later overheard Angie say, 'Well, she'll not work on my line again'.

Note that this is consistent with the peer pressure to be seen as 'trying' that was mentioned earlier and which will be discussed in Chapter 6.

The other way the operators have of exerting some counter-control, and the only restriction on output that the operators may be able to secure, is through a marginal effect on the 'tweaking up' of the linespeed by the team leader (see Chapter 3). Angie bases this on her reading of the relative ease of the line in keeping to the speed. She uses the number of calls for help and the amount of conversation as indications of how hard pressed the operators are. Eventually, even with the experienced operators carrying extra pieces, the line will be pushed until a number of different workers cannot keep the pace and the off-liners are continually needed to help out. At this point the team leader will slightly reduce the linespeed. There were one or two occasions during the research when the experienced operators at the head of the line called for help and did not continue to work at an increasing speed even though it did seem that it would have been within their capabilities to do so.

Clipping and Soldering

The after-bath side of the line offers a slightly different experience of working at Nippon CTV. Since the panels are not actually fixed into the belt there is slightly more space for an operator either to work ahead or to push panels back if the operator drops behind. However, there is no room for storing panels and it is not possible to pile up panels without this action being noticed. In a way the pressure is greater because the off-liners do not help out as they do on insertion and it is very rare for an after-bath member to be able to get help if they fall behind:

> Lesley felt that working on insertion was easier than this side (after-bath). 'If you get behind there, you can call for help. This side it just piles up. No one's going to come and help you out on this side. I've stuck it out and I feel literally exhausted. I mean this isn't hard manual work but it's the tension that gets to you. Nobody likes a pile of work sat beside them. It's the rushing. The work's piling up and you get worked up, don't you? You get tensed. It can be exhausting sometimes.'

There are one or two ways in which individuals are able to cope with their work and vary their work speed slightly without falling behind the line. Dan works on the final tuning and testing of the panels before they go to the final assembly line. Dan has an 'overdrive' speed at which he can operate in short bursts to clear a backlog if he starts to fall behind. He certainly would not, and could not, work at this speed for long and if he cannot put in a burst to get himself out of trouble he will push the panels back up the line. His primary concern is to keep his quality record clear.

> Dan will pile up panels rather than rushing too fast and getting rejects (booked against him). He can get into trouble for passing too many defective

panels but not for having to trolley up some panels if he is under real pressure. His main objective for his own best interests is to keep his rejects sheet 'green'. I asked if this meant he could take a rest when he wanted and trolley up a few, 'No, Ann [the tests senior member] knows if you're just playing up and slacking. She knows all about these tests and she'll know if it's a difficult panel or if the gear is "jigging" [malfunctioning]. We can't get away with that.' Ann regularly sits in on tests to cover changeovers when more than one panel is passing along the line.

Thus, as with the situation of Angie and the inserters, the tacit knowledge of Ann restricts the opportunities for workers to exert counter-control. The other way in which Dan and Sharon (who also works on the test gear) can cope if they are falling behind is by failing a board early in the test routine. Each board has a test cycle of around thirty seconds involving a job manual of twenty-five instructions. Boards which Dan or Sharon fail are passed back to the technical assistants (TAs) who are situated directly beside the test gear. The panels are retested and, where necessary, reworked. If the TAs do not find a fault then the board is recorded as a NAF which, I believe, stands for 'no actual fault'.

Under the quality control procedures, the TAs and the senior member must keep aware of the number of boards tested and the number waiting. The problems that are fixed by the TAs are also recorded on the sheets for the quality department. Things do not run smoothly today and the test gears are constantly playing up. There are also many NAFs being recorded by the TAs. NAFs appear to be a way of coping when the testers are under extreme pressure because of the speed of the line or test gear problems. The full test of a panel may take half a minute or so but if there is no picture up on the screen then the board can be put to one side as a defect within a handful of seconds. Half a dozen boards recorded as defects and then identified as good by the TAs can get a tester back on top of the flow of work with no real harm done. Of course, the number of NAFs is recorded and I have no doubt that Nippon CTV are aware that this may happen. Certainly the TAs see it, but because the test jigs appear so unreliable on occasions there is often room for doubt on the cause of the NAF. [The recording of NAFs was the source of considerable tension between Dan and the TAs in particular.]

The unreliability of the jigs for testing the panels was one of the few examples where the system did not function entirely as expected at Nippon CTV. The resulting uncertainty presented workers with an opportunity for regaining some control over their work situation.

The automated parts checker (APC) at the mid-point on the after-bath side of the line was also prone to unreliability, although this actually made Gilly's job more difficult. The APC determines the speed at which Gilly can pass the panels and those which fail the test take longer. Occasionally the APC would mistakenly record a good panel as a reject and consequently slow Gilly unnecessarily. She shows some discretion in interpreting the results of the APC because of its habit of failing good boards. If she realized that certain fail messages kept recurring and were not accurate when the board was checked manually, then she would ignore the APC and pass the board herself. If she did not do this the boards would very quickly begin to pile up at her work station.

In between the APC and the test gear is the 'mods' (modification) area of the line. With each section linked by the conveyor belt the speed at which they work has a knock-on effect down the line:

> When Lesley and Molly are on their own (on mods) the panels tend to pile up in front of them. This depends on how quickly Gilly on the APC works. Gilly goes quickly and according to the mods people, 'She's a git, so that means mods get plenty to do. The speed available has been increased because of the second APC machine that was recently brought in, but there's still just the two of us here normally.'

In turn, if the mods section goes quickly then the test area gets swamped. Of course, the mods section must go as quickly as they can to keep up with the APCs. Hence, each section, and each individual member of the line, must work as quickly as the fastest station or they will get behind. This situation is different from that on the insertion side of the line where the line itself determines work speed. These pressures create problems between workers; Gilly is a 'git' for going so fast but if she did not work so quickly, the panels would pile up at her station. It was clear during the research period that there was long-term tension between the APC operator and the mods people. Strife between workers was prevalent during my time at Nippon CTV and will form a major point of discussion for the following chapter.

As with insertion workers, operators on the after-bath side of the line displayed a limited degree of informality in how certain procedures were employed. As on the insertion side, individuals needed to act with some discretion over certain rules but did not jeopardize the quality of production *per se*. On the after-bath side, it is Bertha (a senior member) who helps individual members, not so much to avoid being initially booked for mistakes, but to avoid the prescribed chastisement:

> I asked Bertha about the counselling of operators should they have more than 20 rejects in a month. Bertha said counselling would be necessary 'only in exceptional circumstances'. I noted that over half of the operators had 20 plus rejects on the monthly chart displayed for April. Bertha said that not all of those members would have been into the coffee lounge (for counselling). The area where Bertha had shown discretion was in the difference in nature of the jobs, some of which are more difficult than others. She did not think that this was 'fair' and would do her best to ensure that those with the most difficult jobs were not 'unfairly' punished.

Bertha told me that she does not book all of the mistakes that are made on to the display sheets above the operators' heads, 'That knocks the girls down, I want to bring them up and make them happy. It's not fair else.' Bertha is one I would describe as much more of a 'mother figure' than Angie. All the errors, including those from the final line and the APC, are fed in [to the computer] but Bertha told me that she tries to keep everyone on green or yellow if she can.

As noted earlier, this informality may act as a 'safety valve' in releasing some of the pressures which the formal system creates since strict adherence to the formal procedures would result in a large number of operators recording the red 'danger' sign on their individual performance charts. Something similar was identifiable on the insertion side of the line after the regular senior member, Sara, was taken ill. Her replacement as an off-line worker on insertion was a regular Grade Two operator and she told me that she tried to keep everyone below twenty recorded rejects if she could. However, as in the other areas of potential worker discretion, the system has a way of monitoring and restricting such 'misbehaviour'.

The restrictions on Bertha's discretion, primarily, are the TAs who keep their own records and know the reject rate themselves. As far as I could gather, Bertha can ignore the odd mistake, but with the TAs over her shoulder anything too obvious has to be booked. 'I had to do something, I couldn't keep that quiet,' she said of the mistakes Tania has been making. She will keep things under wraps, dealing with it herself 'for as long as I can get away with it. Sometimes it's too big to ignore.'

According to Bertha, Tania has 'an attitude problem'. This first came to my attention when Tania was told off by Angie and told that she was not allowed to talk on the line any more because she had had too many rejects. Tania had been a senior member at Nippon CTV before she left to have a child. She returned as an operator and was stationed on after-bath. The three experienced operators with whom I spoke were all of the opinion that Tania was 'playing up deliberately' in an attempt to get moved because she does not like the cutting and soldering job she has now. Apparently, she would like to be reworking the boards which fail the APC. The speed of this job is not dictated by the line and involves far more variety in activity. All three expected that Tania would be counselled the following day. They were clear that she was 'playing up' and that 'her job is not dictated by her'.

The 'problems with Tania' continued the next day. She was stationed next to a stand-in worker who was covering an absentee. As with insertion, the speed of the conveyor results in problems for members who are not used to doing a particular job. Either this causes a backlog of boards awaiting soldering and inspection or mistakes are made in trying to keep up. Tania, as an experienced worker, was given the responsibility of checking the stand-in's work as well as carrying out her own tasks. Tania claimed that she did not have enough time to cope with her own job and check someone else. Gail (a close friend of Bertha who concurred on what Tania was 'up to') was the next worker on the line and she was inspecting the boards, identifying rejects attributable to both Tania and the stand-in and reporting these to Bertha.

Three or four times Gail reported a succession of rejects to Bertha who then went to speak to Tania and the stand-in. It was clear that Bertha was sympathetic to the stand-in's problems in keeping up on an unfamiliar job but Tania was causing her considerable frustration, 'Oh, she'll be the death of me that one' and 'I'll swing for her', she would say to Gail as she went back to her desk. To Tania herself Bertha attempted some gentle cajoling, 'What's the matter, my love?' but Tania was adamant that they were expecting too much of her and it was all she could do to keep up. It was at this time that Tania was taken into the coffee lounge to be counselled by Angie.

During the research period, the unrest with Tania continued. Tania was not given the job she wanted nor allowed to move from the after-bath side of the line, although she was tried at different stations. The last I heard before I left was that Angie had taken her back into the coffee lounge and given her a warning. Tania had asked for a transfer to another line but this had been refused.

In contrast to Tania's failed efforts, one or two members did manage to avoid a particular job that they did not like. On two separate occasions, Dan told me that he had been moved from the test gear job to stand in for someone but that he had had a very large number of rejects—'200 or something'—and that he had complained that he had had no training and did not really know what was required. This had been enough to get him moved back to the test gear job. Operators who have a regular position at which they are competent can normally ensure that they remain there as long as the senior member or team leader does not, as in the case of Tania, believe that the member is being deliberately obstructive and difficult. Gilly had been moved and could not do the particular job she had been given now. 'I don't care, it's not my job to do this. I didn't ask to move,' she said to me. She could not formally refuse to move but by failing to do an acceptable job she was able to secure a move back to the job that she had demonstrated that she could do well.

What Workers Don't Do

There are occasions when the workers will openly defy the wishes of Nippon CTV management, although these are few and far between. For example, numbers of operators do not wear their blue company jackets—in a conscious act of distancing themselves from the company's expectations.

> Gail has been here five years and feels things have changed noticeably in that period, 'They're much stricter now'. Gail was scathing of at least some of the developments. 'They treat us like children the way they talk to

us sometimes. I mean I've got four kids of my own and there I am being taken into the coffee lounge and being told to wear my blue jacket. And these cards. I mean, you know if you've done good work or not, you don't need these cards. They'll tell you how you've done. It's just laughable. You have to laugh at them, some of the rules. We do. We have a good laugh sometimes.' Gail gave the example of the pink origami swan that had been introduced (at the instigation of a Japanese engineer) to mark a defect-free week from an operator. This was to have been placed on the shelf above the worker but that idea had been abandoned—'We kicked up a stink'.

The workers have also been successful in resisting rather more significant potential changes on the line. Management had tried to introduce two-handed insertion which is the norm in Japan, where there is a standard time of 2.5 seconds per piece compared to 2.7 seconds in the UK.

The company had made attempts to dictate the way in which people work to insert the pieces and insisted that one hand was used to feed the other for insertion. They then said that operators should use the left hand for some pieces and the right hand for others. This had happened before I arrived at the plant but was mentioned to me on more than one occasion. The inserters had refused to do it. Vanessa told me, 'It was alright for some of the parts, but not for all of them. Some you can only do with the hand you use most, you know. But they were stood over us demanding we do it. You can only go as fast as your arms can. They threatened to take us off the line if we couldn't do it. But it was just no good. Some of the girls were saying that they would go home if they made us do that. They were stood over us, you know, threatening our jobs if we didn't. In the end they gave up with that. But we're supposed to do the feeding from left to right. They [the team leaders] can tell us off and warn us if we don't. They shouldn't do things like that. It's not right. It ruins the atmosphere of the place. We're supposed to work as a team down here, but it's no good if it's just us down here. It should include managers. They should try doing these jobs. They just stand there over you, telling you what to do. They just don't understand it.'

The workers are overt in their eagerness for every break from the line. A power cut which stopped the line was greeted with a huge cheer and each break time and the end of the day is anticipated by a countdown of the minutes and seconds leading up to that time. There is a big clock at the end of the P3 line with one of the operators acting as the timekeeper. When the buzzer sounds for the end of the day there is a terrific rush for the exits. On the last day of my research period I recorded the following:

In my last few minutes in the factory I stopped to record, and savour with a smile, the stampede-like exit of the members when the buzzer sounds. I stood beside P3 and within 15 seconds of the buzzer sounding there was only one operator stood anywhere near the line. The whole panel shop [of nearly 400 people] was deserted within two minutes.

Nippon CTV often needs people to work overtime and it is a contractual obligation for all operators to be available for a 'reasonable' amount of overtime (see Chapter 3). In fact there are some people who like to work overtime and there are others who will take considerable steps to avoid doing so. Bertha had managed to be excused from overtime on occasions, 'Sometimes they want the whole line in. You have to give a good reason for not being able to work then. I just say being on the same job will make me ill and I'll be off the next day. That works to get me off if I don't want to work.' As an experienced senior member, Bertha can expect some informal favours from her superiors. Fred Woodhead, the personnel manager at Nippon CTV, described his organization as 'schizophrenic'—'people who have contributed will receive understanding'. However, the company will expect an explanation of the individual's situation and will intrude into the private life of individuals in making judgements on the extent of that 'understanding'.

> Lesley does not like doing overtime and was able to avoid it last year. Her husband works nights and so if she worked overtime they would not see each other. She had been called upon to explain why she was not volunteering for overtime and been advised in the coffee lounge that she should volunteer for some Friday afternoons. She had reluctantly done so but had so far managed to avoid actually doing any. She told me, 'During the high season they do tend to demand the whole line works sometimes.' The consensus on the line was that overtime should be 'a personal choice'. Of those that I spoke to about overtime, several had clearly taken steps to avoid doing any and had been successful. There are always those who need the money to take their place. All, however, had been called upon to give reasons and make excuses for why they were not willing or able to do overtime.

Elsie had been characteristically inimitable when Angie had looked for volunteers for overtime one evening, 'I told her NO WAY. This is my sex night! Me and my man. I don't want to work no overtime tonight.'

There are other aspects of the workplace relationship which demonstrate the perceptions and attitudes of workers toward Nippon CTV and these will be discussed further in Chapters 6 and 7.

WORKING AT VALLEYCO

As discussed in Chapter 4, there is much more uncertainty and chaos on the shop-floor at Valleyco and this gives the workers more space to be able to influence their experience of work than is available to the workers at Nippon CTV.

As was made evident in that chapter, the operators can vary their work speed during the course of a day because their bonus is calculated *daily* on a piece-rate system. Unlike the members at Nippon CTV, the workforce at Valleyco are not kept working 'buzzer to buzzer' and have the opportunity to take informal coffee, toilet, and 'fag' breaks as well as finishing work early 'to tidy up'. At an individual level, the workers will restrict output to avoid increases in job timings or they may choose not even to attempt to earn bonus but just to collect the basic rate. Workers will try and bluff timers to get a 'good timing' for new jobs and they are able to organize themselves informally to aid their work and make things easier for themselves. However, the introduction of group-based pay on the Peugeot cell began to restrict workers' opportunities to act as individuals and has made the inter-worker relations that much more significant.

All for One

The day at Valleyco begins at 8.00 a.m. and the operators clock on and then report to their charge-hand to be given their job sheets which detail what they shall be making. For most workers at Valleyco, the primary control strategy for management is the individual piece-rate system and this is the focus of considerable informal activity on the part of workers as they seek opportunities to beat the system. There are various ways in which workers at Valleyco can work around the piece-rate system at the plant. As recorded in Chapter 4, workers may work ahead of the standard time for a spell so that they can ease off later in the day. They will be careful that the daily total which they return on their work sheets is not above the maximum bonus level, as this would alert the office to the fact that some timings were too easy. The timings themselves are focal points for worker game playing, 'We can con them', as they engage in a battle of wits with the timers. Should workers feel the timings are unreasonable then they may well resort to collecting only their basic pay and work at a desultory rate. Of course, doing so penalizes the workers themselves since the bonus pay is an important addition to a very low wage. Occasionally, workers will try and persuade their charge-hands that difficult timings are unreasonable and request that they ask for them to be retimed. A further way in which individual workers play the piece-rate system is by working ahead and 'banking' the output for the next day's work sheet. Such practice is identical to that reported by Lupton (1963) and Roy (1952). This practice is possible because Valleyco does not have an independent information system recording the work that is actually completed and relies on the self-reporting on workers' sheets.

> I worked with Lesley in assembling the container, I think it was for the Rover 800 on its way to Cowley. Currently, Lesley is the only operator working on this container and she makes 173 per day for her 120 PI bonus. There were three stages to the assembly. My part was to attach two lengths of hose, with butterfly clips, and then tape the longer of these

two hoses to a third hose which has a valve attached and coil these into the mouth of the container. Lesley told me that she had got a good start today because yesterday she had finished her target number for maximum bonus early and so she had made up some sub-assemblies ready for this morning.

On the day from which the above notes are taken, Lesley finished the work needed for 120 PI bonus by 3.00 p.m. with my help. She then started making up sub-assemblies for the next day. Lesley makes the maximum bonus virtually every day. I did not see this form of stockpiling on a group basis and the introduction of group working and group bonuses restricts the opportunity for individuals to beat the system. The inter-linking of workers on a group basis, combined with the reduction of work-in-progress, ties workers' activities closely together and allows management to be able to monitor what is happening far more readily (see the situation regarding the Peugeot cell in this and other chapters).

One or two workers whom I asked about the move towards group working and group bonuses were in favour because, 'There'll be no slackers in this system, if you can't keep up you'll be out. You can't slack when you're part of a team, at the moment you can get away with it.' However, the majority were not in favour and preferred to have personal responsibility for their work speed and their pay, 'I like to just do my job and get paid for that' (see Joy's comments in Chapter 4).

In the Peugeot cell, where group working and group pay have been introduced, the pressure to work as part of a group rather than as an individual was clearly being felt. There is virtually no storage space between work stations and if one operator is working more quickly than another there is soon a pile of highly visible work-in-progress which one of the operators will have to come and clear. This slows down the group as a whole and disrupts the individual operator who has to come and help out. As discussed in the previous chapter, this may also result in the 'slower' worker feeling pressure to work faster in an attempt to keep up. The output figure per day includes only completed final assemblies and any work-in-progress is not counted. The introduction of group working at the Peugeot cell has also resulted in self-policing by workers.

> Mary has been feeding Gwen on work station three and there was some banter between them about how many defective assemblies Mary had passed to Gwen today. 'It was only three today, it's normally plenty more than that. It's normally about 12 isn't it, Gwen?' To which Gwen responded, 'And the rest, aye.'

The effects of this are threefold. First, the near-immediate inspection and return of faulty production negates the opportunity that other workers at Valleyco had for working very quickly to meet standard times and boosting their bonuses at the expense of quality (see Chapter 4). Secondly, prompt inspection prevents prolonged defective production and the build-up of faulty products. Thirdly, a very significant change in the dynamics between workers occurs. On the above occasion, the exchange was fairly light-hearted but there were times when the atmosphere was definitely more frosty, especially between Gwen and Joy, who do not get on. The pressure of supplying fellow workers, who are inspecting their workmates' production, can lead to conflict.

> I noticed a degree of tension between Joy and Gwen today, partly because Gwen was giving me jobs to do. Joy said to me, 'Ignore her. You don't have to do that if you don't want to. Why doesn't she do that herself, the lazy cow?' Joy has had to do all three preparation jobs for Gwen today and this is an example of the tension created between workers by the 'internal customer' ethos.

In the Peugeot cell, the group payment scheme also creates pressure on workers to avoid being absent because the earnings of the line are undermined. Joy told me, 'Even when you feel really rough you think, "Oh, I've got to get in, it's not just me suffering."' Joy said that she would always try and get to work and would not stop working once there 'unless you're really bad [ill]'. This was certainly not the case throughout the plant as a whole which had an enduring absenteeism problem both before and during the research period. A particular problem for many of the women, especially those at Valleyco (who were typically older than those at Nippon CTV), is that they are expected to run households as well as work full-time. A number of them commented that they had to *inter alia* cook dinner, do the shopping, decorate, and carry out a host of other domestic tasks when they got home from work. However, unlike the women workers at Churchmans in Pollert's (1983) study, these women did not believe that working would prove temporary and that their place was 'in the house'. Rather they were resigned to the prolonged hardship of their dual role. Outside the Peugeot and Nissan lines, workers would regularly take a day or two off 'while there's not much happening' or 'to get all the things I need to do done'.

> Jackie, one of the women I sit with at break, has been away for a couple of days now. Her friends do not expect her back this week. I asked if she was poorly but they did not think so, 'just skiving'. Vera added, 'I'd be off too if I got paid for it' [workers at Valleyco must have five years service before qualifying for sickness pay].

If workers cannot avoid being at work they will often take the opportunity to avoid working while they are there:

> During the morning break, one of the operators at the table remarked on how she had gone to the toilet that morning and found the place full of other operators 'having a fag and a chat'. She said, 'I was surprised there was anyone on the shop-floor, the place was packed. All the toilets [cubicles] were empty, mind.'

And One for All?

Where the individual piece-rate was still in operation it was occasionally possible for the workers to combine their efforts and play the system as a group. This was not normally the case because it was more complex and visible to organize a small group to beat the system than for an individual to do so alone.

> At the end of the day I witnessed Kay and the others on the valve line doctor their time-sheets so that no one had a PI of over 120 . . . As with the previous day, I offered to give my production to May who normally works on valves. Today she had been water testing and when Kay (who works out everyone's bonus for the day) calculated her day's PI it was too high. Because Kay had worked out these bonus figures she could then pass some of May's work on to someone else so that that person earned extra bonus.

The workers at Valleyco would often work together informally to make their job easier and to achieve better bonus (see also Chapter 4). This was the case on one of the Peugeot lines where two of the operators were close friends and had avoided the inter-worker tensions that characterized other work relations in that area by working very closely together.

> It was interesting to watch Janet and Mary organize themselves during the day to keep the work-in-progress down. Janet normally works on station one, with Mary on station two, and as far as possible they kept to this. Mary's cycle time was less than Janet's and so she also spent time on station three. I spent the bulk of my time on station four and also spent time on station three. However, the movement of labour was entirely dictated by the flow of products down the line and we moved to where there was a build-up of work-in-progress or to the preceding station once stocks had been exhausted.
>   Whilst I am sure Janet and Mary could do each other's jobs, they deliberately divided the load so that each was kept on their normal station whenever that task was needed. The two operators were never once instructed what they should do, their charge-hand was away and Mark (the unit manager) was around but left them to their tasks. They produced 600 units today and that appeared to be a number that they themselves had decided on. I asked Janet and she told me that that was the number they needed for their bonus and that they worked that out from the previous target when there were three operators on the line. Mark did not appear to have given any instructions, to produce either more or less. The target of 600 was easily met, by 3.45 p.m. (the shift runs until 4.30 p.m.)

However, the impact of group working and group bonuses on the Peugeot line was not typically so smoothly handled by the operators and tensions arose, particularly over the speed of work. The group system began to impinge on the operators' ability to restrict output and protect their numbers because they became reliant on all workers adhering to their unwritten code. This became clear when I asked Mary about the day reported above and why they had decided to stop at 600 units.

It seems that the timings on the Peugeot line are still temporary and so Mary is well aware that it is important for them not to go too fast and cause the timings to be re-evaluated. 'These are only temporary timings at the moment so it's not in our interests to go too fast. See, they think that machine can only do 118 in an hour but, in fact, Janet can do 150 or 160. Well, we're not going to tell them that, at least [not] until we get permanent timings. They've timed all these jobs but they're stalling us. Geoff [Evans] did say something about us being able to earn more than 120 per cent bonus if we did the work. He said, "If you do work extra hard then you'll get paid for it". But I wouldn't trust that. It's a con. They've said that before.'

Then Mary, unsolicited, began talking about the other (Peugeot) line. 'Now take the other line. They're on temporary timings as well, but they're fools to themselves. Well, there's two of them. Have you heard anything about this? Things aren't very happy over there at the moment. It's Gwen, she goes like the clappers all day. They're screwing themselves, it's crazy. They timed her and she did 200 [in a day] and now she's doing 300. They'll look at that and think she can do that all the time. They aren't going to leave the timing at 200 if she's busy doing 300. I don't understand her, she's been here long enough. She knows all the tricks. She knows the time study department and what they're like. It's just greed, I think. It's as simple as that. She just wants as much as she can. I mean, don't get me wrong, we're all here for the money and I like to earn bonus like the rest, but you need to be sensible. They'll change the timings when they know you can go faster. There's friction over there. There have been rows about it.'

Gwen is the final assembler and so she sucks the components through the system, this means the others have to work faster to keep her supplied. I asked whether the others had tried leaving her short of components to slow her down. 'They tried that and there were more rows about it. She makes the others go faster than they want to. I mean, they're not shirkers or anything like that, but some of them want a quieter time of it. They may not want to earn 120 per cent bonus every day. It should be up to them how hard they want to work. They want their "fatigue time", you know, to have a cigarette. Just to have a break in the toilet even. You can't sit there and work for eight hours solid.'

There were one or two further occasions where inter-worker tensions arose that were more than purely personal disagreements. While I was working as a packer on a final assembly line, Pam told me that one of the labourers had been reported to Lee for helping out another of the operators and not doing his own work. Lee, rather than Sally, the line's charge-hand, had then come up and 'ticked him off'. At first I found the incident rather surprising, but through the research period many operators complained about 'lazy labourers'. The labourers are not paid on a bonus system and there was some resentment when the operators were working hard, or indeed, if there was not enough work available for them to earn a good bonus, while the labourers were apparently standing doing nothing. It is possible that this is a conflictual outcome stemming from the male/female divide since the operators are virtually all women and all the labourers are men.

What Workers Won't Do

There were two separate occasions during the research period when workers staged walk-outs due to the failure of the management to maintain a reasonable working temperature during some very cold winter days in February. These were the only acts of collective direct or overt resistance that I was aware of during the research period.

> I was cutting hose again this morning when, at about 8.30 a.m., I turned around and noticed that the shop-floor was all but deserted. The operators had disappeared! I saw Huw and he said that they were all in the canteen because it was too cold to work. He added, 'I wouldn't go down there if I was you. Geoff has already told them to piss off. I know what's good for me and I'm staying out here. Geoffrey is not a happy man.' Undaunted, I braved the canteen. The operators were all sat down in the canteen, most having a coffee. The refusal to work had come because the temperature was below 60°F [15.5°C]. Although most of the shopfloor was OK, the top end was at 56°F [13°C]. Unfortunately, I had missed the process by which the walk-out was instigated. Most, if not all, operators appeared to be in the canteen. One said, 'I'm not cold but I've got to be in here or I'd be called a turncoat' although this appeared to be at least partly in jest.
>   The union representatives went into a meeting with Geoff. The fact that both Lee and Geoff were in their shirt-sleeves drew a degree of ridicule, 'Look at those two, pretending it's not cold!' The union representatives returned to inform us that the workforce must return to work at 9.00 a.m. but that those working on the final assembly lines (at the top end of the plant) could stay in the canteen until the temperature rose above 60°F.

The final assembly lines did not return to work until 10.45 a.m. and even more time was lost the following week:

> Following on from last Thursday, only it took less than a quarter of an hour today, we were all sat in the canteen by about 8.15 a.m. this morning. The walk-out came because the temperature was at 48°F [just under 9°C]

compared to the minimum allowed of 60°F. It was indeed pretty cold in the plant. Several of the operators said, 'Well, you just can't work in that cold even if you wanted to.' In all, two and a half hours' production on all lines was lost this morning . . . There was general discontent at the fact that the plant was so cold after Thursday, especially since the union officials came back to report that the offices were boiling, with shirtsleeves the order of the day. There were many in the canteen sat in coats and scarves. 'You'd think they would have learned their lesson after last week.' Still, the operators were not exactly glad to be sitting around, 'It's costing us money too, of course'. As far as I could gather they were to be paid on a set 90 PI. Maggie, the senior GMB representative, had actually asked if they could go home. This was rejected and, to be honest, I do not think that many of the operators wanted to go home, they wanted it to be warm enough for them to work.

The news came back that management were claiming that someone had turned the thermostat to 0°C. 'Well, they would say that, wouldn't they?' was the initial response, but later, when it was found that two of the heaters were mysteriously turned off, the suspicion of sabotage was confirmed. This rather changed the attitude of the canteen, surprise and dissatisfaction with whoever was responsible took the place of contempt for management. The labourers and maintenance men who had worked on Sunday were called into the office but no explanation was forthcoming and the shop-floor workers were told to look out for anyone other than the maintenance men around the heaters. The message from the meeting was that if the culprit was found, then he or she will be 'out the door', and Geoff Evans was also talking of taking legal action if he found who was responsible.

The consensus of the shop-floor was, 'Well, that's not on, is it'. Geoff Evans then surprised everyone in the canteen by sending the message that he would buy all the shop-floor workers a cup of tea or coffee. The surprise offer was quickly snapped up, everybody helping themselves to a 'milky coffee' on Geoff . . . The fact that sabotage was at least part of the problem and Geoff's coffee round gesture meant that the shop-floor returned to work willingly. 'Come on then, let's show willing' said Maggie as she led the move back to work.

The episode recounted above displays an unusual moment of consensus between the shop-floor and its management. The reaction of the shop-floor workers was almost unanimous in condemnation of any saboteur, not least because the time down had cost most people money in lost bonus earnings. I did not hear any more regarding the incident and, whether or not sabotage was confirmed, certainly no one was held responsible. One of the labourers was given the use of a company car and required to come into the plant early each morning in order to put the heaters on.

SUMMARY

This chapter has begun to explore the way in which the process of management control is part of an ongoing and negotiated set of relations between workers and managers. As has been clear in both case studies, the research settings are characterized by 'negotiated orders', or 'structured antagonisms', between workers and managers which may manifest themselves in numerous ways. Equally, the two cases offer different patterns to these negotiated relations. As discussed in preceding chapters, the workers at Nippon CTV operate in an environment in which the systems and procedures break down only rarely, while there is more uncertainty and chaos in the daily work of the Valleyco operators. Within these differing contexts, the processes of negotiation, accommodation, and resistance vary and result in dissimilar outcomes.

At Nippon CTV workers are rarely able to gain more than momentary respite from the line and workers who are seen as 'not trying' by their peers come under considerable pressure. However, worker camaraderie can also assist individuals when workers identify and correct each other's mistakes. Workers at Valleyco enjoy relatively greater opportunity to regulate their effort-bargain and secure some autonomy. Still, the greater coupling of activities and the introduction of group working and group bonuses has also stressed inter-worker relations here and there is considerable friction between workers at both plants. At Nippon CTV the senior members play an apparently important role in acting as 'safety valves' to release some of the pressures placed on the operators by the company's procedures.

Chapter 6 explores some of the reasons for workers doing what they do, in order to explain why the situations at the plants are as they are. There is further discussion of, in particular, certain aspects of the workplace relations raised in this and preceding chapters regarding worker commitment and their identification with the company, the nature of inter-worker relations, and the questions of choice, coercion, and behavioural compliance.

6

Why Do Workers Do what they Do? Evidence of High Commitment

'We could stop this line if we all pulled together. You know, without us they can't make anything. If we all decided it was too fast and left sets, they couldn't manage then at all. We can only go as fast as our arms can let us, you know. Sometimes, if it gets too fast then we can't keep up. And so we leave sets and they have to turn the speed down. Sometimes they turn the speed up even if we're on target for our production. That's really frustrating. It makes you very angry but there is nothing you can do.'

Vanessa, insertion operator at Nippon CTV.

INTRODUCTION

In the preceding chapters, I have detailed the control strategies employed, how they are implemented in practice, workers' actions, and the informal behaviours of both workers and managers that make up the management–labour relationship within the workplace. As we have seen, the two plants differ quite considerably, particularly in the processes of management control and in the informal behaviours of both the workers and their superiors. While there are numerous similarities between the pluralist control strategies of Valleyco and Nippon CTV, the extent of *de facto* managerial control at Nippon CTV far outstrips that in Valleyco. Of equal significance, worker 'misbehaviour' (Thompson and Ackroyd 1995) has not been eradicated from the workplace situation at either plant. In recognizing the extent and efficacy of the control exerted by management at Nippon CTV, it is important not to overlook the actual behaviours of workers as they seek to survive, regulate, or even beat the system. Cavendish (1982) and Kamata (1983) are just two researchers who have asserted the overriding importance of technical control (in each case, the assembly line) only to proceed to detail how the system is dependent on 'work group self-policing' and/or 'active compliance' with management goals (see Littler and Salaman 1984: 63). To identify Nippon CTV as having secured a significant extension of managerial control in comparison to Valleyco is not to argue that managerial prerogatives and omnipotence are assured under that manufacturing and control system. As the quotation at the beginning of this chapter indicates, the workforce are aware of their potential power for disruption but also appear to feel themselves subordinated to the line. This chapter explores that ambiguity.

While Chapter 5 attempts to identify the choices of action available to workers, and the degree to which some are favoured over others, in this chapter I will identify some of the factors explaining why those choices are made and will again seek to relate worker action to managerial behaviour in a dynamic rather than a unidirectional way in order to capture the actuality of workplace relations. The preceding chapters have described the manufacturing system, the control system, and the degree to which workers *have* to do things, as opposed to electing to. We have seen that compliance may not be assumed and that management may indulge, to a degree, worker behaviour outside that prescribed formally. The extent to which management indulges workers constitutes for labour what Elger (1975) called the 'limits to recalcitrance'. However, the question of why and how workers work is a very complicated and wide-ranging one. The chapter will explore this area in order to allow a more full and sensitive interpretation of the workplace relations of the two plants under study. I disaggregate some of the key dynamics in understanding why workers behave as they do by addressing issues of inter-worker relations, the system and its agents, and examining the importance of communication and quality in exploring the differences that have been evident within and between the cases. First I consider the attitudes and actions of individual workers themselves.

FOR THE LOVE OF THE COMPANY?

Japanese workplaces, and subsequently 'Japanese-style' workplaces, have been put forward as exemplars of 'better' employment relations by many different writers (from Dore 1973 to MacDuffie 1995). A key argument has been that the 'mutual benefit' or 'shared destiny' relations supposedly apparent in Japanese workplaces have engendered greater *commitment* amongst the workforce where, 'Organizational commitment implies identification with an organization and acceptance of its goals and values as one's own' (Lincoln and Kalleberg 1990: 22). It is therefore pertinent to report the observed actions and verbally articulated views of workers in regard to how they enter the workplace situation, particularly with regard to the extent that they have accepted the goals of the organization's management as legitimate and in accord with their own.

To a degree that is perhaps surprising, the workers of Valleyco and Nippon CTV shared many common traits and perceptions regarding their position, their relative affinity with others, and the attitude with which they entered the workplace relationship. Very few in either setting spoke favourably about their job, their management, or the generalities of their position. For most, 'this' was better than nothing as a way of earning. Workers commonly reported that things had been 'better' before, or elsewhere. There were some individuals who felt things were better where they were now and, if they did so, then they normally made reference to the attitude and support of their fellow workers.

The personalities of key members of management and its agents and the personal relations they formed were important in understanding the specific situations of the plants in question. Workers at both plants tended to empathize with those who sympathized with their situation on the shop-floor. A very common complaint at both plants was that management did not understand what was actually required on the shop-floor, did not understand the specific problems faced by workers, and did not spend enough time on, or show enough interest in, shop-floor activities. In view of the very different levels of managerial control and the differences in the manufacturing systems that were in place, the degree of overlap in worker perceptions is very interesting, suggesting that there is a considerable degree of common ground and experience for workers across different capitalist workplaces operating under different management regimes.

A number of workers at Nippon CTV commented on the comparison between their experiences when working on the site with the previous owner and the situation now. One member with over ten years' experience felt that things were much stricter now, even as compared with the earlier days of Nippon CTV, let alone SouthWestern Electronic. In the early days of Nippon CTV, she had felt that there was a greater 'team effort' with 'everyone pulling together' because the workforce then 'was smaller, with a new MD'. She described how the management and workers had felt part of an important project and clearly she felt some involvement beyond her 'fair day's work'. She described how Desmond and others had actually worked alongside her on the line when necessary but 'now there's too much to do upstairs'. She felt there was more 'flexibility' (on the part of management) in those days. She clearly remembered those days favourably in comparison. There were others who remarked similarly:

> June and the rest have been banned from talking to Mick, probably following his counselling yesterday. June informs me that there is to be 'no talking to Mick'. She is very pissed off with the whole thing, clearly resentful that this instruction has been given. She complains about the changes that have taken place. She has been here, I think, since the beginning of Nippon CTV and has worked here before when it was SouthWestern. She identifies that the key changes have been in terms of the quality of production required, and the levels gone to to ensure it is attained, and the discipline, 'Nippon CTV are much much stricter,' she tells me, 'When it was run by SouthWestern, workers in the plant could smoke and drink on the line'. It is clear that June is talking about the level of discipline across the board, not just in terms of eating or smoking.

The perception of why these changes have occurred is very interesting. Very few workers talk on a daily basis about Nippon CTV being Japanese controlled. While workers are aware that the plant is Japanese owned, this does not figure regularly in their complaints about their working position.

> Molly has been here six years and Lesley worked here when it was South-Western. Neither is very enamoured with Nippon CTV or rather some of their superiors. 'The Japs are alright, it's our lot that are the problem. The managers, right down to the senior members, they just can't cope. They can't take the pressure that's put on them. They don't know how

to deal with people. They don't get any training or anything, they need to be taught, you know, how to talk to people. They show no respect some of them.'

This sentiment was repeated by other experienced workers such as Elsie:

Gail and Elsie both said the same about the Japanese, 'They're OK, they are. It's the people in charge here that are the trouble. It's those getting above themselves. The company's OK. Nippon CTV is quite a good company to work for. It's just some of the people here that are the problem.' It seems that Nippon CTV is seen as the umbrella organization, the wage payer, etc., whereas the day-to-day problems, gripes, and dissatisfaction are attributed to the specific managers involved.

In a similar way, at Valleyco, numerous workers remarked that they felt 'things' had deteriorated at the plant, often regarding the working relations between operators. The more experienced workers claimed that there had been a 'better atmosphere' in the past and that the younger workers did not work as hard as they should.

I chatted to an operator from (final) assembly who has worked here for six years. She felt that things were much worse here now. The work is harder she felt . . . and there is now 'a bad atmosphere'. She said that the work has not changed but that there is more of it. The atmosphere has deteriorated because 'all of the older workers left and I don't like working with the younger ones. They're too bitchy.' The woman who told me this was about 35–45 years old and she sat with a woman in her 20s who nodded in agreement.

The Valleyco operators were also scathing of their own managers and their ability, although they detected less of a shift in the nature of discipline and control. The most common complaint at Valleyco was that management did not deal fairly and equitably with the shop-floor and that some workers were favoured over others. Rather as the workers at Nippon CTV detached their day-to-day difficulties from their perception of the company, Valleyco workers hoped that the parent company would realize that some of the managers were 'useless' and replace them.

The majority of workers' complaints centred on management attitudes and the managers' expectations of their workers. This was the case at both plants, although the specific instances were different. Despite the fact that the production management staff at Nippon CTV have desks on the shop-floor and hold most of their meetings there, there were complaints about their not spending enough time among the workers and consequently not having a full understanding of the workers' own positions. 'They don't spend enough time down here to see what it's really like. They should try doing these jobs. If they can't do it how can we be expected to?' Vanessa, in particular, was critical of management in this way, 'I don't think it's fair that they expect us to do some things they couldn't do themselves. They think it's all our fault [when things go wrong] but it will be a part shortage or something.' These are similar sentiments to those expressed by Gladys and Irene on the Nissan line at Valleyco (see Chapter 4), who believe that their managers will unjustifiably blame 'operator trouble' should there be difficulties with production.

One of the senior members at Nippon CTV, Bertha, also emphasized the distance between the management and managers' expectations and the situation for the operators. She included her own position along with that of the shop-floor members:

Not for the first time there was a complaint of a distance between the shop-floor and the management, 'They don't know what it's actually like down here. If they sat there [gesturing to the line] they would realize they want miracles from us.'

The workers at both plants do not appear to share any sense of involvement in the organization and most identified instrumental reasons for working, arguing that they came to work for the money. At Nippon CTV, workers regularly referred to themselves as 'robots' or the 'robot line'.

Janie said she was only here for the money. Vanessa said that was mostly it. 'You can earn more here than working in a shop and that. I reckon that at least 70 per cent of them are only here for the money. It's a job isn't it? You've got to do something to earn a crust.'

Workers did not report a great deal of satisfaction with their situation. Rather there was resignation about what their future held. When I talked to the new recruits during induction, they also reported the need for any kind of job in order to earn.

I talked to Jamie who has an HNC, 'I took 250 exams in three years'... Despite his qualifications (in electronics), he has had several jobs—never earning any more than £3.70 per hour—without finding one he settled at. These jobs included factory work and working in a prison. He seems to have moved jobs of his own accord quite frequently. I also chatted to Ernie, who worked for ten years on the docks and is a carpenter by trade. He felt the induction had been good because it eased people into the factory and meant that he had at least met a few people before he started off. When he was made redundant from his job as a joiner, he tried starting his own business but that had failed. Ernie clearly recognized social relations were important, particularly in this job where he did not feel he was likely to enjoy the work. He needed some sort of job to bring in some money. 'Well, I never thought of factories like this place for a job. Well, tradesmen don't, do they? I never thought of doing something like this. I only live up the road and you've got to do something to bring some money in. If you can have a laugh with the blokes then that makes it OK. See, like on the docks there was a big group of us blokes and it was great.'

Ernie at Nippon CTV was in a similar position to several male workers at Valleyco who had also lost jobs with the traditional employers of the area as those industries were run down. Ieuan in the moulding shop at Valleyco had worked in the mines and at both Llanwern and Port Talbot steel works but he identified the work at Valleyco as the 'most boring' he had done.

The inter-relations between workers are key in the perceived experience of the shop-floor. Workers who spoke favourably about the plant tended to concentrate on their fellow workers as the most significant positive aspect. Of one of the younger male workers at Nippon CTV I recorded:

He is fairly non-committal about the job itself, but he used to work in a food factory of some sort and this factory was at least much cleaner and more pleasant to work in. The job was 'OK' but, 'They're a good group here, that's what it's all about'. By this as much as anything it appeared that he meant that people 'pulled their weight'. If they did not there could be 'problems'.

At Valleyco, I heard of one woman who left to work at Panasonic in Cardiff because the money was better but who had returned to Valleyco, 'The work was OK but she didn't like the girls on the line'.

The individual personalities and actions of workers and managers are important in understanding the detail of the workplace relations in the plants. Many workers regarded individuals of the same formal level and authority in a different way depending upon how they perceived them to act in practice.

Dan does not like Angie, he does not feel that she treated him with respect when he first started on the line. He complained to Joan, the panel shop superintendent, 'I had her [Angie] in the coffee lounge', when he and Angie met face to face to sort things out. Dan put in for a transfer, 'We'd all worked this overtime for her to clear the piles of panels all on the trolleys, but she never even said "thanks".' As Dan put it, she showed no gratitude for him 'saving her ass'. It is the lack of respect Dan feels she shows for people that really bugs him, his transfer request was turned down. He also feels that she 'sticks to the book too tightly'.

At both plants workers took steps to demonstrate at least symbolically that they did not share management's objectives and values. The unwillingness to wear their blue jackets, their reluctance to work overtime, and the way in which the panel shop empties at the end of each shift at Nippon CTV indicate that workers do not identify with the company. At Valleyco, the divisions between management and labour are even more evident, with workers actively withholding effort and regularly voicing their opposition to management. However, as we have seen in the preceding chapters, workers do not simply resist as best they can and do the minimum required. There are a number of aspects to the workplace relations between workers themselves and between workers and managers which can help in understanding workers' behaviour.

INTER-WORKER RELATIONS?

A very clear example of how workers tend to empathize with, and be supportive of, those who are sympathetic to their own position came in the moulding shop at Valleyco where there were two quality inspectors working—Adam and Calum. They carry out the same tasks, one on the morning shift and one on the afternoon shift. However, Adam is extremely unpopular with the setters and operators in the moulding shop and is commonly regarded as 'knowing fuck all'. In sharp contrast, Calum is respected and seen as very effective in his job—'You can't hide anything [of poor quality] from Calum, he'll find it at the bottom of the bag.' However, Calum does not apply the quality levels to the letter and told me that if possible he will let things pass his inspection, 'If it's not alright then I'll stop it. My job is to stop the rubbish. But if they [the operators] say, "That's the best we can do," then I will pass them. It is very rare for me to take things to my boss.' The lack of reliable components, the inconsistent performance of the moulding machines, and the variations in the operators' performance combine to introduce uncertainty and informality at Valleyco in a way that is very rare at Nippon CTV. On the other hand, Adam is seen as petty and stupid, and without an understanding of the machines and their limitations or the problems that the setters and operators have. Adam's unpopularity goes beyond the verbal abuse regularly directed his way.

> I learned today that some of the lads tied Adam up on the last day before the Christmas break and dumped him in a skip. 'If I hadn't found him down in assembly, he'd have been there all Christmas,' Jim the supervisor told me. On another occasion, Adam was tied up and dumped in a box and put on a lorry, 'If the security bloke hadn't found him at the gate he'd have gone to Birmingham.'

The relationships that form between workers and their superiors are only a part of the social situation; to a very significant extent, what workers do must be understood in relation to their interaction with their fellow workers. The practical significance of these relations was particularly evident at Nippon CTV and the areas of Valleyco where some form of group working had been introduced. In these situations, the actions and attitudes of individual workers were seen to have an effect, often directly, on the work experience of other workers. This increased coupling of worker activity resulted in heightened potential for inter-worker tension and disagreement, with a fragmentation in workplace relations among these workers. For example, in Chapter 5 we saw that the immediate proximity of the APC and 'mods' had caused friction between Gilly and Lesley and Molly at Nippon CTV and we also saw the tension between workers in the Peugeot cell at Valleyco in Chapters 4 and 5.

The attitudes of workers to their peers seem to be informed by three factors: their respective personalities and whether they 'get on'; whether the person in question is seen as 'trying' hard enough; and whether the individual's actions have a direct and negative effect on their fellow workers. The first of these is an intangible although Janie (who receives a lot of help from her fellow workers, see Chapter 5) commented herself that, 'They only spot the mistakes of the people they like'. The second and third elements were constantly demonstrated during the interactions of workers. As we saw in the preceding chapter, inserters at Nippon CTV would side with the senior member against a fellow worker if they felt that worker had not been trying.

This situation arose with Katie on insertion as well. She was moved from pre-bath inspection because she had been letting through too many rejects. Vanessa, very much against her will, had been moved down the line to replace her and Katie had been put on to insertion toward the bottom of the line. However, she could not keep to the linespeed. Katie did not receive any sympathy or additional help from her workmates.

> Disruptions to the system cause problems between members as well. Katie, who had seemed quite popular during my first week when I was on insertion, is clearly not the flavour of the month now. Mary, the line feeder, has been given one of Katie's pieces to insert because she kept leaving sets. This has clearly caused resentment. Descriptions of Katie as a 'fat' or 'lazy cow' abounded, with comments such as, 'Look at her, she's not even trying,' or, 'It's no wonder she can't keep up, moving at that speed'. These are not within her earshot. Whether she has been openly confronted I cannot say. She is not joined by any of these members during breaks, but she had not usually sat with them. To be honest, the extra piece Mary had did not seem to cause her undue problems, but that was not the point in the inserters' eyes. It is clear that the failure to work at a certain speed (the speed that the other members feel you should be working at) will lead to peer group pressure to increase speed or at least trigger resentment and conflict. In effect, as long as you appear to try, it does not seem to matter if you are 'hopeless' or 'useless' and need helping. If you are fairly popular, it is not too inconvenient for your fellow workers, and [if it is only] for a short period of time, there is little comment made.

As with the conflicts over work speed at Valleyco, these instances at Nippon CTV indicate that workers have an appropriate level of effort in mind when interpreting their workmates' activities. The vast majority of workers at both plants did not simply avoid activity, nor did they seek to do the minimum, but rather they appeared to have some accepted level of effort which is seen as legitimate or 'fair'. As a consequence, individual workers at both plants occasionally came under peer pressure to work faster. Equally, as we saw in Chapter 5, Gwen in the Peugeot cell at Valleyco is under pressure to work more slowly and any 'rate-busters' at Valleyco come under peer pressure to conform.

These informal personal dynamics are compounded in their importance because of the 'blame mechanisms' which are part and parcel of the quality control system in place, especially at Nippon CTV where every individual error must be attributed to an individual member. Not surprisingly, the most deep-seated rifts along the line were between workers at different points in the quality inspection process and the most directly confrontational behaviour between workers was related to the monitoring and recording of quality. This is similar in some respects to the instances of open hostility between Adam and the setters and operators in the moulding shop at Valleyco reported above, although there the quality inspection is carried out by white-collar specialists.

There was some real internal discontent this morning on the inspection area of the line. Somebody on after-bath had booked Sally and the inspectors for a missing PH07. The pre-bath inspectors and Sally asked the after-bath people whether it was on the floor and had fallen off the board during soldering. 'She just books them straight away,' said one of the quality inspectors before the bath about one of the inspectors in the after-bath area, 'She doesn't even look on the floor for them'. These complaints were from the pre-bath inspectors because this is booked against them. Of course, if the component has fallen off the board, then it should be booked as some form of 'not connected', rather than as a 'missing' component [not connecteds are considered less serious]. Katie looked on the floor for the component and then Sally went and looked herself and claimed to find the component (under the line). The after-bath girls looked less than convinced! They appeared to feel that she put it there herself and then picked it back up again.

The pre-bath inspectors also complained that the after-bath girls were booking a 'reseat' as a 'not connected'. Katie clearly did not know the difference as she had explained to me before that they were the same and had claimed that she was being lenient on the 'reseats'. [In fact, reseats are seen as less important.] In other words, she is being overly harsh because she did not know the difference between the two defects. Katie and Natasha, the pre-bath inspectors, were complaining, 'She's always booking everything and getting other people into trouble for things that aren't their fault'. There was real friction here today. Natasha said, 'I'll drag her by her hair into the coffee lounge if she gets me booked for that.'

Katie then said to Natasha, 'See Angie and bring it up at a morning meeting.' Natasha responded, 'No way, I'm not doing that, I'll try and catch her on her own. You know what she's like, she's always interrupting. We've got to get her on her own and get her to listen.' The people directly opposite on the after-bath testing then appeared to be told off by their senior member. It also appeared that one of the after-bath girls did not book another for something and this further riled Natasha. She said, 'We don't work as a team here, do we?' Natasha used to work on after-bath testing and would like to be back there so perhaps this partly explains the disruptions. There is definite aggravation between after-bath and pre-bath. The atmosphere is decidedly frosty.

This situation had arisen before Katie was moved to insertion (see earlier). She had been warned by Angie about her performance and was under pressure to improve. At one stage she had complained to Angie that she had had to help Elsie who could not keep up because the small panels she was inserting had bent pins. Gail felt this was disloyal to Elsie, and said, 'They've forgotten who helped them when they were struggling. They've forgotten who trained them.' Gail displayed a clear loyalty to the more senior of her workmates. The lack of slack in the system, and the pressure to perform their own tasks successfully, had led to individual workers blaming each other for problems that arose.

A similar situation had developed between Dan and Sharon and the technical assistants (TAs) at the end of the after-bath side of the line. The disagreements were prompted by the high incidence of NAFs, panels identified as faulty by the test gear operators that do not fail the TAs' retests (see Chapter 5). One of the TAs, Hanif, complained to Dan and Sharon that he was finding a number of NAFs which slows his reworking of faulty boards. Dan aggressively stated that he was completely clear of any blame, and by implication pointed out Sharon as culpable. She was clearly stressed and flustered and complained about the number of boards and of how she 'can't be expected to remember every-thing with all these [boards] piling up'. Dan was not sympathetic and this made Sharon more upset. Dan told me that on another occasion he and one of the TAs had nearly come to blows over the recording of NAFs.

It is not just the quality system and its onus on ascribing blame for faults that inform the relations between some workers. The pressure of the manufacturing system, with its unremitting high speed and no informal breaks, exacerbates the difficulties for the workers and further aggravates their own conflicts.

Each panel has a different test gear placed on the testing equipment and these change-overs can take over an hour sometimes. Today I was with Dan when he and Sharon were working on tests. If one of them has to stop for a change-over, the bottleneck builds rapidly. When this bottle-neck builds there can be considerable stress for the operator. There was considerable friction between Dan and Sharon when the change-over was taking place or when the linespeed appeared to increase. The panels come irregularly at this end of the line and when one of the test gears went down there was further shouting and swearing between Dan and Sharon. Dan gets impatient with Sharon because she has not picked up the same speed as him. He calls her 'useless'. She says she 'hates him, he's a pig'.

But she is in a difficult position because she needs Dan's help. This flare-up came when Sharon kept failing panels which passed when Dan retested them. Sharon was clearly rushed and upset by this stage. [The test gear that went down was quickly repaired, as the test support group are constantly on hand.]

The self-policing elements of peer surveillance in quality control are also evident at Valleyco but the lack of an effective and integrated information system means that the divisive and fragmenting 'blaming' behaviour is not such an important factor in inter-worker relations at that plant.

As we have seen in this chapter and the previous one, individual accountability for defects and workers' mutual loyalty can lead to informal behaviour which actually improves the plant's quality performance in line with management wishes. Quality is an important element in the control of labour at the two plants since it has a certain inherent legitimacy. In other words, workers may more readily identify with the goal of good quality. Management, and customers, are able to draw on this legitimacy in attempting to secure compliance from the shop-floor.

BECAUSE THEY'RE TOLD TO?

The communication processes at Nippon CTV are very significant in understanding what happens on the shop-floor and in encouraging workers to do what is requested by management, although perhaps not in the way that some may assume. The various communication procedures are used as a form of 'battering ram' to drive home messages which management wants to see incorporated into the running of the plant. The process begins in the induction programme where Viv, the induction and training officer, talks about the 'law at the plant'. The company commits considerable time and resources to communications in various forms and while workers may consciously discount the significance of these communications they do carry minimally a symbolic effect. As we shall see, particularly in the next chapter, this communication is typically unidirectional and top-down.

Within the first week of my research visit, Mark, the senior production manager, approached me to ask what I thought of their communication procedures. This was the only time a senior Nippon CTV manager sought my opinion on their operations.

> Mark came up to me to find out if everything was OK and asked what I thought about their communication. He told me, 'We're always very keen to learn. Like that change I made today in the order [of the monthly meeting, see later in this chapter]. The feedback I've had so far is that that was good.' He asked me for a report! 'We pride ourselves on our communication.'

All communications at Nippon CTV are very carefully orchestrated and controlled. Every morning the team briefing is produced by management and read out by the team leader, the feedback by the advisory board representatives is written by the personnel department for them to read out, and the monthly meeting is conducted by the senior production managers themselves. Specific campaigns are reiterated time and again at these meetings and are emphasized through banners, printed materials, and publicly displayed records. During my stay at the plant there was a 'clean and tidy' campaign. This cropped up at nearly every team briefing; a huge hoarding was erected in the panel shop which read, 'Keep Nippon CTV clean and tidy' and occasionally gaps were left in the line so that members could clean the space immediately surrounding their work position. My diary notes regularly record the clean and tidy message. On the seventh of the month I noted, 'The introduction of cleanliness and tidiness is a key factor in all communications ... The messages are repeated over and over again, battered into the brain until they stick,' and on the thirteenth, 'The morning meeting was as per usual. The clean and tidy message was up again— bang, bang, until the message is taken in.'

Workers are typically disparaging about these communications. 'Stupid' was their verdict on the clean and tidy banner and an operator asked me what I thought of the morning meetings before adding, 'It's a crappy meeting, they just talk a load of rubbish. I never listen, it's just a waste of time'. However, these communications cannot be dismissed as insignificant. The constant monitoring and reporting of quality performance, the 'Work and check' and 'Reversals will ruin your day' red cards on the line, and the public displays of quality have established in the minds of the workers the importance of quality, both for their own position and the company's.

In contrast, the communication between Valleyco's management and the shop-floor is haphazard, typically informal, and often inconsistent. Where the quality messages appear to have been most effectual in influencing operator behaviour (the Nissan and Peugeot lines), it has often been the influence of the customers themselves as much as the internal management which have succeeded in communicating what is required (see Chapter 4).

At Nippon CTV, the monthly meeting is the time when the senior managers report to the shop-floor directly. These extended extracts from my diary indicate the style and direction of the communication, the key significance of quality messages, and the impressions of the workforce to that presentation.

Today was the day of the monthly meeting; far out. We all trailed into the canteen at about 8.45 a.m. Johnny Logan [an Irish ballad singer] is playing on a stereo system and the lights are dimmed. There is an over-head projector displaying, 'Welcome to monthly meeting for June' and instructions to fill the seats from the front. Somebody turns to me and comments, 'They ought to play something more lively.' These meetings are seen as boring and sleep-inducing for most of the operators that I spoke to (there were a number of jokes and comments about having a nap or taking the chance for a rest). The monthly meeting is held in the main canteen area where the seating is rearranged to form rows facing forwards and at the front there is a main stage. The operators are broken into two groups (for the meeting) and we all entered with the majority of the insertion people from the panel shop. In front of us there is a lectern with a microphone and PA system. The whole meeting lasted about 45 minutes.

First of all, Desmond, the production director, stepped up and he spoke for about five minutes. He ran through the production levels for the last month in brief detail. The target for production was missed by only three television sets. That is out of a target of 44,000 and he 'thank[s] everyone for their help and efforts in managing this achievement'. Basically, the message appears to be that this result is OK. Sat beside the overhead projector is Marcia, she changes the slides for Desmond as he talks. But, quality was not up to target. Desmond makes this point and stresses its importance. 'We *must* have quality and quantity.' Desmond shows us some charts that show that Nippon CTV is up to number three in the UK for sales, from position six or seven about six months ago. But he warns us things must continue. Desmond calls for 'care and concentration' in order to improve the quality performance. Desmond exhorts people, 'We need care, commitment, and concentration.' Desmond is a man of around 50 to 55 with a very honest and appealing face. He speaks in an earnest manner, stressing the importance of what he is saying. The message is spelled out that quality is in need of improvement. Desmond sounds a bit like an unhappy, but kindly, headmaster. There is very much a feeling of stern admonishment, a 'could [must] do better' tone. This is with a 'we' sense in that it means 'you' must do better for 'us' to succeed.

Following Desmond, we had Mark the production manager for the final assembly area. He is smoother and more relaxed on stage. He goes into detail about the performance of the previous month. First, he tells us of how he had a quality meeting 'offsite during the Friday of last week' (when the plant was on holiday). At that meeting, a member of *management* (as he put it) said that he 'always banged on about quality, why didn't it come at the head of each presentation?' So Mark decided it should and therefore today he began by considering each final line's actual and target quality performance. This fits neatly with Desmond's speech, demanding increased quality as well as continued quantity. The target percentages for quality on the final assembly lines vary from 90% to 95% and the achieved quality varied from 80.8% to 94.8%. A couple of lines were up on target, the others were down. Some were down by a considerable margin. 'This is not acceptable,' was the message. Mark discussed each line, what they had been making, any reasons why quality was low, and where improvements were necessary. 'I don't normally like to single out particular areas where there has been poor performance, but today I'm going to because we really must try and improve.' He proceeded to mention specific task areas and therefore, by implication, specific individuals. Those that had done well, he congratulated and the congratulations may have been only a few words, but there were one or two 'magnificent efforts' and 'I really think that is a great effort and a great achievement'. There is a lot of hyperbole at these meetings. Mark made it clear that it was *he* who personally thought this and that, but he also developed the 'we' needs. Occasionally, *he* would think something and almost dare 'you' not to. He would say '*I*' and let it stand in the air, he never actually said '*don't you?*' but it had a '*and so should you*' ring to it.

The quality performance was broken down for each final assembly line by machine shop, chassis, panels, components, and a couple of others. Each had an increase or decrease in performance on the previous month with a percentage attached. 'Operator productivity was up, but that includes quite a lot of overtime. Operator efficiency was down.' Mark also wanted final packing to improve. By the sound of it, he had been down there on the shop-floor and discussed this with those involved. 'If there is a scratch on a case or a piece of tape on it, then the next person to see that will be the final customer. That will be their first impression of Nippon CTV and it is first impressions that count.' One of the reasons for poor performance was defective bought-in materials from Singapore. 'They say that we can't match what they can manage in the Far East, but it seems that not everything is brilliant quality from there either. And I don't know about you, but I think it's a good effort to be able to do better than Singapore on this one.' This was said in the manner of, 'Go on then, tell me it isn't so'. This is the step towards Mark's goal of '96 and 98% quality, that's what I want to see and this [using the example of one of the good lines] is a step toward it. Let's keep going in that direction.'

Clearly, some of this information was of specific interest or rather specifically aimed at the shop-floor operators. However, I don't think people were really concentrating. They may have been listening for their own area, but there was an awful lot of information divulged that was not of interest to anyone on, say, P3 insertion. Mark went on about wooden cabinets for one line and a hold-up on corner brackets on another. There was that sort of detail. The tuners were of 99% quality which Mark described as 'an excellent effort'. He then proceeded to run through the next month's (i.e., June) schedules. There was a groaning and rolling of eyes from the audience as he indicated that the target was 55,000 TVs for this month. This was about the only response detectable in the crowd except for a few yawns during the whole 45-minute meeting. Mark ran through some other points including that a Japan Audit Unit is coming soon, they only come once every two or three years and, 'They report straight back to the President' and therefore, they are 'very important'. So extra effort was needed, uniforms had to be worn, no sweet papers lying around, etc. This brought Mark on to the next point. The latest Nippon CTV slogan is 'Keep Nippon CTV clean and tidy'. This is displayed on a big canvas banner in and around the plant which Mark described as 'like in Japan'. Mark proceeded to talk about tidiness. There is now a 'yellow card system' where any director will put yellow cards on or next to anything they are not happy about regarding tidiness as they wander around the shop-floor. I believe this was a total productivity idea [the plant's suggestion scheme, see Chapter 7]. Mark also gave the sports and social club a mention, with a big push for participation, because it is in trouble through a lack of attendance. He told us, 'In Japan they like to mix business with social events. We could do that here. *I* think it is important, so anyone with anything to add, or to say what they want, come along.'

He proceeded to tell us about where the televisions are actually going, 'There is still a market out there. We've got confirmations for production right up to next January.' This instils confidence and keeps people aware of the end market of the product. It was quite common to hear of Nippon CTV's good performance in the market-place, and this was stressed along with the need for continued effort to keep things going. Mark told us that we would be building to stock for this month and next. Then we would be flat out, straight out the door. No building to finished goods stores then. June and July would be the only two months for that. Nippon CTV has moved up to third place (in UK sales). 'Let's see if we can make one or two shall we?' This was a typical example of the exhortations to keep the company ('we') on the up. Mark stresses that there is job security because of the sales going well *but* that it is quality that makes all the difference. 'That's the most important thing. We're still taking people on. We're still interviewing. There's a market out there for our TVs, our sales people have made a really great effort. But we've got to back them up with the sort of quality product that they can sell. It's up to you to secure your own jobs into the future.' That's the message.

The lights dimmed back down and we filed back out of the canteen. As far as the operators were concerned, there was little discussion of the meeting, except some comments about the new monthly targets. The targets include a quality target which was in the region of 90% to 95%. We wandered fairly slowly back. There was certainly no rush to get on with making Nippon CTV number one or number two! Basically, people did not appear that affected by the meeting, at least not explicitly. There were a few eyes rolled at the output targets and the quality message was the same as normal, I suspect. People were fairly muted and said very little about the information itself. The panel shop went in at 8.45 a.m. and the final assembly areas had either been in before us during yesterday, or were due in afterwards.

Later in the month, I asked Dan about the monthly presentation and he told me that Nippon CTV also have a six-monthly presentation which includes a lot of financial information on profits, sales, and expenditures, and so on. Dan said, 'You think, "Why tell us this shit?" Then you think, "Well, at least they are telling us, lots of firms don't." ' It is in the area of quality control that the communication procedures seem to have been most effective for Nippon CTV, although this is underpinned with punitive measures for recalcitrance and it is difficult to disentangle the different reasons workers have for expending effort and attention on securing quality.

Certainly Nippon CTV's managers are careful to maintain the quality message and the procedures at the plant are consistent in underlining the importance of quality. If the finals area finds more than three examples of the same mistake in one batch then someone from the panel line must conduct a 'batch check' on all the panels in that batch (normally between 400 and 600). This is very time-consuming and puts the individual worker (usually a senior member) behind on their own tasks. Hence the senior members also have a vested interest in ensuring the quality of their line's production. This practice demonstrates the impact of self-policing and shows how Nippon CTV's quality system places responsibility for the quality of work with those building the product and also aligns the self-interests of the workers with those of the company. Dan told me that on one occasion he had been required to batch check 1,000 panels because there had been more than three mistakes. Dan must sign off each board that he tests with a coloured chinagraph pencil. He had been identified as responsible for the failure to detect the faults and he told me that he was videotaped when he retested each panel.

Unlike Nippon CTV, there is very little by way of formal communication between management and the shop-floor at Valleyco. There are no formal morning meetings and no regular meetings between the shop-floor and senior management apart from those conducted between Geoff Evans and the union stewards (see Chapter 8). Informally, the charge-hands may act as a conduit for information between management and the shop-floor although this was dependent on the style and personality of the individual charge-hands.

> I talked to Heather about employee involvement and basically was left with the same opinion [that I had formed earlier], there is very little in the way of formal communication between the management and the shop-floor. Heather said that she herself was very interested in what went on and so would go out of her way to find out what was happening. As Heather put it, 'I'm nosy, I ask, and then I tell my girls.'

Where attention had been paid to communicating with the workforce at Valleyco, specifically on the Nissan and Peugeot lines, it was the message regarding the importance of quality which had been most evidently received and enacted by the workers concerned. The power and influence of the customers has also emphasized the significance of quality and is utilized by managers as they seek to legitimate their requests of workers for improved performance.

> Mary pointed out that the wiper blade must be in exactly the right place when assembled. She said that quite often it had slipped out of the jig slightly but that Mark had told them that it must be in exactly the right place. He had told them that this was a 'Peugeot requirement'. The way she said this it almost sounded like an order from God!

The exhortation to perform at higher levels of both quality and productivity are regularly legitimated by management at Valleyco by reference to the necessity of meeting customer demands (see Chapter 4). As at Nippon CTV, in such instances the implicit (and often explicit) reference was that the workers' jobs depended on their ability to meet these expectations.

BECAUSE THEY HAVE TO?

Throughout the research period, the actions of the workers at the two plants regularly demonstrated that they had reported accurately on their feelings about the management. As we have discussed, there were innumerable instances when workers, either individually or as small groups, would demonstrate the distance between their goals and those of the firm. These actions were often deliberate symbolic acts to demonstrate dissatisfaction and dissonance (for example, not wearing the blue jackets at Nippon CTV). The implication of these actions is that workers are acting in ways that may accord with management requirements because they *have to* do so under the system of manufacturing and control employed at the plant, particularly at Nippon CTV where workers' choices over action are so restricted. Even in the area of quality control, where management may arguably lay claim to a greater level of legitimacy in the eyes of the workforce, there were instances where workers demonstrated that their expectations were not in line with those espoused by management.

> When the rush was on during the afternoon, and Dan was pushing the panels back because he could not keep up, one fell off and smashed. His comment, 'Well I don't care, do I?' Everyone knows that they are monitored for their quality performance and this is explicit and that is what everyone seeks to be 'OK' on. As long as Ann, his senior member, does not think Dan is slacking, he will go at a speed that allows him to keep his quality high. The presence of the senior members keeps the pressure to work constant and high, but the operators focus their efforts on appearing to do well as management measures it. A smashed panel on the floor, at least an individual one, is not booked against Dan but had he rushed to keep up and let through a faulty panel, that would have been.

I should point out that I never witnessed any wilful sabotage at Nippon CTV and Dan did not smash the panel deliberately. However, he was very pragmatic in his approach and stuck to surviving the system as defined by management. The key significance of quality to Dan was his personal quality record, not that of the line or the plant. Rather like the way in which Dan could buy some extra time by failing good panels (see Chapter 5), this practice could only possibly go unnoticed if it was used irregularly. This also indicates that it is vital for management that their rules are consistent with their overarching objectives. A second instance at Nippon CTV also helps to demonstrate how quality fits in with the attitude of the operators. This happened on my first Friday at the plant when I was working on insertion next to Vanessa:

> Oh disaster and calamity, I put in the wrong piece. Well, it was a capacitor with funny stripes up the sides and it is difficult to tell them apart. Vanessa noticed and chaos ensued. Trying to find out what I had done and still keeping inserting bits, the boards suddenly seem to speed up. Vanessa called for help but there was no one there. She took a board out of the belt! But it's 12.15, the buzzer goes, she stays maybe an extra 20 seconds to mention it to someone and sort one board out; her friend is waiting. The stampede exit. Sharon is there an extra two minutes and I mention it to her. Within two minutes the whole line had disappeared, 'We'll sort it out Monday'. Angie, of course, is still there. Nobody is the least bit interested in sorting it out. If you chain people to the line (almost literally with the earthing wire that inserters wear to remove static) then when the release call comes, they are off.

The diary notes from the following Monday read as follows:

> Vanessa found just two wrong components from the Friday mistake. Apparently they were the right value but they still needed to be changed. The wrong 'bombs' came from the contingency trolley, so although I should have checked it, it was really Sara's fault. She had taken the inappropriate component from the contingency trolley that is used to stock up any shortfall from 'b' stations.

It is interesting to note that in my diary I have adopted the same 'blaming' mentality as the workforce, a mistake had been made and it must be someone's fault. Vanessa had not forgotten to check this when she arrived on the Monday morning. The mistakes would have been down to her had she not been able to redress the problem before the boards reached the pre-bath inspection.

Vanessa had two rejects in the whole of May and has never been into the coffee lounge to be counselled in the seven years she has worked at Nippon CTV. She had worked as an off-line member but when she returned from long-term illness, 'I just couldn't cope with it'. She is clearly a model member and so it is not surprising that I was put with her when I first joined the line. She trains up new recruits when they join and is the longest-serving member on the

P3 line. However, Vanessa often drives home to have her lunch, 'I just want to get away from the place,' even though the break is only forty-five minutes and she does not live particularly close by. Vanessa is typical of workers at Nippon CTV, in that she takes a quiet pride in her work and is very clear on the need to maintain quality, but at the same time she clearly distances herself from the company and could not be said to have accepted the values and goals of the organization.

The workers at both Nippon CTV and Valleyco were very restricted in terms of choice of employment in the areas at the time of the research (see Chapter 2) and discussions which focused on the dissatisfaction felt at working at the respective plants did not usually include the possibility of leaving. The operators normally restricted themselves to bemoaning the specific job or work position that they had, contemplating the possibility of a move elsewhere on the line or, at Valleyco, the prospect of taking a day off. At Nippon CTV, the discontent was normally directed at the individual task rather than the job *per se* and most seemed to consider themselves trapped at the company through lack of alternative employment.

> 'It's a life sentence in here. You're here for four weeks, but I'm here forever,' Janie said to me. Vanessa commented, 'The only way out of here is to get pregnant.' There is much joking up and down the line to this end, but with a bitter edge. Basically, the operators feel as though the choice is to work or not. And once they are in Nippon CTV they seem to expect to stay, 'We're like robots'. There is lots of banter and joking, a lot of it with sexual innuendo. Somebody commented, 'You've got to do something, you'd go insane in here else. You've got to have some fun somehow.' Vanessa said, 'I don't stay in here a minute longer than I have to unless I'm doing overtime. Then it's my choice.' This is certainly borne out by the stampede to leave at the end of the day.

Workers have a certain resignation over their situation, especially at Nippon CTV where there seems little opportunity to voice dissatisfaction in any meaningful way that might engender change (the role played by organized labour at the two plants is discussed in Chapter 8).

> There was a real horror story today from the 'borrowed' member [on mods]. Last Thursday, she had gastric flu and had been very ill. She had wanted to see the doctor when she got to work (that's what Personnel tell them to do, come to work and ask for the doctor [see the induction programme in Chapter 3]) but he could not see her. They had then taken her up to [a local] hospital but they could not help her there. They had then made her sit on the line working. When she had complained that she felt sick, they gave her a yellow bucket to throw up into. She had finally got to see the doctor and had been given some medication and sent home. By this time it was 2.45 p.m. She was still ill and did not come in on Friday.

On Monday, she was taken into the coffee lounge and warned about her time-keeping and attendance. I have no way of knowing for sure that this is true, but I have no reason to disbelieve her. I was told it in a matter of fact, not sensationalist, way. Neither of the two experienced operators that were also there either disputed it or even seemed surprised by it. They were 'disgusted' at it, but it did not appear to be seen as unusual by them.

SUMMARY

This chapter has explored why workers act as they do at the two plants. Throughout the chapter we have considered whether workers at the plants identify with the goals of management and accept them as their own; the data suggest that this is far from the case and that workers at both plants share a sense of resignation at their position. In this and previous chapters we have seen that workers regularly express verbally and actively demonstrate their alienation from management, although the specifics of their actions vary between the two plants. In both plants workers are openly critical of their managers but there is some ambiguity in how they perceive the wider company.

Consistent features in both plants were the way in which workers empathize with those who are sympathetic to their situation, and that they are supportive to those fellow workers who are perceived to have made a 'fair effort', who are 'trying' in their jobs. This suggests that workers have a view on what it is legitimate for managers to expect from them, and that this is negotiated informally amongst the group, with 'rate busters' and 'slackers' (or, in this study, 'flyers' and 'lazy cows') both coming under peer pressure to conform. The complex and contingent nature of inter-worker relations indicates that worker collectivity or loyalty may not be assumed and there are certain developments under new manufacturing practices which appear to further complicate this issue. We have seen in this and previous chapters that the removal of buffers, a quality system which highlights individual accountability, and the incorporation of peer policing can place extreme pressure on inter-worker relations, leading to fragmentation.

The significance of communication, especially regarding quality and workers' security, cannot be overlooked in understanding why workers do what they do. We have seen that Nippon CTV stresses certain messages and behaviour and backs this up with both internally consistent procedures and symbolic actions in order to reinforce these points. Many workers perceive that quality is an issue which has an inherent legitimacy, and they take some pride in their work. Managers capitalize upon this, particularly when it is linked to customer expectations and, ultimately, jobs.

The message that comes from the workers themselves is that they face simple and stark choices: to keep their jobs they must conform to management expectations. The economic environment and the labour market make the jobs a necessity for most. It seems clear that the majority of workers take the choices that are in their interests in order to keep their jobs; they do what they have to.

The next chapter considers the participation of workers in the organization and in the wider function of the production systems at the two plants. It also considers the extent to which management at the two plants actively seeks to involve the workers in areas beyond their manual tasks.

7

More than a Pair of Hands?
Worker Involvement in what they Do
and how they Do it

'Let's have something done around here that's done for pride.'

Desmond, Nippon CTV's production director.

'How can you expect no defects with the speed this [line] goes? You haven't got time to take pride in your work. You are always just trying to keep up.'

Molly, Nippon CTV operator.

INTRODUCTION

As has been discussed previously, the debates over the role of labour have been central in discussions regarding contemporary manufacturing management. One of the key elements which proponents claim distinguishes this model is the active participation and involvement of workers in problem solving and decision making (Kenney and Florida 1993; Womack *et al.* 1990). Further, it has been argued that various HRM practices are integrated with a superior manufacturing system to create an environment of 'shared destiny' in which workers are highly committed and involved and actively participate in solving management's problems to the benefit of all parties (MacDuffie 1995).

The purpose of this chapter is therefore to focus specifically on the extent and form of worker involvement in the plants' operations beyond day-to-day task execution. In particular in this chapter, I will discuss the degree to which, and the formal and informal means by which, management seeks to involve workers and the workers' own actions with regard to both task execution and task design (Klein 1991).

THE EXTENT OF WORKER INVOLVEMENT

In the induction programme at Nippon CTV (see Chapter 3), every new recruit was introduced to the importance of quality in the plant's operations. The quality manager, Bobby Best, made a lengthy presentation introducing the history of total quality assurance and explaining how Juran and other Americans had taken the ideas to Japan. He told the recruits that 'Japanese goods used to be cheap rubbish'. He continued by telling them that the quality department certified suppliers' quality and that the plant did not have inward inspection. Best indicated that this approach and procedure might be different from those at other places where people had worked. He also mentioned the importance of market research, the role of quality engineers in monitoring and inspecting the internal manufacturing processes, and their intention to achieve 'quality by design'. Finally, he emphasized the strictness of the final inspection procedures before goods arrive with the customer, stressing that the processes were geared to 'customer satisfaction'.

When describing individual roles, Best mentioned his own tasks in planning internal production and in the examination of process faults. Turning to the operators' jobs, he stressed the importance of the manuals and said that these should be followed at all times. These were so important that, 'If you don't have a manual you can refuse to work'. The talk had begun with the use of rough examples to consider the savings that were possible from improving quality. Best told the group that 90 per cent of rejects are due to internal factors rather than faulty components and that an average rework costs £4. He then informed the recruits that the removal of internal mistakes would save over £250,000 because the technical assistants on each line would no longer be needed. However, there was no mention of worker involvement in solving problems nor were problem-solving activities such as suggestion schemes or quality circles discussed. The only direction regarding operator responsibility for quality centres on working to the manual (for more on the induction programme see Chapter 3).

In contrast, at Valleyco the management has sought to encourage workers to take responsibility for the quality of their own work and to be more proactive than merely identifying and correcting their own mistakes. However, this has been attempted in a haphazard and inconsistent way which has not met with the widespread acceptance of the workforce. One of the few remaining inspectors on the shop-floor told me,

> 'They say that the operators should look out for any defects, but they've got their numbers to make and so they are interested in speed.' . . . She was critical of the quality control department and management in general, 'The management don't know what they're doing'.

The inspector was sceptical about both the competence and the sincerity of management regarding quality. She told me that there were problems reported with a new air and water testing machine for jets—'It probably fails too many!' The lack of faith and trust in management at Valleyco was a persistent factor for shop-floor workers.

As discussed in Chapter 4, the charge-hands and operators in the machine shop were particularly critical of the quality control department. Despite the fact that the machine shop had been introducing new equipment, the responsibility for checking defects and identifying the reasons for these had been left solely with the workers. Far from seeing this as an opportunity for further involvement in their work, the operators were resentful: 'They [the QC department] should take samples during the day, we're only the operators, it's not our job.' Of course, this contrasts with the situation on the Nissan line in particular where individual operators have accepted the need for quality and taken on those responsibilities in a very conscientious manner (see Chapter 4).

At one time, the plan had been for there to be a regular Friday meeting held fortnightly by Geoff Evans; there had been one almost a year ago, and then nothing. Subsequently, there was no regular formal communication between management and workers at Valleyco. This is in stark contrast to the situation at Nippon CTV (see Chapter 6) but workers at the two plants still hold many of the same perceptions. In particular, workers perceive that there are large gaps between themselves and those they refer to as the 'ties' (at Valleyco) or 'upstairs' (at Nippon CTV) and in the knowledge of management regarding the actual situation and difficulties on the shop-floor. Workers and charge-hands throughout the Valleyco plant are very critical of management. When management has attempted to communicate with the operators, there has been a failure to get its messages across. I attended a mass meeting in the December before the research period began at which time the introduction of the business units was presented. In January, the operator and the charge-hand I asked about the units criticized the presentation:

> I asked Helen [an operator in the motor shop] about the business units that are to be introduced. She did not know what I was talking about, despite the meeting held in December at which I was present. As I had suspected at the time, there was too much information and Helen and Paula had clearly not taken in the key points. Their foremost memory was of being bamboozled by the accounting figures they were presented with, 'It's too much for me, it all goes over my head'. This was echoed by Paula who complained about accountants and engineers dominating the meeting. Having said this, Helen also complained about the lack of information and communication presented by management, 'They just don't explain things to us'. This was directed at her wish to know how their individual tasks fit into the whole of the business and exactly why they should do this or that and not [to be given what she regards as] meaningless accounting figures.

These sentiments are similar to those expressed by Nippon CTV workers in relation to the monthly meetings held by management at the plant (see Chapter 6).

Most operators rely on informal communication, rumour, and gossip to provide them with information, particularly at Valleyco where there is little formal collective communication. Some of the charge-hands at the plant do go out of their way to try find out what is happening, and why, but the extent to which they do so depends on personal characteristics. Even in the units such as the Peugeot cell, there were frequent criticisms from workers regarding the lack of involvement and communication. The perception is that they (the shop-floor workers) have no input into the running of the organization or any decisions taken, '[We have] no involvement at all'.

At Nippon CTV, there are a number of formal meetings which might offer opportunities for two-way communication, but in practice they do not. As reported previously, the morning team briefings always end with the team leader asking, 'Any problems?' but on only two occasions did anyone speak up. Both times this was to ask whether there would be any more replacement heads for the air-powered clippers. This is of concern to the after-bath members because the manual clippers make their hands ache (there had been a rumour that their use is to be discontinued because they are too expensive). Similarly, the monthly meeting ended with an invitation to ask questions or raise points:

> While we were chatting I was informed that there would be a meeting with management tomorrow morning (the monthly meeting). Mark and Desmond will be there. 'Mark's OK, he talks to you and that. Desmond walks around a bit but he doesn't talk.' 'You might find it interesting. They talk about targets and schedules and sales and stuff.' Vanessa's friend says that she falls asleep when she is there. I'm told that it normally lasts about half an hour and Janie said, 'Great, we've got half an hour off tomorrow. That's the way I look at it.' Vanessa said, 'At the end of the meeting they ask if there are any questions. But they've made up their minds already. They don't want to hear about it. Sometimes nobody [even] asks if we have any questions.' There is no feeling of involvement or participation on behalf of the workers.

Group communication at the Nippon CTV plant tends to be unidirectional and focuses on how the plant's performance has compared to the targets, how individual lines have performed, and what management thinks of these performance levels. On occasions when the performance level drops, management may take additional steps. These involve communication, but only in the sense that workers are told that they are not doing well enough and that managerial controls will be tightened.

> 'Six months ago all of the insertion group had to go into the coffee lounge for a telling off about quality not being good enough. There was the threat that people would lose their jobs if there was no improvement. Talking was completely banned. And the team leaders were like watchdogs.' Vanessa continued, 'We were told we were sending through as many bad components as good. Some boards had as many as 13 defective insertions on them.'

At Nippon CTV, the onus is very much on workers carrying out their specified production tasks. Following the induction programme, new operators are sent straight out on to the shop-floor to join their teams. A number of members complained that they had been 'just dropped in' on the line and Vanessa told me that she had been left to 'sink or swim'. Dan said he had had to learn the job very quickly, while Sharon did not feel that the training had been adequate, 'I was just dropped in and expected to get on with it'. She had not been able to keep up on insertion and she had been counselled. Subsequently she had moved to tests and now seemed more confident that she would keep her place in the company; it was clear from the way that she spoke that she had expected to be laid off before she found she could manage on tests (see also the case of Trini, Chapter 5). Sharon told me that there was the opportunity for rotation on overtime but that otherwise this was her position and she would keep to it. There was no evidence of systematic job rotation in the panel shop area. Workers work in a position in which they can be expected to keep up with the line and there is no expectation that they will regularly move to different positions on the line, much less different sides, unless people are ill and positions need cover. However, they must move if so requested by the team leader.

After a year's employment at Nippon CTV operators who have a good performance and attendance record may apply for Grade Two status. To achieve this, and to secure the concomitant pay increase of more than 10 per cent, operators must learn different jobs and work in three different areas of the plant.

Gail (on the after-bath side of the line) had to have a time on insertion and in final assembly to get upgraded, 'You have to show your flexibility'. Since being upgraded she has gone back to the job she did before, 'I'd need retraining now if I went back. It was a waste of time really.' But it did show an operator's ability to learn different tasks.

The speed of the line itself negates the possibility of regular rotation:

Exactly what flexibility means in practice was emphasized again today because some people are out ill. The replacements, even if they are experienced, just do not have the necessary speed to keep up, 'It takes practice to get the speed'. Even the senior member, Ann, is not as quick as Dan or even Sharon when she has to stand in. To keep up the speed, the actions have to be automatic, there is no thinking time. While Ann is working out which panel it is and what test is next she is slipping behind the pace.

As discussed in previous chapters, operators are loath to move from a job that they are used to and which they can manage (this was just as much the case with the workers at Valleyco, especially if they had a job on which they knew they could earn a good bonus). Equally, team leaders do not want to disrupt their line unless necessary and operators cannot engineer a move simply by under-performing (see the case of Tania, Chapter 5). This is stressed to new recruits during induction:

At the very end, the importance of communication particularly regarding problems was stressed. The new members were urged to 'Show willing and communicate' if they encountered problems. Viv seemed to anticipate that any such problems would involve a person having to do a job they did not enjoy and her advice was as follows—'It's no good thinking, if I'm bad at this they'll move me. We won't, you have to show that you're willing to try. It's no good just giving up and waiting to be moved.'

Team leaders do not allow any discretion to operators regarding their position on the line,

> There was another incident of interest today, Jon had decided to move himself (on after-bath) and had swapped jobs with a female operator, with both of them happier where they had moved to, he told me. He said that he had decided to do this himself but that they had been moved back.

The team leaders and managers at Nippon CTV do not allow for any significant individual operator discretion over tasks or organization. Right from the instructions regarding working to the manual in the induction programme, the onus is firmly on doing what the system requires without thinking or questioning. Operators are not expected to make genuine contributions beyond maintaining their own performance at an acceptable level. Any change or idea workers may elect to incorporate informally is likely to focus on their own discrete task, either to make things easier for themselves, such as feeding components from one hand to the other during insertion, or to improve their recorded performance in the eyes of management.

> The four mods workers are penned in between the APCs and the technical assistants' equipment and they seemed to work together as an informal team quite successfully during the day. Lesley and Molly were described by Bertha as 'excellent workers'. Lesley had a reject yesterday—a short circuit which was the first reject she had had this month—and she had immediately responded by changing her handling of the soldering iron.

Of course, by improving their personal performance regarding quality the operators are also matching management's requirements and this is facilitated by the feedback on quality problems which is almost immediate and specific to an individual operator. From management's viewpoint, close surveillance and rapid feedback ensures there is no stockpiling of faulty production. (Contrast this with the situation at Valleyco in Chapter 4.)

The situation for some workers in Valleyco is rather different from that at Nippon CTV because the manufacturing systems there are less stable and controlled and management is not so aware of the detail of the processes involved. The uncertainty of the system, the relative size and variety of job tasks, and the attendant tacit skills of the workforce allow workers in certain areas of Valleyco to retain knowledge and potentially to make a genuine contribution to improvement activity should they choose to make management aware of their ideas (and if management should choose to listen). This was particularly the case for the setters in the moulding shop, but throughout the shop-floor I became aware of ideas and improvements that people had made, typically without telling management.

Setting a machine in the moulding shop might take upwards of one hour and involves mounting the appropriate tool to the moulding machine, often using clamps and blocks because many of the new tools do not fit the old injection machines. Once the tool is in place, the machine is run and adjusted until the mouldings are at an acceptable level. This involves adjusting the injection pressure, temperature, and moulding time. The setter's job is one that comes only with experience, the men themselves describe it as 'highly skilled'. These workers have far more opportunity to develop an involvement and pride in their work than do the line members at Nippon CTV or the operators at Valleyco whose job cycle will be measured in seconds and repeated identically for hours at a time. They also develop specialist knowledge in their work which they are careful to keep. Derek, the assembly area setter, told me one day about a setter who formerly worked at the plant, when it was owned by Connor Industries:

> Derek told me about someone who used to work at the plant whom he called John 'stop it'. 'He wanted things to run perfectly but I told him, "You'll soon learn. You never get perfection in anything in this world, you can only hope to get an acceptable level." I told him he'd soon see that I was right after he worked here for a bit, that he'd soon be "Connorized". Anyway, he came up a few months later and said, "You were right." He was "Connorized".' This man had previously been in the [Royal] Navy and, according to Derek, was used to getting anything he needed 'on the tax payers' money, but it's not like that in business'. John had also told Derek he ought to write things down but Derek told him that, 'I prefer to keep things in my head where no one can get at them'. John was made redundant and according to Derek, they just took his notes out of a drawer and knew all that they needed to know to do his job, 'So in effect he wrote his way out of a job'.

In speaking to me, one or two operators at Nippon CTV publicly bemoaned the lack of opportunity to take pride in one's work. The recorded quality of their work is the only aspect of differentiation between workers, with output determined by the linespeed, and a number of operators did take a special interest and pride in their performance:

> Molly and Lesley complained about the speed of the line, particularly because it detrimentally affects quality, 'How can you expect no defects with the speed this [line] goes? You haven't got time to take pride in your work. You are always just trying to keep up.' And, 'We could all do a perfect job if we had time to check our work properly.' This was something that they both felt very strongly, this lack of opportunity to have any pride in their work, the discarding of their own conscientious attitude to work to be replaced by rules and surveillance.

Vanessa was another who set herself personal goals beyond meeting management's expectations. She told me, 'I've set myself a personal target of four defects per month.' In such instances, workers are actively engaging with their work to an extent that goes beyond the minimum required by management's own controls.

There was no quality information fed back onto the line yesterday but Vanessa knows exactly what she has done. Indeed, she appeared to be arguing about whether she had made any mistakes yesterday or not. She said under her breath, 'They leave it until you forget what you were doing.' Vanessa would know every mistake and even dispute the ones that she was claimed to have made. However, these would not be changed.

The system at Valleyco informally relies on the co-operation of operators in taking responsibility for *more* than their designated job tasks (as does management at Nippon CTV when experienced workers are required to take extra pieces to carry the slower workers when the team leader tweaks up the linespeed, see Chapter 3). As we have seen in earlier chapters some of the workers, such as those at Valleyco who are in lines and cells supplying Nissan and Peugeot, have taken responsibility for their activities, particularly regarding quality. Following the reorganization of lines and responsibilities which left a single charge-hand running several lines, I asked about the increased span of control:

I asked about whether Sally, now she is in charge of so many lines, had any trouble with the R8 [Rover] line and maybe needed a lead hand there. I was told, 'The girls on R8 aren't the sort to send out defective work or anything. They seem to get on with it themselves. They're the sort that will sort things out for themselves.'

These examples of 'responsible autonomy' (Friedman 1977) centred on small numbers of workers who had an increased group awareness and an identification with a certain product, customer, or line. The workers on R8, Nissan, and Peugeot products had adopted a commitment to quality that occasionally went beyond that which the vagaries of Valleyco's manufacturing systems and management allowed.

Janet had noticed a quality problem with some of the main links she assembles into the wiper. There were bubbles in the paint and she had rejected some before noticing that a lot of the others were similar. She called for Mark [the Peugeot cell manager] and the inspection department passed them. I heard her say that Jacques [the most senior French manager at the plant] had said they were OK to use. Janet was not impressed by the quality of these parts, 'Well, it's on their backs, they said to use them. I wouldn't want them on my cowing car,' she added.

PROMOTING PARTICIPATION?

In the preceding section, we have considered the practical extent to which workers are involved in their organizations with regard to how and whether their activities extend beyond the minimum expected of them in producing goods ('task execution'). This section discusses whether workers, team leaders, and charge-hands are encouraged to provide inputs into the improvement of the systems in which they work and how this is done ('task design').

At Nippon CTV, senior management does expect its team leaders and middle managers to contribute to the improvement of the manufacturing system at the company, but even the training officer admitted that the training provided for these members is limited.

> I spoke briefly to Cheryl the training officer this afternoon. She only joined Nippon CTV six weeks ago and has clearly been surprised by what she found. The training officer post was a newly created position and since Nippon CTV does not provide job specifications [a practice that Desmond described to me later as 'elastic boundaries' which ensure no one can hide from responsibility behind arbitrary demarcations] she had clearly had difficulty in actually working out what she was to do. She described the current position on training as 'none, or *ad hoc*' and her first aim was to try and develop a strategy, or at least a record, of who had had what and who thought they needed what. To this end, she had asked individual departments or individual managers to provide a 'training gap analysis' on where they were and where they thought their training should take them. This, of course, had elicited many different levels of response (not least in terms of resources required) and Cheryl herself had received 'no input, no briefing' from more senior members of the personnel department. At present, she said, 'Senior members and above get virtually no training.' I expressed my surprise to her at this lack of training at Nippon CTV and she agreed that she too had been surprised when she arrived.

The 'sink or swim' approach to new arrivals appears to be used for office staff as well as shop-floor workers. Indeed, a number of middle managers spoke as though they felt rather isolated and did not identify themselves with the company when speaking. During the induction, the personnel manager gave the example of when she had herself forgotten to clock out at the end of an overtime session and had not been paid for a Saturday she had worked. She also spoke of 'the company', 'they', and 'Mr Nippon CTV' when referring to the strict rules on absenteeism. There was a similar style of speech from Bobby and Viv during induction, and Bobby even said, 'Well, me and you, the proletariat,' in describing his and the recruits' position in the company. There was a clear divide between the managers at this level and 'the company' and some of those to whom I spoke sounded trapped. The way in which they spoke indicated that they felt neither on one side of the fence nor on the other, while definitely feeling subordinated by, and to, the corporate entity.

This is particularly significant at Nippon CTV because it is with the senior members, team leaders, and middle managers that the expectation for improvements lies. Senior management has clearly focused its attention on members above operator level in looking for progress on quality and efficiency issues. The plant management had recently organized a series of presentations by departmental managers to senior members and there was also a two-day training programme for nine senior members during my time at the plant. Following these, there was a meeting between 5.30 and 7.30 one evening at which the senior members were required to put forward their suggestions for improvements.

> I asked about [whether there was] a suggestion scheme and Molly thought they had tried one and 'Got back a load of abuse. People just said what they felt.' Lesley added, 'They weren't really interested. They don't want to hear what we have to say anyway.' She also said something about how management have already decided what they are going to do before they actually ask the operators.
>
> Dan also mentioned that there had been an attempt at initiating a suggestion scheme. He said that the team leader had come round but no one had said anything. He added, 'If they ask me, I'll tell them. I mean, they asked!' I did not get the impression that management would be taken by many of Dan's suggestions!

In fact, the plant's Total Productivity (TP) programme, which was intended to generate improvements, was not proving successful during the research period. The documentary records which I have from members of management show that there were only eight suggestions made and recorded from October to the following June for the whole of the panel shop (see Figure 8).

As well as attempting, unsuccessfully, to elicit worker suggestions, the assistant managing director of Nippon CTV (the most senior Japanese member of staff at the plant) had started quality circles, with small meetings being held throughout the plant, but these did not prove successful either. They have started again, but only on selected lines, and the quality circle now includes a quality control representative, someone from engineering, and only one or two members from the line itself. Mark (the senior production manager) headed one for P3, and Ann (the test gear senior member) and a senior member from a small panel line were involved. Apparently, the quality circle was to also have included Dan but he could not be spared from the line. Dan said that he respects Mark 'because he's worked his way up' and he said, 'I tell him why [there are problems on tests], is that there's not enough people on the line. We just can't keep up sometimes.'

The only member of P3 apart from Angie to make any suggestions to the Total Productivity programme was Sharon, the senior member on insertion, who had previously been a team leader herself. She told me that TP suggestions must be submitted to the team leader who then passes them on to engineering who make an evaluation of the suggestion. There is no financial benefit available to the person making the suggestion. Sharon had made two suggestions and complained about the length of time that it had taken to hear anything

REF NO	AREA	START DATE	IMPROVEMENT PROPOSAL	RAISED BY	TARGET DATE	PROGRESSED BY	STATUS
E11	Panel Shop	910618		J. Wilkinson	910723	J. Lowe	To be investigated
P186	Panel Shop	901025	Fit perspex to P2 and P3 lines from a/bath-test	P. Ford	910515	J. Lowe	P3 being progressed
P201	Panel Shop	901025	Hinge cradle-return conveyor foot-covers P1, 2, 3 & 6	S. Monkton	910501	J. Lowe	Being investigated
P202	Panel Shop	901213	Fit deep handles on solder bath glass	N. Wills	910515	J. Lowe	Being investigated
P215	Panel Shop	910501	Install conveyor belt on P1 to return loft and spider jigs	C. Kelly	910815	J. Lowe	Being investigated
P216	Panel Shop	910508	Provide a trolley to transport T803 transfer	S. Trevelyan	910717	J. Lowe	Trial with Rolicage
P218	Panel Shop	910508	Provide an automatic cutter to trim long leads on PCBs	C. Kelly	910909	J. Lowe	Not acceptable to NCTV
P220	Panel Shop	910605	Fit a 'press for attention' lamp and switch for all positions on P3	S. Trevelyan	910827	J. Lowe	

FIG. 8 Total Productivity Suggestions from Panel Shop, Nippon CTV

back. One of her suggestions was that each operator should have a light above their head which could be switched on if they needed help. As an off-liner, she said it was often difficult to tell which inserter was calling for help. The other suggestion was that the larger components which are placed lineside near the solder bath should be on wheeled trolleys so they can be moved more easily. Suggestions from anyone below the team leader level appeared rare, but Sharon told me that team leaders 'are expected to make one per week'. However, she told me that these 'tend to dry up'. The company's records on suggestions indicate that the contribution from team leaders is well below the expected level.

At the Valleyco plant, previous owners had offered financial rewards for suggestions made by the workers but this practice was discontinued when Valleyco took over and there was no formal suggestion scheme or group problem solving activity during the research period. Previously, Derek had made money (15 per cent of the saving to the company) when he had thought of a way of avoiding having to buy a new tool which would have cost £6,000. He had been offered £215 and an engineer had claimed that the company had not intended to buy a new tool, but Derek insisted that he get the saving on the new tool and he commented, 'I don't know why he was so bothered, it wasn't coming out of his pocket'. Derek said his ideas were 'all about saving me work really' but that Valleyco had said that 'any ideas that were good for the company were good for us too, but I don't see it like that. If there was no money, then where was the incentive?'

However, some workers had been prepared to make further suggestions, almost always ones which made their job easier, but found that management often failed to follow up or fund their ideas and had even claimed the better ideas as their own. In the moulding shop, Jim told me that many of the little developments that have helped the setters and foremen have come from the shop-floor. He mentioned quick release pipes and variable clamps which had been introduced but he also said that a request for washers had been turned down because of the expense—£400. In the end, the setters had had to make their own makeshift ones with scrap steel and a hack-saw, and one of them bemoaned the 'shortcuts' which he felt were dangerous.

On another occasion, Len had an idea that would have made a big improvement on a job I was doing. This job involved removing a cap from its sprue using a jig which had a guard attached. To retrieve the cap I had to fish under the guard with a screwdriver and Len described to me a way of designing the jig that would have made this much easier. Margaret's response was, 'They won't spend money on anything as sensible as that, Len.' When I asked her about suggestions in general she said, 'Well, there's no incentives are there. There's no reason to put anything forward, nothing gets done. If the ideas are any good, management claim them as their own.'

There was a widespread lack of trust and confidence in management at Valleyco which negated any possibility that workers might actively participate in the organization. When the current managing director, Robin Bennett, arrived he had unsuccessfully attempted to improve shop-floor relations; he held some meetings, spent time on the shop-floor, and learned the workers' first names in an attempt to break down the divisions. He encouraged workers to speak up.

> I chatted to Vera during the afternoon and she was as anti-management as normal. She told me of how Robin Bennett had arrived and said that anyone should be able to talk to anyone else without any fear, and that any problems should be raised. Vera had reported a problem to Bennett and, 'Within minutes there were about ten blokes out here from the office wanting to know who had been talking to Robin Bennett'.

The shop-floor workers at Valleyco were universally critical of their management, sceptical regarding their competence, and frustrated by their attitude. A number told me that they hoped that the take-over would herald a new regime, 'I hope Valleyco [corporate] management have got their heads screwed on and then maybe we'll get some new management here,' and they were disappointed that there had not been more changes at the time of the change of ownership, 'We had thought we'd get some new managers when we were taken over'. In part, the frustration is that they do not have the opportunity to make comments or suggestions which might improve their situation. This view was shared by the charge-hands who were equally sceptical regarding the contribution of their own ideas. I overheard Heather and Sally during a lunch break, discussing with others the moves to reduce stock and introduce an internal JIT system:

> The women were of the opinion that such production methods were not universally useful, 'Well, they work on some sections but not on others. Not that you can tell them. They don't understand it, do they? They're as thick as shit. They ought to come down and work on the line for one day. Then they'd see what it's like. But there's no telling them is there?' This led to further comments about the lack of communication, one said with sarcasm, 'I've a good mind to demand another fortnightly meeting!' [the meetings on a Friday, of which there was just one, nearly a year ago]. 'It's the only chance we get to say anything, isn't it? Well, the only chance when there's witnesses. Otherwise they just say, "Why didn't you tell me about that before?" or "I never knew that".'

The situation for team leaders is very different at Nippon CTV where management expects each one to make at least one suggestion per week. The problem for the team leaders is finding time in their hectic week to actually identify a problem, a solution, and to write it up into a TP suggestion. The team leaders work very hard at maintaining their reputations with Marcia and Joan (see Chapter 3) and Marcia in particular makes her expectations clearly known. However, as mentioned above, the plant's records indicate that team leaders have been struggling to find the time necessary to work up any suggestions that they may have. During the day I spent shadowing Angie she did take some time to work on her suggestion for that week,

At this point (after the morning coffee break at around 11.15 a.m.), Angie spends about 20 minutes working up her TP suggestion for this week. This involves identifying problem areas that need special attention on the manuals above the heads of the members with coloured marker pens. Angie tells me that she has plenty of other ideas that she would like to work on and put forward but she just has not had the time so far. With how busy she is kept by the line, Angie does not have the time and space to work up these suggestions into a usable form. The constraints on her are resulting in her just putting forward any idea in the meantime. She seems literally to have plucked the idea from quickly studying the line and then writing it up. She works on the idea for 20 minutes and it basically involves just colour coding the individual manuals with areas for special attention during the course of inserting components into the board.

A few minutes later, at 11.45 a.m., Angie joined the rest of the team leaders for their regular morning meeting with Marcia and Joan. At the meeting, Marcia noted that she had not yet received any TP suggestion sheets and insisted to the team leaders that they be in by 4.30 that afternoon. One of the team leaders whispered to me, 'I could do with more people but that's not really the idea.'

After lunch, Angie had to deal with a problem with a 'wrong value' at a change-over and ended up having to collect small panels by the armful from P4 to keep her line running. The whole day was fraught with an almost constant need for firefighting to keep things running. Some time after 2.00 p.m., Angie was able to return to the need for a TP suggestion.

Despite spending some time on the TP idea this morning, Angie was trying to think up an idea on the spot for this week because the idea that she has had she has not had time to complete. She checks with one of the after-bath TAs and Bertha about rejects and whether there is anything to recommend there. Angie asks Bertha, 'Have you got any TP ideas?' and Bertha replies, 'Not off the top of my head'. She is looking harassed and says to me, 'Just take her away'.

In the end, the problems with the small panels from P4 persist and Angie is unable to complete a TP suggestion for that day. According to Joan, the panel shop superintendent, this week has been particularly problematic for Angie, 'She's had it the hardest this week,' and the end result is that she just does not have the time to make a considered and well-planned suggestion.

The charge-hands at Valleyco typically have less opportunity to influence situations than they would like.

The lack of co-ordination and communication between the offices and shop-floor was starkly illustrated today. I worked with Heather on a new jig that has been made to manufacture a new product for Jaguar—a power wash jet and hose assembly. Jaguar dictated exactly the dimensions and materials to be used, sending Valleyco a detailed drawing from which the engineers at Valleyco drew up the design of the jig. The jig was actually made by a contractor. This jig was then presented to Heather and the operators. This was the first they saw of the jig and their first involvement with the new part was to attempt to use a jig designed solely by the engineers. This lack of involvement of the people actually required to use the tool was apparently typical. Not surprisingly, Heather and the other shop-floor workers are resentful at their lack of opportunity to have an input on such new projects and this ill feeling is compounded by the fact that the engineers often overlook problems that might have been identified by involving the operators earlier. In this particular case, the jig did not work successfully because when the tubing was turned around, it twisted and the components were consequently not square with each other. Jaguar insisted on a tolerance of only 3 mm. from square.

Since this problem was immediately noticed by Heather, the engineers were subjected to a few choice phrases when she talked to me. She said, 'I really enjoy working on new projects. Taking things from scratch and really getting to grips with them.' Heather used the jig and had discussions with several different engineers. She made notes of what she thought should be done and this included angling the board at 45 degrees to make it easier for the operators, 'It's not fair for the girls to be uncomfortable. It's about time they were taken into consideration with these tools.'

Heather had a conversation with one engineer and they agreed that a clamp to hold the piping straight would solve the problems. Then the chief engineer arrived and I joined in this conversation. He said that the tool started in the wrong place. Instead of clamping the plastic moulding and pump caps in place and manipulating the tubing, he said they should clamp the piping first to avoid it twisting and then add the components with the aid of a 'mechanical advantage', i.e. a small press. This seemed to make sense and I could not help but wonder why they had not done that in the first place. Still, from what I could gather, they were stuck with this jig and whatever amendments could be made to it. Heather then [spoke] about setting the tool at an angle and about how the operators' comfort was of importance. The chief engineer was dismissive. He said, 'You keep telling me they all work differently anyway,' and he then just walked off. It was a very rude gesture and Heather was not pleased, 'He'll just take something you've said in the past and throw it back in your face and walk off like that'.

Megan, one of the charge-hands on the Peugeot lines, also complained that she was not able to take her own decisions and run things her own way. When the unit was originally formed, the two charge-hands (Megan and Joan) and the cell's quality controller ('Duane the brain' as he is sarcastically known by the shop-floor) had visited an identical line in France and seen it in operation. Megan had learned the jobs there and then been responsible for explaining what was necessary to the operators on her line. However, after that, her role had been increasingly diminished to virtually that of any operator because the unit manager, Mark, took over all responsibilities for the Peugeot cell. She was previously the charge-hand on the instrumentation line (which has been sold off) and from what she said she was responsible for running that line, with a great deal more responsibility than she has now. The responsibility and opportunity to do things her own way and take decisions is clearly something she misses.

A further contrast between the two plants is the active role of management at Nippon CTV in co-ordinating and undertaking problem-solving activities. Managers are regularly seen out on the shop-floor and the operators are used to having their activities scrutinized at first hand by management. In fact, I learned that when I first arrived people thought I was a member of Nippon CTV because it was not unusual for members of management to come down and spend time around the lines. Additionally, office staff will spend time lineside studying processes in great detail. While I was at the plant, the F1 assembly line was studied daily by two technical services staff members who spent an hour or more each day focusing on a particular part of the line which had been targeted for TP improvement. It is interesting to note that, despite this attention, the shop-floor still feel that management fails to understand their situation and their problems (see Chapter 6).

That management has directed its attention at the senior members and above when seeking suggestions and improvements has, at least in part, been born of necessity due to the operators' unwillingness to contribute. Joan told me that there was some lack of confidence in the local management on the part of the Japanese parent company because of the limited success of the TP programme.

There is a TP meeting every Tuesday and, at the one I observed, the lack of involvement of shop-floor members was a point of concern. Marcia had only one suggestion from the more than 350 members in the panel shop. The meeting of thirteen staff, including the three production managers and three technical services managers, discussed the use of rewards to encourage suggestions. However, there are bad memories of two previous failures—the 'SMART' campaign with its 'smartie' badges and a bottle of wine to reward good suggestions and 'PIP' (productivity improvement programme) 'which never got anywhere'. There was an idea that a bar of chocolate might be awarded for any 'constructive suggestion' or that good ideas might go into a draw for a colour television. In the end the meeting broke up without deciding anything amid sarcastic mutterings implying that it had been a waste of time.

In the panel shop, Marcia had to make her own suggestions to team leaders:

In the meeting between Marcia, Joan, and the team leaders, Marcia makes some suggestions for the team leaders on how to improve quality on batches of panels that the line has already made ... Marcia tells her team leaders to refer to the previous quality sheets from each batch the next time that model is being run. She then says, 'What do you do about it?'

She wants the team leaders to display above the heads of the individual operators what they did wrong last time. Then anyone would be able to look at the computer read-out and 'see if we're having the same problems again'. One of the team leaders has delegated this to her senior members and they then feed the information back while the technical assistants write up the red cards for display on the next batch. Marcia stresses, 'We must keep on and on and on with this quality. If it's not emphasized to members we're not getting anywhere.'

Marcia's objectives for the panel shop (see Figure 9) include ensuring that her superintendent and team leaders encourage 'all members to think of ideas, improvements, etc. and uphold the concept of TP' and the members of the TP meeting also expressed a desire to see greater involvement.

In practice, management appeared to have been forced to settle for trying to keep people aware of quality and thinking of ways in which it might be able to encourage workers to improve their quality performance. Joan told me that they were planning to introduce a shield to award to the line which makes the best improvement in quality over a month period. This was planned for the high season, after the summer holidays. Joan told me that the possibility of identifying individuals as 'star performers' was discussed but the decision was taken to focus on the consistent quality improvement of a line over a month. At a meeting of the production managers with Desmond it was this consistency that was stressed. Apparently, Tuesdays and Thursdays are 'good days' for quality, as compared with the rest of the week. Joan privately expressed the concern that the shield would soon become 'old hat'. P1 had had some improvements on quality recently and Marcia had bought the line some sweets. Joan felt that this was appreciated as a token gesture by the shop-floor. Desmond was not convinced by these rewards and said, 'Is that the real way to go? Let's have something done around here that's done for pride.'

SUMMARY

This chapter has explored the extent of worker involvement in the planning and developing of what they do and how they do it. It has also provided information on what managers expect from the shop-floor and on the degree to which the two sets of workers are encouraged to become involved and to contribute their ideas.

We have seen that at Nippon CTV there is virtually no formal involvement of operators in problem-solving activities, either at a group or individual level. Equally, there is evidence that managers have not actively sought to encourage worker involvement or participation and, from induction on, workers are expected to conform to prescribed standards and activities rather than actively participate and show discretion. The plant has active and well-orchestrated communication processes but these concentrate on a unidirectional, top-down flow

MANAGEMENT OBJECTIVES 1991

TO. Mr. D. Sweeting   From: Mrs. M. Thompson

CC. Mr. M. Baker   Date: 5-06-91
Mr. J. Wilson
Mrs. J. Morris

Panel Shop Team Leaders.

1.   Efficiency/Manning Levels

Target for 1991 104%

1.1   Daily efficiency charts to be displayed and discussed regularly with the team, by Team Leaders.

1.2   Team Leaders and Senior Members to achieve improvements with line balancing and fine tuning.

1.3   Reduction of After Bath members: Study of what the job entails, how much of its necessary etc trials to be carried out on effectively of cut backs.
(Implementation begun)

1.4   To improve quality on insertion to reduce the necessity of inspection on after bath.

2.   Quality

2.1   Identify members with quality problems, Team Leaders to set up re-training schedule with Senior Members. Progress to be monitored until improvement made and maintained.

2.2   More training for Senior Members on the necessity of good quality and efficiency and the importance of their role in achieving these.

2.3   Encourage members to make suggestions and improvements by offering a prize or gift.
(Implementation)

2.4   Monthly reject charts to be displayed, against 90B achievements.

2.5   Individual reject charts displayed above each member, highlighted in colours for good, caution, danger.

2.6   Senior Members and T/A's have regular discussions to help reduce rejects and feedback on problems.

2.7   Keep White/Yellow/Pink sheets in batch order for easier comparison when checking rejects.

2.8   Re-balance After Bath so each member only doing one type of job i.e. Soldering or Cutting not both.

2.9   With the reduction in reject's the T/A's will be able to do quality checking around the Panel Shop.

2.10   34 members re-training for doing Solder Pads, and only one type of solder bit used. Training to take place for mods.

2.11   Quality targets set for each Panel Line and charted by Team Leader.

P1   3.5%
P2   0.6%
P3   3.0%

Fig. 9 Management Objectives for Panel Shop, Nippon CTV
Note: This typewritten memo is reproduced without any amendment or correction.

P4   0.5%
P5
P6   0.8%
P7   3.0%
P8   2.25%
P9   0.1%

3.   T.P. Improvements

3.1   Clean and tidy schedule for each line.
This to be checked regularly by Team Leaders with appropriate check list (to be formulated).

3.2   Superintendant and Team Leaders to encourage all members to think of ideas, improvements etc and uphold the concept of T.P.

4.   Absence

4.1   Trial to take place in latter part of June, when members returning from sick will remain in the coffee lounge to be interviewed by manager.

4.2   Normal procedures followed on returning to work with appropriate disciplinary action taken. Team Leaders displaying absence charts and encouraging members to consider the team.

5.   Off-Standard Hours

5.1   Generally these are beyond our control, but we shall continue to communicate with the relevant departments to try and get standard time added wo the model i.e. Weights, Tieing of Leads, Glueing, Tape.

5.2   With appropriate action being taken on poor quality and more and more feed back has reduced the number of batches being reworked.

6.   Non-Productive Hours

6.1   To reduce the amount of lost hours on line breakdowns, the bath support members will be encouraged to oversee the maintenance members who respond to problems, in the hope that they would be able to do minor repairs.

6.2   Bath supports spend time cleaning extraction tubes on irons, when required. One member released to do this job would allow supports to do more maintenance, and take preventative measures where they know problems might occur.

6.3   Team Leaders will be encouraged to cut waiting time to a minimum, take preventive measures where possible, where they have pre-warning of possible problems e.g. shortages etc.

6.4   Instead of stopping for 15 minutes on Fridays for clean up we now use the toilet gap and take two extra cradles so that each member in turn clean up.

6.5   Use one T/A to look at at Test Gear problem and see what improvement can be achieved on break downs.

6.6   No casual absence taken without appointment card or letter seen and then copied on to the leave form.

Marcia Thompson
PRODUCTION MANAGER

FIG. 9 (Cont.)

of information and do not constitute mechanisms for involving workers. The formal improvement activities at Nippon CTV are not working well and it appears that, as a further example of workers demonstrating their disaffection with the management, they are unwilling to engage in any discretionary improvement activities. There is some evidence that even team leaders and middle managers feel disenfranchised and disinclined to participate, or are so busy that they cannot contribute as they might otherwise. In contrast, some workers do demonstrate a sense of pride in their work by setting personal targets for quality that exceed management's formal requirements. However, these workers are often frustrated by management's actions in speeding up the line to the detriment of the quality of their work. Certainly, some of these workers might be persuaded to contribute to improving the organization if there was a different management regime in place.

At Valleyco, there is a mixed picture although the intentions of management seem even more constrained than at Nippon CTV. There are no formal problem-solving activities and there is no regular and formal communication between the management and the shop-floor. Like so many things at Valleyco, the situation is inconsistent and haphazard, with informality pervading these activities. That said, there is evidence that on some lines, especially those with a specified and visible customer, workers are prepared to become involved beyond the minimum and to take additional responsibilities. Moreover, the evidence suggests that these workers may work more efficiently and effectively. Overall, though, plant management seems either unwilling or uninterested in allowing workers to make constructive contributions, despite the fact that some workers may be prepared to do so. The uncertainty and informality has allowed some workers, especially those with wider-ranging job tasks, to be able to develop tacit knowledge and skills and to feel a sense of ownership over their position. These workers have made changes, often to make 'things easier' and to improve their bonuses, without telling management.

Chapter 8, the final chapter presenting data from the two case plants, considers the role of organized labour.

8

The Role of Organized Labour

'They [the union] are a waste of time and money. They've got "Nippon CTV" written across here [indicating her forehead]. They won't fight for you or if they do take up your case they always come back with the same answer, "Well you have to see their point of view over this".'

Molly, Nippon CTV line worker.

'Don [the chief shop steward] and me have a good working relationship. He tips me off and I tip him off about things. But we are not in each other's pockets.'

Marcia, panel shop manager, Nippon CTV.

INTRODUCTION

The role and significance of trade unions in the 'new' workplaces has been widely debated (Ackers *et al.* 1996) and opinion has been varied. In reviewing the significance of trade unions within current debates regarding HRM and new industrial relations, Guest and Hoque (1996: 12–13) identify three strands of work in the American literature. The first is concerned with the relationship between business strategy and HRM strategy (for example, Tichy *et al.* 1982; Miles and Snow 1984) and Guest and Hoque conclude that this perspective is driven by business and market considerations and treats trade unions as irrelevant if they are mentioned at all. The second strand they term the 'Harvard view' of HRM (Beer *et al.* 1985) and they interpret this as basically a repackaging of 'personnel management'. Within this view, 'stakeholder interests' are acknowledged but trade unions are relegated to a minor role. This work was extended by researchers at the Massachusetts Institute of Technology who presented a more comprehensive framework which, Guest and Hoque (1996) recognize, made explicit both the influences of the wider economic system and the potential role of trade unions (Kochan *et al.* 1986). Kochan *et al.* celebrated 'new' industrial relations and presented a positive view of trade unions by focusing on cases where successful collaboration between unions and management had resulted in significant change. They presented a case for such collaboration. The third strand of literature identified by Guest and Hoque presents HRM as an approach which is concerned with the full integration and utilization of the workforce (see Delbridge and Turnbull 1992). This approach is best reflected in the work of Walton (1985) and his 'control to commitment' argument (see Chapter 1). Guest and Hoque (1996: 13) recognize that, 'With its focus on an integrative, unitarist perspective, in which emphasis is placed on commitment to the organization, the role of trade unions is called into question'.

However, the role of trade unions has consistently been reported as a significant aspect of the 'Japanese' model although commentators have disagreed over the influence and impact of enterprise unionism in Japan. Dore (1973), for one, has characterized enterprise unionism as a part of the more advanced unitarist relations to be found in workplaces in Japan, whereas Gordon's (1985) historical review of the development of labour relations indicates that the post-war climate of apparently harmonious employment relations came after a period of bitter conflict which ended only when the balance of power tipped decisively in favour of management. Still, there is no doubt that the enterprise union is a fundamental institution of post-war Japanese employment relations for the core workforce. These institutional arrangements have underpinned much of the debate over the transfer of the 'Japanese' model (Ackroyd *et al.* 1988; Elger and Smith 1994).

In his research on Japanese manufacturing organizations in the UK, David Grant (1996: 205) identifies an 'overlap' between 'Japanization' and 'new industrial relations' with regard to the importance attached to 'the issue of committed and cooperative workforces who identify with the interests of their employing Japanese transplants or emulators'. This is consistent with the arguments put forward by proponents of co-operative or partnership-based relations between management and trade unions (Kochan *et al.* 1986) and new industrial relations is often presented as engendering a move to high commitment from workers since it entails 'the replacement of the class struggle with the struggle for markets. No longer us (the workers) against them (the management), but us (our company) against them (the competition)' (Bassett 1986: 174). In turn Grant (1996: 209) argues that:

Where transplants are unionized, their approach to employee relations will have generally led to their signing of new-style agreements with a single union. These agreements are based on a spirit and intention which seeks to move industrial relations from a conflictual process to one based on cooperation and trust. In this context, new style agreements can be seen as attempting to facilitate reductions in 'them and us'.

However, as we have seen, particularly in Chapter 6, the workforce at both Nippon CTV and Valleyco do not identify their interests with those of the organization, nor do they display an internalization of management's goals as their own nor an acceptance of management prerogatives as wholly legitimate and uncontested. In short, workers report the persistence of a conflict of interests between management and labour.

Consequently, within the context of these debates, an important aspect of this study is an exploration of the role played by organized labour in the two plants. The environment for employee relations in the UK has been changing rapidly over the last fifteen years with changes to the legislative framework, differing economic circumstances and the decline of permanent full-time employment in the labour market, and the increasing significance of foreign-owned firms in the UK (see Blyton and Turnbull 1994: chapter 3). In turn, the situation and the role of trade unions have come under pressure and close scrutiny. The Workplace Industrial Relations Surveys (for example, Millward *et al.* 1992) have provided evidence of the trends and structural changes being enacted on shopfloors in the UK (that is, the 'form') and studies such as this one provide the opportunity to put 'flesh on the bones' and develop a more accurate picture of the dynamic tensions which are shaping these developments (that is, the 'content'). As we shall see, a number of the trends identified at a macro-level in the UK are prevalent in the research sites, *inter alia* union mergers and the development of general unions, single union agreements, and consultative bodies which circumvent union organization. The role of organized labour in the workplace is also key in beginning to understand how the developments associated with the 'Japanese' model will interact with the changing institutional context. In particular, our concern is to reflect upon the outcome of a 'partnership' approach from the union at Nippon CTV and to compare and contrast this with a more traditional adversarial stance from the unions at Valleyco.

THE UNIONS AT VALLEYCO

There are two trade unions recognized to represent shop-floor workers at Valleyco, the General, Municipal, and Boilermakers trades union (GMB) and the Amalgamated Engineering and Electrical Union (AEEU). The GMB is the bigger of the two at the plant and acts as representative for the interests of most of the semi-skilled shop-floor operators. The AEEU represents the skilled trades workers, some shop-floor operators, and also the labourers. In fact, there is a division along gender lines in relation to union membership at the plant: virtually all the men are in the AEEU and all but ten of the women are in the GMB. There are five stewards at the plant—three women from the GMB, and two men from the AEEU. The convenor for the AEEU, Lloyd, is by far the most experienced and the others take their lead from him. The GMB stewards are inexperienced in their role; there were some redundancies and the previous stewards volunteered to leave. Kate, the moulding shop steward, told me that she 'sort of got pushed into it because no one else would do it'.

During an interview, Lloyd explained the local organization of his union. There is one full-time official for the area, the 'district secretary', who is now responsible for a far wider geographical spread than was previously the case. Lloyd put this down to 'decreasing trade union density and a decreasing number of firms'. The union at the plant is a part of a branch which has a part-time official, appointed by the union and paid 'a minimal sum'. There used to be meetings every Friday at the branch—'The branch is a meeting place of working class people'—when Lloyd would pay in the contributions and chat to the branch officer. The contributions are now taken directly from the wages of the members and branch meetings have become less frequent, at first being held fortnightly and now monthly. According to Lloyd, this has fragmented the branch as a social organization: 'There used to be a full house in a pub or club, fifty people or so. Now it's a handful. It's decimated the branch set-up.' Lloyd takes new members to the house of the local branch officer rather than have them wait for the next branch meeting. The GMB organization is slightly different in that the plant acts as the branch, rather than being a member of a branch which covers all workplaces in the local area, and Maggie is the branch officer as well as the convenor. There is a full-time GMB officer in Cardiff, the nearest city.

As convenor at the plant, Lloyd is responsible for the paperwork on each member of the union. When Lloyd, who is a machine shop technician, first arrived at the plant the union took only skilled workers as members. This has changed, 'We need as many [members] as we can' and there are no qualifications needed. Lloyd has members working in the tool room, in the maintenance and quality departments, and as setters. In the last few years, storemen and labourers have also joined and this created some friction with the GMB. Lloyd had wanted all the 'indirect' workers in the same union, 'to give strength in numbers'. Now he has about sixty members, and there are about 100 still in the GMB. Lloyd told me that this represents about 95 per cent union membership of shop-floor workers. Apart from the shop-floor unions, office workers are represented by the Association of Scientific, Technical and Managerial Staffs (ASTMS, now the Manufacturing, Science and Finance Union). Recently, staff members of the MSF approached Lloyd about moving to the AEEU because their official has left the plant and they do not have an elected representative.

The number of stewards depends on the number of union members and the different areas or trades represented. Lloyd had initially resisted taking direct workers but the branch officer had told him that he 'must take anyone wanting to join'. He has eight direct workers as members and felt that he would soon need a steward to represent them. Lloyd described himself as 'having the final say' and taking 'ultimate responsibility' for issues and decisions affecting the union and its members. There are annual elections for each of the steward posts.

The stewards meet monthly for a joint shop steward committee meeting. This was run years ago and then abandoned due to the ill feeling between the unions. For a period, Lloyd had basically run union activities himself but the new GMB stewards 'are very keen' and Geoff Evans, the operations director, had given permission for the joint committee to be resurrected. The stewards are also scheduled to meet Geoff monthly, although in keeping with the erratic nature of communication at the plant the meetings are 'not always actually held'. Informally, Lloyd and the other stewards will make contact with Geoff when necessary.

Lloyd said that any formal dealing between the union and management, such as disciplinary action, would begin with a meeting between the supervisor, the individual, and their area steward. If there was no agreement, then Lloyd, as convenor, would become involved, along with higher management. If there was still disagreement, then the local full-time officer and the plant's managing director would be brought in. Similarly, he said, the annual wage bargaining was conducted initially between the stewards and Geoff Evans but, following a failure to agree, the full-time officer and Robin Bennett (the managing director) joined negotiations. Lloyd told me that they had not yet managed an on-site agreement while he had been at the plant, and that they had always involved the local officer in their negotiations.

The annual pay negotiations used to involve only the convenors of the two unions, but now each steward participates 'to give them experience'. Lloyd is the only one of the five stewards with previous experience and the others rely heavily upon him, including the GMB stewards, who will bring him in on issues pertaining to one of their members. Lloyd said that relations between the two unions had been very bad: 'It was daggers in the back between the two. There was very bad feeling. They would down tools if one had half a penny more than the others. It [the wage claim] was the most secretive thing out. They would never show each other their wage claims. They would take industrial action and we wouldn't support them. Then if we had to strike, they didn't support us.' Lloyd had been able to turn this around and promote more openness and solidarity: 'With the way I am [as a person], it moulded us into a one-bodied machine rather than two separate units.' Now, before the wage claim, Lloyd and the other stewards sit down and discuss things jointly. 'We gain because of the increased numbers when we're joined with the GMB. In fact, we probably gain more because of that. Maggie will come to me if she has a problem because of the strength in numbers.'

The annual pay negotiations each year are due to be completed by 1 April and preparations begin at the end of January or the beginning of February. The stewards of the two unions consult with their members independently, looking for advice and suggestions. They draft a basic wage claim which is taken back to the members for approval. Then the two unions come together and discuss their relative claims and 'try and mould it so they are as similar as possible'. There will be differences because the indirect workers are on a set wage while the direct workers are paid by results (the piece-rate system described in previous chapters). Once the unions are agreed, they submit their claim to management. In the first instance, they meet with Geoff Evans, normally at the end of February. Geoff makes an introduction 'to save time and misunderstanding' and they discuss the issues so that he 'fully understands our claim'. Geoff then takes this to the managing director and an offer comes back to the unions after about a week.

There is a meeting at which the management presents its offer. Lloyd said, 'The offer is often well below expectations. We have struggled to keep the rises above the rate of inflation because that dictates our standard of living.' Lloyd gave the example of the previous year, when the union had asked for '12 per cent plus strings' and had actually wanted 10 per cent: 'Because of the bargaining position we're in, we ask for more than we'll accept. They never come back with an offer that's anywhere near it.' If the stewards think that the offer is acceptable they then take it to their members and it is discussed separately in the different work groups. Lloyd said, 'We will recommend acceptance but it's up to them.' If they think the offer is inadequate, then they do not bother to go back to their members 'because we know what they're looking for'. The shop stewards will then reject the offer and 'try to get as much as we can'. The previous year the management had gone away and improved the offer to an acceptable level. The stewards and the local full-time officers had met with Geoff Evans and the previous managing director and then addressed the workforce recommending acceptance. Lloyd said that years ago, the company never wanted the full-time officer involved and 'we could have 20 meetings on-site before they allowed the officer in. Now they prefer to get him in because they know they won't get acceptance [from the plant stewards without him]. They often ask for him to be brought in, even without a "failure to agree" notice.' Lloyd said that management felt that an on-site agreement was unlikely and 'want to save time' by bringing in the officer early. He also felt that this reflected the 'softened attitude of trade unions'.

The previous year the claim had included a call for an improved 'status scheme and an increased time-keeping bonus', what Lloyd called 'strings'. The original offer was a 7 per cent rise plus a bonus payment. The improved offer had reflected small further increases for select groups in the plant. Lloyd said that the managing director had described the basic wage of the labourers as 'immoral' and that 'he couldn't live with himself while that was the case'. They had been offered an extra £5 per week for the previous year and a further £5 per week for the following (present) year. Lloyd said that the maintenance and storemen had received 'token payments' of around £3 per week, while he, as a technician, was 'one of the few who didn't get an extra payment'. The pay offer was broken down by work group (which helped fragment the shop-floor collective) and Lloyd described what he called 'an interesting case'. The toolroom workers were paid at a lower level than some other groups and Lloyd said that he 'begged and asked the maintenance men to join with the tool room and act as a group to push forward their [the tool room's] claim'. The toolroom workers are Grade One skilled men, as are the maintenance workers. Lloyd said that in most plants 'maintenance typically command respect as intelligent men, they often have the best [union] representatives'. Lloyd tried to group the tool-room and maintenance men to increase their bargaining power but the maintenance men ignored Lloyd's pleas and did not elect a representative, 'God only knows why they didn't do it'. The tool-room workers went ahead with their claim and won a £4.50 addition to their basic weekly pay. Eight months later, the maintenance men 'decided they didn't know about it' and complained. Lloyd had clearly taken the brunt of their discontent; they complained that he had failed to act in their best interests, a claim that he strenuously denied. He felt that the maintenance group had 'a lot of trouble makers, some bad personalities'. Lloyd had clearly been very upset by it: 'I felt ill about it all but the tool room supported me. Fair play to them, they stood by me.' In the end, the managing director offered the maintenance men £4.50 extra per week as well, but Lloyd was disparaging, 'There's no guts in them [the maintenance men] to try out people with power. They're all hot air.'

Lloyd said that the anticipated wage claim was part of the annual budget submitted by the plant to their French owners. He was not sure how autonomous the plant might be but, 'I would say the French will have a big say. I doubt if Robin Bennett is in a position to say "yea" or "nay".' Lloyd said that since sales and profit would be down on budget, he was resigned to the likely effect on the wage claim for that year. There are no links between this plant and any others owned by Valleyco. Apparently, a previous owner had wanted joint negotiations and a uniform agreement between the two Welsh plants in the group but the meetings never happened, 'It was "them and us", a dog eat dog situation' between the unions of the two plants. Lloyd added, 'With the government regulations on secondary picketing, we couldn't support each other anyway.' Lloyd said that he relies on the full-time officer to take everything into account because, 'We're isolated from other plants'. Lloyd was conscious that the financial position of the company was paramount in settling pay claims: 'He [the full-time officer] and I feel that if a company has a good profit level then they can afford decent pay claims. Otherwise they can't.' Lloyd said that he would expect the officer to be 'fully familiar with the financial position'. However, by this, Lloyd meant the going rates locally, in the companies the local officer covers, not the financial position of Valleyco. He admitted, 'We don't really know anything about the financial position of the plant.' Lloyd said that occasionally Geoff would show him some information 'but normally we don't know'. Apparently, Geoff had shown Lloyd the trading position that day. Of course, the position is a bleak one, and this strengthens management's arguments. Lloyd said there was a legal requirement to disclose financial information but he was very sceptical about what that information would mean in a large multinational. There is no requirement to provide plant-specific information. Lloyd said that management's willingness to provide information 'depends on how far down the road we get, especially if we're recommending industrial action'.

Lloyd said that since he had been at the plant there had never been industrial action over a wage claim. He said that the changes in the labour laws meant that 'we cannot risk' industrial action. These developments have severely restricted the unions. Lloyd said with resignation, 'We've no strength at all really.' Lloyd described ballots which had been held on strike action but said that these had been used to try to force a better offer from management: 'I go back to Geoff and say, "Right, we have an OK for strike action, any thoughts?" And then they may slightly improve their offer by half a per cent or something and we accept. It's more a moral victory. We can use the threat but we can't afford to strike.'

On the Shop-Floor

In practice, the role of the stewards as the communication link with the shop-floor is inconsistent. There were numerous occasions when the stewards were called in to see Geoff for various reasons, including discussions on a 37-hour week, the possibility of redundancies, and the appointment of a new personnel manager. However, on other occasions, management used the charge-hands to carry information back on to the shop-floor. In either event, the shop-floor had to rely on the informal grapevine to carry the news because there were no formal meetings or presentations. On a number of occasions, the call for the stewards to meet with Geoff was met with speculation and rumour over the reasons. These groundless conversations were often more widely communicated than the out-comes of the actual meeting.

During the last few weeks of my research period at the plant, demand for pro-duction dropped dramatically and suddenly. The plant management announced that the plant would revert to a four-day week and suggested that the work-force take their September holiday early in the form of the days they would be laid off when the short working week was introduced. The majority of the work-force did not want to give up their holiday entitlement, particularly since the management could give no guarantees regarding the future need for redund-ancies. When the plant management was trying to come to an arrangement over lay-offs, Geoff resorted to speaking directly to the workforce. Geoff visited the full-time officer in Cardiff and Lloyd told me, 'In all fairness to Geoff, he went down to Cardiff to discuss it with our blessing. He was clearing the air and informing them of the situation to avoid any confrontation.' The shop-floor had heard that Geoff had been to Cardiff and their view was that it was 'probably to see if he can force us to agree'. A number of the experienced shop-floor workers were worried when they heard that Geoff was to speak directly to the workforce. Megan said, 'He's a big bullshitter and he's liable to talk them into anything.' They were also worried that Geoff would insist on a show of hands. Megan said, 'I don't want that. Some people will be too scared of Geoff to vote the way they feel.'

The following day Geoff spoke to the assembled workforce. He told them that he wanted them to give up their September holiday and take the pay early, in lieu of the five Fridays which would be lost because of the lay-offs. He informed the workforce that sales were currently 33 per cent down on the predictions used to set the half-yearly plan. He said that the budget had anticipated a £50,000 profit to June, and added, 'This was to be the first time in a long time that we would have made any money' (which contradicts what he told me in an interview the previous year). He appeared to have written off the first half of the year and was keen that the plant register a stronger second half. He wanted the week in September to be available to meet increased demand which he was hoping would come following a predicted cut in interest rates that would stimulate the market. He confessed he was guessing but described this as his 'crisis plan'.

Geoff spoke in what appeared to be fairly honest and accurate terms regard-ing the problems facing the plant, but his reputation and past experience counted against him. His normal arrogance was concealed but not forgotten and the shop-floor had not forgiven past perceived injustices; I was told that he once refused to accept four different ballot results until he got the result that he wanted and that in the past he had persuaded the workers to forgo pay awards because 'things would be much better later' and they had ended up with only 4 per cent over three years. Even though Geoff could not control the economic forces that were largely responsible for the plant's predicament, as Megan put it, 'There'll be plenty of people all over the factory saying this is down to Geoff Evans, "It's all his fault and he's trying to pull the wool over our eyes". They've been fed so much bullshit over the years they just don't trust him.'

During this episode, the union also came under fire. There was a body of opinion that believed the stewards were not telling the shop-floor all that they knew. In fact Megan, whose husband is a steward, said, 'I don't think we get told the whole story of what happens in those [union/management] meetings'. While many people were keen to see as many 'working for as long as possible', that is, they were eager to stave off redundancies, the proposal to give up the September holiday was rejected two to one. Even Joy, one of the first who would leave if there were redundancies, said, 'I don't think it's right for them to mess around with our holidays. I mean it took our fathers and grandfathers long enough to earn them.' Lloyd took the view that 'those looking to be here in the long term or so, wanted and needed a break because July to December is a long time.'

Lloyd said that his members had been approaching him in the weeks prior to the lay-offs: 'They're telling me they're expecting redundancies. They know they have no work so they're not going to fight it. They're prepared for it and they're expecting it two or three weeks before it happens. They're aware of the recession and they know what it might mean.' During this time, there were reports of lay-offs and redundancies at the big car makers almost every night on the television news. Lloyd described the whole situation as 'dog eat dog' and he reluctantly recognized that all he could hope for was that ultimately the number of people keeping their jobs would be greater than the number who lost theirs. He was not so concerned about the lay-offs if, by that means, they could avoid redundancies. He said that, 'because the women's wages are so appalling', most of the shop-floor would only be about £5 worse off on a four-day week.

While the unions were ultimately powerless to resist any lay-offs and redundancies they did attempt to actively represent their members' best interests and the workforce saw their representation as credible. As reported in Chapter 5, on two separate occasions the shop-floor temperature fell below the minimum acceptable level and on both those occasions the stewards led their members off the floor and into the canteen. An identical situation is described by Cavendish (1982) in her case study, but there the workers were told to keep working and given two pence to buy a hot drink; the union did nothing beyond asking for the boilers to be repaired and the workers had to work through the day. At Valleyco, there were two sit-ins while the union refused to work until the shop-floor temperature reached an acceptable level. Despite the difficulties at Valleyco, the unions were also continuing to negotiate a reduction in the working week to thirty-seven hours. Lloyd claimed that management had been 'putting us off' and that he had secured Geoff's agreement for the implementation of a 37-hour week during the previous year's pay settlement. He told me that he had it minuted, 'I've got it there in black and white.' As far as Lloyd was concerned this represented a 'contract'. However, he would rather see his union try to legally enforce this than have to take industrial action. Indeed, the attitude among many on the shop-floor was that strike action was undesirable. One worker told me, 'I don't believe in strikes, they don't do anybody any good.' Most workers at Valleyco simply could not afford to go on strike.

The shop-floor workers typically had a high regard for Lloyd but the other stewards were not well respected. Maggie came in for considerable criticism when I asked operators about the union. Ieuan, in the moulding shop, said she 'looks like the back end of a cow and is about as useful', while she was variously described as 'thick as shit' and 'useless' by other workers. Even Kate, one of her stewards, said that she was 'too reticent to push for things'. I was told by Vera that when the union stewards had been called in by management and told that the working week was to be shortened, 'Lloyd said he was the only one who didn't seem happy at what had happened [that is, at the prospect of a "few days off"]. Lloyd said he was the only one who didn't smile when the news was announced. He couldn't see Jac's [the other AEEU steward] face but the others were all grinning from ear to ear. Lloyd said that he felt a pain here [indicating the stomach area] when he heard it. He felt sick to the stomach.'

In turn, Maggie was very disaffected with management at Valleyco. One day when I spoke to her she had just been trying to negotiate for the radio to be turned on each hour to hear the news of the Gulf War (which broke out during the research period). Normally, the radio was on for an hour in the morning and an hour in the afternoon. Management had refused and she said, 'Everything's an uphill struggle here. They won't give us anything.' She referred to the management at the plant as 'pompous and arrogant'. The refusal was met with acrimony and management relented to the extent that the shop-floor workers who had relatives involved in the war were allowed into the offices to listen to the news every hour.

The agreement for the radio to be played for an hour, morning and afternoon, was part of the pay deal from the previous year. One day, it was left on for longer than an hour and one of the workers quipped, 'That must be our pay rise for this year!' The shop-floor were not happy with Maggie's role in those negotiations. Helen in the motor shop was scathing, 'The priorities are all wrong, she goes in there and the first thing she'll ask about is the radio. I want more money, I don't care about the radio.' Many of the workers recognized that the union was in a very weak bargaining position and that the stewards faced a difficult job. Helen described the pay claim for that year before commenting, 'Geoff Evans will fall off his seat laughing and Robin Bennett will have a heart attack'. However, like most of the shop-floor, she felt Lloyd and the others had made an effort on their behalf, 'Well, they're militant enough'. In fact, Helen was sympathetic to Lloyd's problems because her brother had formerly worked at the plant and had been a union official. She told me that she used to get very upset because the workers would call him a 'bastard' and so on behind his back. She said people would just listen and say nothing when her brother spoke about the situation at the plant and then would complain to each other when he had finished, 'But they wouldn't do the job themselves. They have the chance to speak but don't take it.' While Helen was not wholly satisfied with her representatives, particularly Maggie, she would not do the job herself either.

The shop-floor recognized that the odds are stacked against them and their representatives. The majority of workers were resigned to a reluctant pragmatism in their dealings with management. They were also aware that outside forces had a significant bearing on their position. During the period leading up to the lay-offs, there were days when there was no work and workers sat around reading magazines; and the recession and its effects on Britain's motor industry were constantly in the news to underscore the fact that it was not just Valleyco that was suffering. There was an increasing awareness that the customers of the plant were very influential in the internal affairs of Valleyco. This influence was plain for workers to see during the frequent visits which representatives of customers made to the plant (see for example the Nissan visit described in Chapter 4). These visits often involved a number of car company people for at least half a day and they would investigate anything and everything. During one visit by twelve representatives from Peugeot, two young men left the main group and, in the words of Heather, went 'off everywhere, searching through every bit of paper and every shelf'. They even asked Lloyd for all of his union papers and searched through them. These visits by customers not only emphasized to the shop-floor that they faced both their management and the pressures of their customers in any negotiations but also symbolized the level of power and authority held by the customers over the plant and its workers.

THE UNION AT NIPPON CTV

The arrangements for organized labour are rather different at Nippon CTV from those at Valleyco. Before the plant was reopened under Japanese ownership, the company negotiated with different unions and signed a single union agreement with the Electrical, Electronic, Telecommunications and Plumbing Union (EETPU, now the AEEU). This agreement was in place before staff were recruited and all employees were informed that this was the only union that the company would recognize. The union signed a 'strike-free agreement', with a commitment to pendulum arbitration. The company runs an 'advisory board' at which elected representatives are informed of the company's trading position and of management decisions and policies. At the company advisory board (CAB), the opinions of the representatives are sought in order to incorporate these into management decision making.

The senior shop steward at the plant is Don Pendleton. He has been at the plant 'since day one' and was a steward for two years before becoming senior steward, a post he had held for two years at the time of my interview with him. He is a grey-haired, bespectacled man with a friendly and conciliatory manner. He speaks with a strong local accent and exudes an air of care and concern. He described the beginning of the union at the plant:

> 'There were 2,500 people employed here and they were all made redundant. Nippon CTV says it wants 300. It's an ideal situation where you can get a new agreement. You would agree to anything then to get that job. That agreement was signed before anyone worked here, between the EETPU and Nippon CTV. Then, when we were interviewed [for a job], we had to agree with conditions like flexibility and they could do that because they were starting a new company. It's very different from trying to introduce it at Ford's.'

The union has seven stewards at the plant: one in the machine shop, two in the panel shop, two in finals, one in stores, and one in maintenance. There is one senior shop steward (Don) and one deputy. Don is also the representative of the new facility on the other side of the city and visits this once a week. There were only twenty-seven people working there at the time of the research. The union has a full-time official, the area representative, in the city. He acts as the secretary of branch meetings for the plant. The plant has its own branch. Don explained that the Nippon CTV branch is out on its own because it is the only 'strike-free agreement' in the area and so there could be a 'clash of principles' with other local union branches. He told me, 'We are absolutely self-contained.'

On the first Monday of each month there is a stewards meeting, held on-site during work hours. The full-time official attends this meeting as well as the branch meeting for the whole factory. The EETPU had arranged one or two meetings with other stewards with strike-free agreements to facilitate the 'passing of ideas'. Don told me that there were seminars to explain how things have been going. The last meeting was held nearly twelve months prior to our discussion, in Swansea, and Don said twenty-one company branches had been involved.

Apart from the restricted interaction with fellow members of his own union, Don and his colleagues have also had some contact with the company's Japanese trade union. He explained, 'Each company has their own union [in Japan]' and representatives of Nippon Denki workers' union had visited the plant and Don had spent an hour with them. This was two and a half years ago and Don commented, 'They're probably a lot stronger than over here because if you get expelled from the union then you can get expelled from the company. You can't work there if you're not in the trade union.' Don told me that he had not discussed the agreements the union had in Japan, 'They were more interested in conditions here and what we put up with in comparison with what they put up with.'

Don was keen to emphasize the fact that he felt the situation of his union and its role were the same as anywhere else, 'As a union we are just like any other. We do have problems but we don't have to discuss things with any other trade unions. We're the only one here. We have elections for shop steward positions every two years. It has got to be seen that you're not backing off from management or you don't get voted in.' He continued, 'CAB gives the opportunity to discuss things initially and to sort out your problems before they become problems. That's because it's explained and doesn't just go straight up on to the notice board with people waving their arms and complaining.'

Don briefly recalled the expulsion of the EETPU from the TUC. When the EETPU had been instructed to withdraw from its no-strike agreements, the then leader, Eric Hammond, had refused. Don told me he had said, 'We can't change it because no one will trust us in the future. We couldn't go against our word, we can't rip up agreements already made.' Don concluded, 'We said, "We're not breaking up agreements we have already made."' The eventual expulsion was a result of the 'wisdom of the TUC', he added sarcastically. There is no form of organized opposition to the union at the plant. The only occasion when organized opposition might occur would be during elections, when individual shop stewards might come under threat. The senior shop steward is voted in by the other stewards, 'We have a ballot vote on all issues for the EETPU'.

Don said that there had been no change in the formal agreement but that the communication levels have gradually improved: 'In the Japs' opinion, the more you talk to the workers the better. This was very strange for people to talk to the bosses about their job. It was really new for the gaffer to come to you and explain things and ask for your opinion. They didn't always take it but it was nice to be asked.' In terms of dealing with managers about specific points during his time as senior shop steward, Don told me, 'I always try to stress that things are never in black and white because this gives us a chance to talk about each case individually. I like to keep it very open. It is very rare that distinct lines are made—only in terms of stealing or fighting.' Don felt that over time he had been able to play more of a role in what takes place, 'I've been able to become more involved. Managers approach me first to discuss what should happen. Then I can sound out the case in the first instance. I'm involved in mediation at a very early stage.'

However, the effectiveness of Don in this role is unclear. The example he gave of this process did not appear to support any notion that he had been able to moderate or modify management's actions. He talked about the displays of workers' quality performance above their heads in the panel shop, 'They brought those cards out and I didn't like it. We didn't like the idea of embarrassing people to improve their work. I went to Marcia. It was more self-pride. I thought it was very Japanese and didn't like it.' Still, that procedure progressed as desired by management and the cards remain in place. Don told me that a member accompanied him in his meeting with management, 'She was satisfied and explained things to the girls on the line. They've accepted this thing now.' In terms of difficulties that he had experienced in dealings with the company, Don identified absenteeism as the main problem, 'They're pretty keen on it, these Japanese'. Don felt that absenteeism accounted for the vast majority of difficulties (he mentioned a figure of 97 per cent) but claimed, 'We don't have many [problems]'.

Don gave a further example of where the trade union and Nippon CTV had worked together, namely, in the introduction of 'high season' hours. Under this arrangement, members work a $37\frac{1}{2}$-hour week for the first seven months and then a $42\frac{1}{2}$-hour week for the rest of the year. Payment is made on the basis of a constant 39-hour week. According to Don, management approached the trade union and said, 'We would like to change the hours'. The trade union had then sounded out the attitudes of members on the shop-floor and Don said that they had liked the idea of Friday afternoons off. Don described the mutual benefits thus, 'It's ideal for management because everyone is giving $3\frac{1}{2}$ hours overtime at the flat rate [during the high season], but it's good for us because we have less time at work in summer.' Don said that this had been combined with an adjustment on overtime payments since the stewards had felt that there should be an extra payment made for overtime after a certain level. Following pressure from the stewards, an amendment was made whereby the first six hours of overtime per week in the high season are paid at time and a half and after that, it is double time. Don claimed that this 'didn't get as far as CAB. The trade union met management and then it was put to CAB.' This was unusual because the agreement was struck with the stewards prior to the proposal being passed by CAB.

Company Member—Union Member

Despite Don's insistence that the union is a viable independent representative for its members, the shop-floor workers were widely critical of the union when I spoke to them. Molly and Lesley said, 'They're a waste of time and money. They've got "Nippon CTV" written across here [indicating her forehead]. They won't fight for you or if they do take up your case they always come back with the same answer, "Well you have to see their point of view over this...".' They summed up their feelings, 'I mean this toilet gap is disgusting. It's degrading but the union does nothing.' Lesley even mentioned 'back-handers' at one point in the conversation.

Dan told me that he had been wrongly blamed over some graffiti that had appeared on the test gear. An operator who had subsequently left the company had actually been responsible, but both Dan and another operator had been suspected. They had been taken into the coffee lounge and threatened with the sack. Eventually, when the other operator left and the graffiti stopped, they had been informally exonerated but no one had apologized to them. I asked about the union in this episode and he said violently, 'A pissing waste of time'.

On another occasion I spoke with a member from a different line who was transferred to P3 for the day. She had been at Nippon CTV since the start and had worked at the site under the previous owner. She described the 'new union' as 'not much good' and the union arrangements as, 'No strikes. They [management] sit in the coffee lounge and explain things [to the union] and then lower the agreement.'

During the research period there were incidents which indicated that the workforce may have been correct in suspecting that the union was unlikely to be able to provide effective independent representation. During a day spent shadowing Marcia, the panel shop manager, I asked her about the union and she told me that she and Don 'have a good working relationship. He tips me off and I tip him off about things. But we are not in each other's pockets . . .' Later that day, Don and Marcia met to discuss an appeal made to Don by one of the panel shop members over a decision by Marcia to stop her booking days off:

It is 4.30 p.m. Don comes to see Marcia about a person on the line. This member has booked holiday which is tagged on to the end of the summer shutdown vacation. Apparently this is not allowed and hence she has been told that she cannot book those days. She has asked to Don to approach Marcia and see if she can make an exception. Marcia says, 'CAB agreed in the last two or three years that no one can have extra time off then [at the beginning or at the end of the summer holidays] unless they are marrying or there is a bereavement. I am just going by company policy. I would have argued for it but she could have changed the dates.'

Apparently, the problem is with a holiday booking and somehow Marcia knows that the member could have changed the holiday dates. Marcia continues, 'I am upholding CAB, I can't change that, there is nothing I can do.' Don tries to play up that the member is a good employee, 'She is a good worker this one. She has five years' experience and I have talked to her team leader and there have been no problems. I just ask you to reconsider in this case.' Marcia replies, 'It is a bloody palaver but the rules is the rules.' Don tries to get Marcia to support him if he takes the case 'upstairs'. 'I would ask you to make an exception or she will take days off sick next time. She has made it worse for herself because she is genuine.'

Marcia agrees to take this upstairs, 'I will see if I can catch Desmond in a good mood, not like this morning over that absentee [see Chapter 3].' Don says, 'So I can go back to her and tell her that you will reconsider. That you will support her case with Desmond.' Marcia says, 'Tell her I will have another word but the rules are the rules.' Don: 'Thank you very much.' Saving his face? Marcia then turns to me and says, 'I will stick to what I put, he won't ask again!'

When I saw Don later he told me that Marcia would take the case 'upstairs'. He told me that he has said to Marcia, 'I'd like to think you'd support this'; moreover, he has told the member that Marcia will support her but that 'company policy is this . . .' In other words, Don has protected himself and partially covered Marcia by deflecting the blame 'upstairs' to 'company policy'.

When I asked Don about criticisms from the shop-floor, he said, 'I just say, what kind of a rise did they get at their company where they had the full power of the trade union behind them? We got 9 per cent.' He continued, 'I point out that people join a union for the right to work not the right to strike. You can pay your money through a union and the first you hear of them is when they stick a banner in your hand. You think about it. With all the new legislation brought in, how many successful strikes have there been in the last few years?' As further justification for his union's position, Don indicated the pendulum arbitration clause of the agreement, 'I think our situation is better where we have this pendulum thing and then if management is wrong then they will lose. If we lose, then we have to accept that we were wrong. I think it takes the fire out of things if you know an outsider will come in and look at things fairly.'

I asked Don about the arrangement where the trade union agreed not to strike. He replied, 'There is no sanction of industrial action at all. But if a line puts down their tools there is not much we can do about it. We just say we won't lead our members out. Anyone stopping work, would not be supported by the union. We go and say, "We can't start to negotiate until [you] are back at work." We have never had that in ten years and I believe that is because of communication.' Don acknowledged that if things did disintegrate totally then the workforce could just walk out irrespective of any union agreement. However, he agreed that this was not a likely scenario. Despite the scepticism on the shop-floor, membership of the union is high. Don told me that over 500 people, out of more than 600 who were eligible at the time were members. Anyone below director level is eligible and Joan and some management staff are among Don's members.

In his eagerness to present the union in a good light, Don made certain statements which, it emerged, were inaccurate, as, for example, in relation to membership. The membership of the union at the time was 514 but this was out of a total of 1,001 employees, of whom 892 were classified as direct employees. He also exaggerated the role that the union plays as an independent negotiator with management. The company handbook states that 'The AEEU (formally [*sic*] EETPU) recognizes that all collective issues will be raised at CAB in the first instance and will only be taken up by the TU if they cannot be resolved by CAB advice.' It continues, 'The AEEU can exercise influence over CAB by having its stewards elected onto CAB. . . . The AEEU recognizes that it is in the best interest of harmony to pursue its objectives ideally within the CAB and to only move outside CAB where in its view it has no other option.' Moreover, the handbook indicates that the company will conduct a 'salary review' with effect from 1 April each year and during the induction programme Claire told new recruits, 'They [the union] can represent your interests as an individual if you have a grievance or whatever. They don't get involved in what we call "collective bargaining issues" such as pay or hours, that doesn't involve them.' In interviews, management confirmed that pay was set in accordance with the upper quartile level for similar factory work in the local area and that Nippon CTV was the second or third best payer in the industry across Britain.

The shop-floor workers were clear that it was the CAB which provided the most important avenue for them to be heard. One described it to me as, 'the crucial thing . . . This is where everything is brought up.' She added that there are elections on to the CAB and that 'the union try and get shop stewards on it'. She described the pay as 'quite good' and added that she believed in 'a fair day's work for a fair day's pay'.

The Company Advisory Board

The CAB has thirteen members including the managing director, who acts as chair, and Don as the senior shop steward. The others are elected representatives from the various sections of the plant: one each to represent the machine shop, stores, maintenance and technical assistance, engineering, administration, superintendents and team leaders, and the air conditioner plant, and two each for the panel shop and final assembly. The union has four of its seven stewards on the board. Each meeting is also attended by a number of senior managers who make presentations and play an active role during the meetings. CAB is responsible for discussing all issues regarding rules and procedures but is not to discuss issues relating to specific individuals.

Don described a possible scenario where a proposal may be acceptable to those present on the CAB but not to the trade union. If that situation arises, then Don will take the issue to the shop stewards and ask them for their opinion. If the trade union then says 'no' and management will not agree to change the proposal then the issue goes to pendulum arbitration. As Don emphasized, the CAB is an 'advisory' board and 'can only advise management'. A 'failure to agree' between union and management sends the issue to an independent arbitration service (ACAS) who will find in favour of one side or the other; Don gave no examples of this having happened. In practice, Don described a process in which both sides keep talking until their positions are practically level, 'not because either side backs down but because they see the logic of what the others are saying'. This process takes place under the auspices of the CAB and Don says again, 'We can only advise them'. The managing director then takes this advice to the board of directors and asks them, 'Will you take these revisions?' However, Don was keen to underline the fact that he felt the trade union arrangement here was not extraordinary, 'We're just the same as any other trade union, it's an advantage to be there when they're making rules'.

During the research period I was able to attend one of the monthly CAB meetings as an observer. The following notes, taken directly from my diary, detail the meeting and the process by which the decisions were communicated back to the workforce.

The meeting is held in a smaller room beside the training room. There is a round table with 13 places set. Don made the point of the symbolic round table. This meeting is for the air conditioner plant as well as this one. The room is actually named the 'CAB room' and along the back wall are extra seats for observers—there are six observers from the air conditioner plant here. Different people are invited to observe each meeting. I do not know how they're picked, randomly from the shop-floor is my impression. The MD chairs the meeting and tells the observers, 'Feel free to participate in the meeting'. None of them says a word throughout and no real attempt is made to bring them in on discussions. They and the other members are reminded that the matters discussed at the CAB are 'confidential' until the 'brief back' that is orchestrated by personnel. Despite what Don had told me (about how seriously the meeting was taken by the company), the MD was not at the last CAB, he had been in Japan, and he informed the meeting that he must excuse himself at 3.20 today. [The meeting started at 2.30 p.m.] The personnel director chaired the meeting from that point.

The meeting began with a presentation from the MD who used an overhead projector to put up slides reporting the stock levels and sales in May. Nippon CTV (UK) was 9,000 units above budget in stock, however, budget sales were 17,000+ as opposed to 20,000+ actual. The MD also reported the figures for Germany, France, and the level for Europe as a whole. Overall, Nippon CTV was 23,000 units above budget for stocks in the whole of Europe by the end of May. Nippon CTV (UK) is holding its market better and has moved to number one in some areas/product groups. The MD informs the meeting, 'We're holding prices to maintain profitability' and says that Sony and Nippon CTV are holding up best during the current difficulties. He tells the meeting that the retailers who actually sell Nippon CTV's products do have the ability to offer special offers on CTVs or VTRs, or to offer package deals, 'Once they're sold they [Nippon CTV (UK)] can't tell the retailers how to run their business'. However, he added, 'I think in the longer term there will be a move to ensure there is not a supply to retailers who make ridiculous discounts.'

There were further figures on the board regarding Nippon CTV (UK)'s performance, for example, its budgeted sales were 17,200 and its actual sales 16,751 units. Nippon CTV (UK) is called a 'customer of Nippon CTV'. For Europe as a whole, Nippon CTV (UK)'s performance is minus £38,000 (an actual loss) as against a budget of minus £137,000 which puts the cumulative performance for the year so far at minus £145,000 as opposed to a budgeted performance of minus £150,000. Then the air conditioner market is considered, Nippon CTV (UK) is the only customer for the air conditioner plant.

The other managers that are to give presentations appear to be making up their notes as the MD makes his presentation, implying that this has not been high on their priority list.

Now it is Desmond's turn, and he presents figures for the performance in May and the plan for June. Nippon CTV fell 3 units short of their 44,000 units plan in May. The schedule for June has 85 batches totalling 55,829 units planned. Desmond is currently predicting a shortfall of around 300, and he attributes this to integrated circuit chip supply problems. The target for July is to be 53,600 units. He then produces a table of 'Nippon CTV operating parameters'. These include figures for efficiency, overtime, absence, labour utilization, and the finals acceptance rate for quality. They are as follows:

Efficiency:	target: 101.2%	actual: 102.1%
Overtime:	target: 5.0%	actual: 8.4%
Absence:	target: 3.5%	actual: 3.6%
Finals acceptance:	88.75%	
Labour utilization:	84.2%	

Desmond proceeds to inform the meeting that the labour utilization figure for June will be very bad 'with excess hours the problem'. The average for the year thus far is 81.25% for labour utilization. Desmond speaks in a very earnest fashion, his body language adding to the plaintive tone in his voice. He is 'not so happy on acceptance'; it has dropped from 90.5% to 88.7%. While he identifies this as 'partially due to start-up problems on F1 and P7', he adds that this is 'a very worrying situation. There has been an increase of 0.5% on major faults that are due to silly mistakes, people not concentrating and not doing their job properly.' Desmond is admonishing the meeting now and he is emphasizing that this is a grave matter, his whole persona communicates this, 'We must improve or we're not going to stay in business. I'd like you to take this message back to your constituents . . . and we're going to be hard on these people. This is really serious now, ladies and gents. If we see people not fulfilling their job properly we will have no hesitation in disposing of their services.' Desmond is making sure no doubt remains in people's minds. He wants his message to be taken back to the shop-floor. And the message is that people must concentrate hard, avoid mistakes, or the repercussions will be serious. Desmond completes his presentation by pointing out that any major fault is 'immediately identifiable to a customer. Just one, in a house, in a new TV set and we're in trouble.'

Then, back to the Chair who announces that there will be a Japanese visitor on the 2nd and 3rd of July. He is the group executive that the AV division reports to. A big cheese. He will be reviewing the refurbishment activity amongst other things. The Chair points out that the stocks are too high in Europe and that they have been 'asked to cut back by 20,000 units' on production. I assume this is across the plants. He reassures the meeting that there is a full firm order book to the end of November.

He next discusses the plans for extension to the plant and informs the meeting that there has been strong resistance from local residents. Nippon CTV [has] been in close discussions with the local authorities, 'The feeling from [the city] planning council is this is par for the course. We do pursue a good neighbour policy. We are willing to compromise if possible.' The extension is planned for a school site across the road from the main plant and would raise capacity from 800,000 CTVs at present to one million units. Nippon CTV [has] been 'in discussion with Mr Ikeda' over the question of 'how big we can go here before needing another site'. Apparently, forecasts for 1996/97 suggest that Nippon CTV may need 1,000,000 set capacity level. Nippon CTV certainly has the backing of the local authorities, the meeting was told the representative of the city council had threatened that Nippon Denki 'would pull out of Torport' if the proposals were not accepted. However, the MD pointed out that, 'He was trying to speak on our behalf and there is no possibility of that happening.' In fact, he further reassured the meeting that the mood was 'rather the opposite when I was in Japan'. There then followed a brief general report from the air conditioner plant which noted that management [was] 'looking for uniformity in your holidays as soon as the project was up and running'.

Following that, the personnel director ran through the employment data for the last month. The employment figures for May were given as follows: direct employees—892, indirect employees—109, giving a total of 1,001 members, with trade union membership at 514. He reported 11 new [company] members. The meeting was then informed that the projected labour turnover was 30% for the year and that it stood at 35% for May. The expected end of year figure for direct workers was 25%. The labour turnover figures [excluding temporary workers] were presented, broken down by length of service and reason given for leaving. There have been 40 resignations and eight dismissals for the year to date.

There were further charts displaying direct manufacturing overtime levels, these were plotted monthly for 1989–91. Currently, the overtime levels are exceeding the previous year with a predicted figure of 9.5% for June. Then there was a chart displaying sickness and absence figures, and these too were plotted monthly for 1989–91. The personnel director asked whether the attendance award scheme was working. The graph appeared to run between 4% and 6% over the year, which represented a decrease on 1989 levels.

Next, there followed a detailed discussion of the proceedings of a special CAB meeting held two days earlier. This was described as a 'follow up' on the special CAB which had discussed proposals to alter the sickness pay scheme. The current scheme costs Nippon CTV around £300,000 a year. The meeting was informed that Nippon CTV has 'a common culture, to treat staff and shop-floor alike with the scheme based on service against entitlement'. The amendment to the scheme was that there should be no entitlement to sickness pay after a second absence during any 12 month period. There would be a requirement for self or medical certification of illness for periods of absence of five working days or more and there should be a 'clear 12 month period elapsed since the second absence'. The CAB meeting was informed that this had been 'agreed by [the special] CAB'.

Further details were outlined. There was to be 'no standard entitlement' after the second absence and the member was to be advised by their departmental manager that 'any further absence may lead to formal disciplinary action'. A third absence would then result in an interview by the departmental manager and the member may receive a first written warning with a freeze on grade movements for six months. There was a question from one of the shop-floor representatives on the board about whether floating days might be given in lieu of days lost during a holiday period when people were ill. The board was informed that there would be no entitlement and this was firmly underlined by Desmond, 'I'm convinced this is the right way to go'. He told the meeting that he had 'checked with industry competitors, Matsushita and Sanyo, and they didn't pay for holiday illness'.

However, during further discussion, it becomes clear [to me] that these suggestions represent a change from the current practice and not all the board members are happy about it. Desmond is keen to see this amendment through, 'The disruption [to production] is quite considerable'. He further claims that 'People have abused it' and that there had been problems with sickness payments and so on. There is a short continuation of discussion but few remain in favour of (or at least continue to articulate their support for) maintaining the payment for holiday illness. Previously, floating days were given in lieu if the claim was supported by a doctor's certificate.

There is a discernible pressure, particularly from Desmond, to push through full acceptance. Indeed, the strategy used by Desmond was to point out that 'At the last meeting, CAB raised no objection', and to push the fact that these proposals were accepted at the special meeting. Desmond pushes this by emphasizing that this was in part compensated for by an extra 1 per cent in the pay deal. 'Oh, I agree,' comments the MD. Next, Desmond pushes the point that the costs of funding automatic pay for sickness are high. He continues by telling the meeting that he is very worried about the disruptions to production. This point is supported by Joan who explains the problems regarding the juggling of labour for team leaders when members are out. One shop-floor representative, who was not at the special CAB meeting and I think is a stand-in, is still expressing discontent. Desmond next points out the number of people involved in taking advantage of this entitlement at present. Desmond then concludes the discussions by talking of the stress of 'members who do actually come to work and have to bear the strain of these fairly cute people around who do buck the system'.

The trade union official, Don, has more or less said nothing during all this except to agree with Desmond and the MD that the special meeting had already agreed these proposals. The amendments are accepted with one vote against (that of the stand-in from stores). The board is informed that they should brief their constituents at tomorrow morning's coffee break. There will be an extra five minutes to allow them to do so. The MD, who has been conspicuous in the way he has phrased certain things, comments, 'I will take this to the board as the advice of CAB' and then excuses himself from the meeting and the personnel director takes the Chair.

There is a question from one of the shop-floor representatives about the procedure following the second absence and the personnel director responds, 'After a second absence the departmental manager will . . . we don't put "warn", we put "counsel" the member concerned'. The argument is put forward that it should be made clear that following a second period of absence the return to work will be accompanied by a formal verbal warning. Desmond now argues that this should not be inflexibly always the case. He feels there should be some account taken of extenuating circumstances or 'where there has been abuse'.

Nippon CTV [has] broken down the patterns of absenteeism and the third and further absences account for about 20% of the total number of days lost. Hence, cutting all payments on this would save an estimated £60,000. The proposal is that each member should have a full 12 months clear of any absence before being entitled to sick pay again. Desmond pushes home this point, 'It's got to be that tough to make any significant savings'. This means anyone forced into having unpaid absence must be free of any absence for a full 12 months before requalifying for sick pay. If someone is out unpaid in May then they must last until the following May. This appears a little less clear and decided and there is talk of extenuating circumstances although this is met with a disbelieving, 'Who's claiming that?!' from Desmond.

The discussion moves to discipline procedures. For once, the meeting is not pushed forcibly in a particular direction by senior management and this topic is opened up for discussion from the shop-floor representatives and Don. Desmond concedes that, 'We have to accept people's word on whether they are well enough or not, but when there are witnesses to the contrary . . .' The Chair pulls this to a close, 'Is everyone happy?' 'No, but we'll have to accept it,' responds Don. In fact, Don seems to lead from the front in terms of accepting things. Whether this is because he is completely ineffectual and disinterested or whether it is the resignation of a man who knows through experience that there is no point in pushing things beyond a very limited level I cannot be sure. Still, whilst he expresses discontent here, his whole demeanour is hardly that which suggests real unhappiness. Whichever reason it may be, Don is not going to be the person who organizes, or indeed, attempts to organize a change to the current status quo.

The logic of the changes to the sickness pay scheme is to try and push people to take floating days rather than report in sick and retain their holidays. Should they do this, they will be allowed to continue in the attendance bonus scheme. The cut-off for the attendance bonus is July 8th, if someone receiving a bonus is absent following that date then the money is 'clawed back' from the next month's pay. And 'This is then advised to the company'. George, the personnel director, asks the representatives of the air conditioner plant, the observers, if they are happy and whether they have any queries. They do not respond as to their level of happiness but there are no questions.

The Chair runs through various pieces of information. The company handbook is currently being reviewed, giving details of the rules and procedures of the company. There is a discussion of the money to be given through the company payroll to charities. The CAB representatives are currently discussing this matter with their constituents. Nippon CTV is spending £26,000 on improvements to car park lighting and security arrangements, for example, closed circuit television monitors. The timing for the summer shutdown for next year is discussed. Personnel have checked with schools either side of the river and they close somewhere between Wednesday 22nd July and Friday 24th July. The proposal is to 'pack up' on Thursday 23rd July and start up again on Tuesday 11th August.

There is a review of the health and safety situation of both the manufacturing sites during the last month. There has been one 'significant accident' with a woman falling and breaking her arm. There have been two near misses, one involving a fork lift driver and the other involving the collapse of part of a contractor's roof scaffolding in the machine shop. The personnel manager acknowledges that it was 'pure luck that no one was injured'. There has been one minor incident at the AC [air conditioning] plant, a contractor was again involved. A sub-committee has been set up to look at eye and ear protection in the machine shop. Protection for ears is now necessary because the sound levels have increased.

The sub-committee to consider the restaurant facilities has stalled, there have been too few volunteers to serve on it. 'Is it worth running it?' someone asks. The issue is adjourned until the winter. One point regarding refreshments is raised; the machine shop runs two shifts from 6.00 a.m. to 2.00 p.m. and 2.00 p.m. to 10.00 p.m. and there is no hot food available for the 36 people involved. This problem will be considered and the provision of a microwave or some such measure discussed.

The charity sub-committee has a number of requests to support certain calls for donations. The donations requested range from between £25 and £100 or for items such as a radio or cassette player. These are all accepted. Two members that are currently ill have been sent baskets of fruit.

The Chair opens up the meeting as a 'round table' for any other business. There is some discontent in the stores area. A new member has been recruited to come in at team leader level. This person is a woman with no factory experience, and the men in the stores area are not happy, 'She's being trained for a job by members who didn't get it'. The Chair responds, 'You can't talk about an individual in CAB.' He informs the stores representative that the matter must go to personnel, in private. 'When it becomes a matter of general principle it comes to CAB.' He adds that 'it must be pushed up to director level first.' There is a question about the votes cast in the CAB election. The actual numbers were not published 'to avoid embarrassment to those not elected'. There is a question about whether smoking is allowed in meeting rooms. These are the only points raised by the table. The representative of the AC plant asks about the provision of safety trousers and jackets.

Everyone is thanked for their attendance and the meeting is closed at 5.10 p.m. As we left the room, I mentioned to Desmond something about the changes in the sickness pay scheme. He responded very determinedly, 'Your job is to come to work'.

The content of the CAB meetings is not to be discussed by any of those attending until after the morning briefing which each of the shop-floor representatives makes to their constituents the next day.

Coffee break time around 11.00 a.m. It is the day after the last CAB meeting. The proceedings of the meeting are disseminated to the shop-floor by the elected representatives. However, they do this by reading out a sheet prepared by Fred Woodhead, the personnel manager, who is secretary of CAB. He condenses down the discussions and outcomes to a single side of A4. The members of CAB are not allowed to discuss proceedings until after this report back to the plant. To allow this process, the morning coffee break is extended by five minutes. However, by the time the representative (a shop-floor member herself) has run through the detail of the markets report and the plant position on inventory, sales, etc., the buzzer has gone to return to the line. Sharon has somehow discovered that there have been moves to change the sickness pay scheme. While the representative mentions this as a change from current practice, alongside information on charity donations, she makes no description of those changes. As people begin to drain their coffee cups and return to their positions, Sharon shouts out a question about the nature of these changes. She is told, as people are already disappearing out of the coffee lounge, that it would take 'too long to explain' but that the details would be posted on a notice board.

I had a brief word to Sharon who appeared to already know the nature of the changes. She was scathing of the way the representative had handled the feedback process and she added, 'Most people won't read the notice board and won't know about this until they're ill'.

As discussed in Chapter 6, communication at Nippon CTV is carefully orchestrated and tightly controlled by management; the feedback report read out by the representatives is produced by the personnel department and the morning briefing by the team leaders is read from a sheet produced by the production department. In this way, management is able to script the communication which passes down on to the shop-floor. By focusing attention on the details regarding the plant's business performance, the information that actually has an impact on the shop-floor workers is effectively hidden from them. As a consequence, the majority of the workers leave the 'brief back' unaware of the change in the rules of the sickness pay scheme and its implications for them.

SUMMARY AND IMPLICATIONS

This chapter has discussed the structure and character of organized labour at the two plants. This is important in the debate over the nature of contemporary manufacturing management and the 'Japanese' model and the role of organized labour therein, and is also significant in providing insight into the implications for workplace unionism of recent developments in the economic and legislative context of industrial relations in Britain. By inspection, it appears that the two workplaces are very different. Valleyco has two recognized unions for shop-floor workers which engage through a steward system in collective bargaining over pay and conditions. The unions are members of their local organizations. In contrast, the union at Nippon CTV has signed a single union agreement with a no-strike clause and a commitment to pendulum arbitration and does not engage in collective bargaining over pay. The union at the plant is isolated from others in the region. Moreover, the union at Nippon CTV espouses an ideology of partnership, while the unions at Valleyco maintain an ideology of conflicting interests. Therefore, in accord with Kelly's (1996) axis of militancy-moderation, we may recognize the Valleyco unions as displaying 'militant' characteristics and the union at Nippon CTV as 'moderate'.

Despite these clear differences, the situations of the unions at Valleyco and Nippon CTV share a number of characteristics. The evidence from Valleyco suggests that the pressures on traditional unions, particularly legislative and economic, have eroded their opportunity for independent action which is actually effective in securing improved conditions for their members. While the AEEU has formally agreed not to strike at Nippon CTV, strike action seems no more likely at Valleyco. For one thing, the workers could not afford it financially.

The union officials at Valleyco appear to regard themselves as less effectual in shaping management action than does the senior steward at Nippon CTV. It seems that the pressure on the traditional unions—high local unemployment, decreasing contact with other local union stewards, economic recession, and falling demand—may have left them as toothless as the 'new realist' deal between the AEEU and Nippon CTV.

However, despite these difficulties, the unions at Valleyco have managed to engage in meaningful, albeit limited, bargaining with management and were able to resist pressure to give up their September holiday and were able to ensure that the shop-floor temperature was at the legal minimum before work commenced. In these instances, the unions demonstrated that they and their members do not share management perspectives and that the union officers were willing and able to put their members' position. The members themselves realized the difficulty of their situation and that of their stewards but continued to actively show their desire for independent collective representation of their interests.

At Nippon CTV, the union does not have a formal independent route for communication and negotiation. Certainly, management at the plant ensures that the shop-floor workers are far better informed about the company than those at Valleyco, but any shop-floor or union influence is filtered through management channels of representation. This influence seems very limited. The research shows that the CAB places the balance of power squarely with management and the 'brief back' episode demonstrates how this process may actually assist management in making surreptitious changes to the formal regulations at the plant. The union members at the plant do not appear to believe that their union offers effective independent representation. The evidence suggests that even informal attempts to influence management by the stewards founder on the company's hard line in upholding its procedures. This form of new industrial relations, however, has clearly not won over 'hearts and minds' and the shop-floor workers are critical of their own union representatives. The plurality of shop-floor interests is underscored by workers who feel that they are suffering due to a lack of effective formal representation.

The Challenge for the Union Movement

The two cases presented here demonstrate the way in which workplace relations may be constituted under new forms of management and production. These cases also present further information which emphasizes the threat that these developments represent for workplace unionism and therefore the union movement. Workplace unionism and the pressures under which it must operate have been receiving increasing attention (Millward *et al.* 1992; Terry 1994). The research reported here suggests support for the widely held notion that the internationalization of capital has been matched by a decentralization of production (Lash and Urry 1987) which has resulted in localized bargaining and a process of 'disaggregation' (Hyman 1992):

The new strategies of management . . . must be understood as a new discursive framework and strategic orientation that attempts to isolate and erode the relatively autonomous collective traditions in industrial relations, reconstructing worker representation and
loyalties around the effort of the individual, the 'needs' of production and the identity
of the firm (Clegg 1989; Guest 1989; Garrahan and Stewart 1992; Martinez Lucio and
Weston 1991). Therefore, changes in management practice are deemed to contribute to
an undermining of traditional worker representation in the workplace. (Martinez Lucio
and Weston 1995: 237.)

The two cases presented here are instructive since one is an example of
the single union agreements that have proven increasingly popular with foreign
direct investors into Britain and the other is a brownfield site with 'traditional'
collective bargaining. Despite the structural and historical variance, the two plants
have both been subjected to a number of similar pressures toward fragmentation. Blyton and Turnbull (1994: 129) note that:

In each and every case [of a single union agreement], however, there is arguably a much
diminished influence for the trade union. Not only do such agreements approximate to a
new form of 'enterprise unionism', virtually excluding *external* trade union influences and
any wider social, economic, political or legal agendas that the union, let alone the union
movement, might be involved in, but the union has a greatly reduced *internal* role.

For the workers at Valleyco, the situation has become increasingly similar to
that at Nippon CTV, largely through the impact of external economic forces
and the breakdown of historical union structures. The workers at both Nippon
CTV and Valleyco do simple standardized tasks and are replaceable; the local
labour markets are full of potential replacements; economic restructuring of the
local economies has decimated male full-time employment and resulted in many
women's key, but arduous, dual role as sole 'bread winner' and 'home maker';
the increasing coupling of workers' activities and responsibilities, with an attendant (and contradictory) necessity for individual accountability and blame; the
localization of bargaining and/or the incorporation of the union into management communication structures; the competitive market-place and the dominance of the 'customer'; and the fact that both plants are a part of far bigger
transnational corporations, have all combined to fragment the labour collective
and undermine the independent and effective representation of labour through
the traditional union structures on the shop-floor.

However, the two cases also demonstrate that, despite the above pressures,
the shared experience of exploitation (the 'gap' between the shop-floor and the
company) persists and, perhaps through the process of 'factory consciousness'
(Chung 1994), continues to provide a dynamic for workers' sense of the collective; the attitude of 'them and us' persists (Kelly and Kelly 1991). Despite this,
and for the reasons listed earlier, the workplace unionism at the two plants is not
able to deliver an effective and successful representation of the collective. In part
the fragmentation of labour through the 'blaming' processes of the quality system may be responsible for this, although as Hyman (1992: 129) notes:

Unions as collective organizations are inevitably rooted in a heterogeneity of immediate, localized experiences and aspirations; *spontaneously* these are as likely to be in conflict as in congruence. The construction of broader solidarities has always required a deliberate and precarious *effort*, a mobilization of bias by leaders and rank-and-file activists; and success, when achieved, has usually proved temporary and partial.

Overall the unions at both plants face considerable problems. The new realist position of the AEEU at Nippon CTV has allowed management the 'reassertion of their prerogative' (Purcell 1991) *but* the ideology of partnership and co-operation has not eroded workers' perceptions of conflicting interests. In these circumstances, the union has become isolated from its members, the stewards have been incorporated into the management process, and the workers overtly bemoan the lack of a more militant stance from their union. As a consequence the union's position is essentially fragile since it fails to 'build on the only reliable foundation, namely its membership and their willingness to act' (Kelly 1996: 102). Indeed, these findings add strength to the argument of Kelly (1996) who concludes that the appropriate course for unions is that of militancy since this better serves union members' interests. The case for militancy is strengthened by Graham (1995), who reports similar findings at a Japanese car transplant to those presented here, in that the 'Japanese' model 'neither engages workers in managerial aspects of their jobs nor provides an avenue for real involvement in decision making' and that, 'When workers did manage to have input into decisions affecting the quality of their lives, it was because they went outside the model's boundaries and approached the company as its adversary' (Graham 1995: 137).

Further, this research would suggest that, following Martinez Lucio and Weston (1995), the challenge for the union movement lies with those above the shop-floor level. In countering the assumptions of the impact of disaggregation (see Amoroso 1992), Martinez Lucio and Weston argue that the outcomes are not definite, but rather, that there are opportunities for trade unions, most notably in the way that informal 'networks' between different plant and office union representatives have been evolving (see also Wainwright 1994). Still, the evidence which Martinez Lucio and Weston present of how and where this is actually taking place is limited. Moreover, they also note that the internationalization of capital has resulted in increasing pressures to fragmentation for labour as workplace representatives compete with each other (see also Mueller and Purcell 1992). Therefore, it seems that the challenge for trade unions is to organize themselves and act collectively on an international basis and they can only do so if regional, national, and international representatives of the labour movement play a strategic and developmental role. If labour is to be able to rally an effective opposition to the successful establishment of managerial prerogatives as represented by the Nippon Denki Corporation and its ilk then it must surely seek strength through global co-operation of its members; 'global' capital must herald 'global' labour response.

9

Management and Labour on the 'New' Shop-Floor

INTRODUCTION

In this book I have reported the workplace relations and management practices of a Japanese-owned consumer electronics plant and a European-owned automotive components plant. Through the use of an ethnographic research method it is possible to explore how management seeks to implement JIT, TQM, and team working, to understand the role of labour in shaping these management initiatives, and the impact of these for both management and labour in practice. The particular strength of this form of research is in providing detailed accounts of the social relations on the shop-floor in contemporary manufacturing. From the enhanced understanding that such detail allows it is also possible to draw some more general observations from the two cases.

The Japanese transplant's management has been far more successful in establishing internal process control and integration than is the case for Valleyco. In part this is because the transplant has been buffered from its external environment and hence uncertainty from market fluctuations or unreliable schedules is removed. The European-owned plant is constantly reacting to various sources of uncertainty such as poor supplier quality, changes in customer orders, and internal system breakdowns. Neither plant is successfully integrated into a value chain with tight process control in the manner of the exemplars of best practice from the literature.

The Japanese transplant has been at least partially successful in establishing the technical systems of JIT and TQM, and, in appearance, its work organization and HR practices closely match the best practices identified by Womack *et al.* (1990) and MacDuffie (1995). However, as we have seen, the effect of these is not to encourage mutual responsibility and high commitment but to extend management's control and to restrict worker opportunity for autonomy. As a result workers have very little involvement beyond the routine of their job tasks and are active in distancing themselves from management and in refusing to contribute discretionary effort. The system at Nippon CTV is quite effective in undermining worker resistance and managing the labour process but at the cost of employee involvement in any continuous improvement and problem-solving activity.

In contrast, management at the European-owned plant is struggling to retain control over its processes and the shop-floor activities resemble a form of 'directed chaos'. The uncertainty in Valleyco allows workers to regulate their effort-bargain and to secure a measure of counter-control; however, management is attempting to maintain its systems and is reliant on some discretionary co-operation from workers, particularly when uncertainty in customer scheduling creates 'rush jobs', panic situations where labour is required to work particularly quickly to meet unanticipated customer demands.

In practice the Japanese transplant is more successful and efficient in the management of the labour process and its manufacturing operations but this control is effected without winning over workers' 'hearts and minds'. Conflict remains a central feature of the shop-floor relations at Nippon CTV and the unitarist assumptions of the proponents of new management models are demonstrated to reflect an inadequate conceptualization of the 'new' shop-floor. Equally the research findings do not support the rhetoric of multiskilled and empowered workers engaged primarily in problem solving and continuous improvement.

The Nippon CTV system is superior in its combination of technical efficiency and social control, primarily through the marginalization of the uncertainty that blights the manufacturing practices of many organizations. This superiority is achieved through the avoidance of traditional bureaucratic dysfunctions and through the extension of managerial control. The process control of the plant's JIT system also restricts the opportunities for worker resistance. However, the system at Nippon CTV does not include a recombination of planning and execution, heightened worker autonomy and skill, nor worker-manager reciprocity; it cannot be considered a radical departure from traditional capitalist shop-floor relations. Therefore while the *form* of HRM and work organization at Valleyco and Nippon CTV may be different, the *content* is readily recognizable.

MARGINALIZING UNCERTAINTY

Nippon CTV has managed to secure control over its processes and successfully sought to decrease the instances of uncertainty in the everyday running of operations. Management has been able to all but eradicate informal negotiations over day-to-day working because it has decoupled its internal operations from the external sources of potential disruption—market-place fluctuations and variable and unpredictable customer schedules; and variable reliability (in quality and delivery) of suppliers and internal systems. The proof of this is evidenced by the exceptions—the problems that quickly manifest themselves on the shop-floor whenever either 'external' or 'internal' suppliers fail to meet management's expectations or when technology is not as reliable as it might be. Nippon CTV's success in securing *internal* control stems from its decoupling of processes from external sources of uncertainty. At least in the case of its British operations, it has not secured the greater control and influence over its supply chain and the market-place which has marked certain Japanese corporations (Ohno 1988; Womack *et al.* 1990).

Crucially for the labour force, the reduction in uncertainty also marginalizes the significance of *informal negotiations* between management and labour over the 'rules' governing those operations (cf. Blau 1974). As a consequence, labour loses the opportunity to secure some leeway in relation to the formal written systems in place (for example, Brown 1972) and management is not caught up in negotiations over those procedures, nor required to justify instructions to workers within the system on a regular basis (see Armstrong *et al.* 1981). This marginalization of uncertainty is a salient factor in the situation at Nippon CTV: uncertainty, and the scope for informality which that brings, is fundamental in understanding the patterns of negotiated order at any workplace. The contested nature of this negotiated order is ignored by proponents of high commitment HRM but is central to the findings of a number of studies which report on workplace relations in detail (for example, Armstrong *et al.* 1981; Gouldner 1955; Hamper 1992).

The situation for management at Valleyco is in direct contrast to that at Nippon CTV. Both internally and externally, the Valleyco managers are struggling to maintain some sort of control over their systems. The unreliability of supplier quality, the unpredictable variation in customer orders, the malfunctioning of equipment, *inter alia*, result in the breakdown of the formal systems. Valleyco management and the workforce are then necessarily caught up in persistent informal negotiations because the formal systems in place simply do not work; the result is a form of directed chaos. This does not appear to be uncommon. Many other authors have reported the chaotic nature of shop-floor activity (for example, Juravich 1985) and the fact that management in general is 'opportunistic, habitual, tactical, reactive, frenetic, *ad hoc*, brief, fragmented and concerned with fixing' (Thompson and McHugh 1990: 137) or what Blyton and Turnbull (1994) call '*un*strategic'. The porosity of the formal system can be exploited by workers as they seek to wrest some degree of control over their work experience from management. And, it should be noted, worker resistance may be a *source* of uncertainty for management.

Chapters 4 and 5 provide numerous examples of how workers at Valleyco exploited the limitations of management control. A number of these relate to the piece-work system of remuneration and control, for example systematic soldiering, building a stockpile, or bluffing the timer, and these features have been reported by numerous studies into workplace relations (for example, Roy 1952, 1955; Lupton 1963). There are also examples of how unreliable quality from suppliers can result in managerial inconsistency, thus undermining management as it seeks to legitimate its position regarding the need for high-quality performance (as seen in Chapter 6). In such circumstances, management falls back on the fragmented and *ad hoc* approach reported here and elsewhere. This, in turn, may necessitate further informal compromise and thereby give further opportunity for worker influence as patterns of order are continually renegotiated as a part of the social processes of the organization (Elger 1975; and also, for example, Crozier 1964; Dalton 1959).

However, the evidence suggests that management can effectively reduce the impact of uncertainty in certain circumstances. Management's relative dominance at Nippon CTV is secured in large part through greater *process discipline and control*. For example, the moving assembly line determines a relatively uniform work speed, the reduction of internal buffers of stock and time imposes a rigidity and discipline to production schedules, and the close monitoring of quality with individualized accountability at each stage of the production process maintains pressure to conform to management expectations and ensures that defective production is identified almost immediately.

Moreover, in a context where management ideology dominates, informality becomes the realm of management through which it actually extends control by, for example, the 'tweaking up' of the linespeed and the reproportioning of work levels which go beyond those specified in the standard times and work manuals of the formal system (as indicated in Chapter 5). This represents at the plant what Armstrong and Goodman (1979) identified as 'managerial custom and practice'. Informally negotiated settlements on the shop-floor at Nippon CTV are predominantly over the extent to which management may extend control beyond that formally designated. Following Armstrong *et al.* (1981), the 'legitimising principles' which underpin these settlements at Nippon CTV are founded largely upon a 'world view' which accepts managerial prerogatives, particularly regarding 'the product and its efficient manufacture'. The necessity for quality in order for the plant to survive in the increasingly competitive market-place is a fundamental factor in management's attempts to legitimate its actions at both workplaces.

The efficacy of the manufacturing system at Nippon CTV is such that little authority needs to be exercised by way of direct instructions under forms of 'personal control' (Edwards 1979). As a consequence, Nippon CTV operates with increased spans of control and a smaller number of direct supervisors than is the case at Valleyco and control is underpinned with a highly effective monitoring and surveillance system, particularly for quality performance. The opportunities for extending control which these systems offer management has been noted elsewhere (Delbridge *et al.* 1992). This situation is in itself reliant on a relatively smooth, reliable, and (managerially) preordained set of shop-floor activities. The formal monitoring and control systems in place record information on how the system matches with what is anticipated. In contrast, the system at Valleyco is heavily reliant on personal relationships and informal solutions to *unanticipated* events within that system.

However, there are pockets of the shop-floor at Valleyco that share the characteristics of managerial control present at Nippon CTV. In some areas of Valleyco's operations, management has begun to adopt the principles of JIT and TQM. Management has not secured the marginalization of uncertainty to the same level as at Nippon CTV but certain lines show similar traits with work-in-process inventories brought down, and individual accountability up. As discussed in Chapters 4 and 5, the tighter coupling of internal processes, and hence workers (underpinned by group performance-based pay), with a decreased reliance on informality and increased clarity and visibility of responsibilities has resulted in intensified pressures for workers, for example to attend work when feeling unwell or to work faster in order to keep up with others on the line.

In both of the case companies there is evidence of the way in which management has established process discipline and control in order to marginalize uncertainty. This was especially the situation at Nippon CTV, where an 'internal' or 'bounded' JIT system was proving particularly effective. Through marginalizing uncertainty, management reduces the number of occasions when workers are able to engage in the informal negotiations which offer opportunities for labour to secure some counter-control and to influence the effort-bargain. At Valleyco, the systems were not reliable and, as a consequence, while management sought to direct the chaos, workers were able to take advantage of the informality to improve their situation.

EFFICACY AND EFFICIENCY

The preceding section has indicated the extent to which the manufacturing systems at Nippon CTV are facilitated by the marginalization of uncertainty. The subsequent process discipline and control severely limits the opportunities for workers to engage in substantive informal negotiations over their work and consequently limits their ability to successfully secure greater control of their situation. This should not be confused with a position which might be regarded as technologically determinist, for there is no guarantee that these systems will provide such outcomes. Hamper (1992) provides a vivid account of how an assembly line may not be enough to secure managerial control of the shop-floor (see also Cavendish 1982; Linhart 1981). Nor should these findings be taken as evidence for the primary importance of the technical aspects of contemporary manufacturing. The requirement is for research which may provide insights into the interface and interaction between the technical and social aspects of the workplace. A key element of management control as a social process at Nippon CTV is that it is consistent with the technical requirements for efficient production.

In the terms of Gordon (1976), the rules and procedures at Nippon CTV are consistent with the twin objectives of efficient capital accumulation (*quantitative efficiency*) and the subordination of labour and the continuity of capitalism (*qualitative efficiency*). Unlike examples of an 'unstrategic' management of production where the control of labour appears as an end in itself (rather than a means to the end of efficient capital accumulation), at Nippon CTV the dysfunctions of certain control procedures are circumvented (see Delbridge 1995).

For example, the case studies presented by Roy (1955) and Haraszti (1980) both detail situations under piece-rate systems where workers are prevented from making goods because of the bureaucratic procedures by which they are controlled. As Edwards (1979) has noted, piece-work systems encourage workers to actively deceive management and to regularly restrict output. This is a key feature of the shop-floor reported by Roy (1952, 1955) and is central to the situation on most of the lines at Valleyco. In the case (in a socialist state) reported by Haraszti (1980), the bureaucratic rules governing the piece-work system were flouted by workers with the tacit agreement, or 'indulgence' (see Gouldner 1955), of management who understood that workers were forced to 'loot' in order to meet production plans.

The cases reported by Haraszti and Roy and the situation at Valleyco demonstrate the complex nature of workplace relations and the manner in which the contest between management and labour may result in managerial action inconsistent with economic rationality. Research by Cavendish (1982), Hamper (1992), and Kamata (1983) documents the way in which working on a mass production assembly line also includes these facets of the workplace relationship between management and labour. In contrast, at Nippon CTV, the incorporation of the objectives of JIT manufacturing and the company's style of TQM facilitate the presentation of a coherent set of priorities to workers which allow for a more complete combination of the control of labour with management's economic goals.

The system at Nippon CTV works in such a way as to 'square the circle' of qualitative and quantitative efficiency. The research data presented in this study indicate that on occasions worker 'misbehaviour' (in supporting each other to avoid being booked for mistakes) may actually result in an improved position for management (in the form of better quality). While there is a danger in exaggerating the omniscience of management, at the very least the 'unintended consequence' of the control process in this instance is consistent with the economic efficiency of the system. Moreover, as will be reviewed later in this chapter, the pressures of the system, for example with regard to worker self-policing, exert a fragmenting influence on the shop-floor collective which is consistent with the reproduction of the social relations of production.

The efficacy of the management system on the shop-floor at Nippon CTV may be emphasized by considering what impact a 'work-to-rule' by the shop-floor might have. In most organizations, a 'work-to-rule' is an effective form of resistance since the formal rules are insufficient for management to secure efficient performance. At Nippon CTV, the impact would be likely to prove almost negligible. The shop-floor might achieve a slight reduction in output should the more experienced workers refuse to accept the extra pieces they are expected to take on when the linespeed is tweaked upward and less competent members fall behind. At best, they may be able to resist the speed-up and restrict line efficiency on the grounds that the standard times for panels should be adhered to. We may contrast this with the situation at Valleyco, where management regularly must call on its workers to make 'extra efforts' in order to meet 'rush jobs'. If workers refuse to work above a certain speed, then the plant may fail to meet the delivery deadline. Valleyco's customers impose enormous punitive fines on suppliers which fail to deliver reliably and if Valleyco proves unreliable then it may lose business. Of course, the loss of business would threaten workers' jobs and hence there is some common interest between workers and managers in meeting their customer demands (Cressey and MacInnes 1980).

MANAGEMENT INDULGENCE AND THE LIMITS TO CONTROL

Although, as explained above, the Nippon CTV management system is much more co-ordinated and effective than that at Valleyco, it is still important to recognize the limits to management control (Thompson and Ackroyd 1995; Hyman 1987). Uncertainty has not been eradicated and, at Nippon CTV, unreliable technology (exemplified by the test gear and the parts check machine) can offer opportunities for workers informally to secure some additional influence over their position. Equally, as we shall see, there are degrees to which workers may successfully resist and regulate their effort. Still, uncertainty may actually result in an increase in pressure and stress on workers. As we shall reflect in a later section, the pressures result in a fragmentation of the shop-floor collective while workers' choice is marginalized to a considerable extent.

If management at Nippon CTV has secured advantages over more traditional organizational arrangements, equally, the contradictions claimed of modern capitalism—flexibility and decentralization versus tightening regulation and control (Muetzelfeldt 1989; Blyton and Turnbull 1992)—are not readily apparent as constraints to management at the plant. In essence this may be explained by the *lack* of decentralization to be found in the control systems at Nippon CTV. This is clearly facilitated by the stability and reliability of the shop-floor through the marginalization of uncertainty discussed above. However, a consequence of this is that workers do not make contributions beyond those formally expected and monitored, nor can management expect to draw on good will. The strict formal system results in workers acting in pursuit of their own best interests, for example in resisting overtime work and failing to participate in discretionary activities. At Valleyco, on the other hand, management may have to rely on at least some workers making additional efforts in times of crisis, for example on 'rush jobs'.

In direct contrast to the arguments for high-commitment HRM, workers under the 'high surveillance—low trust' regime at Nippon CTV are not given discretion and they are not expected to contribute beyond 'doing what they're told'. The system does not rely on workers making 'extra' efforts (neither in the conception nor execution of tasks) except that they must attempt to keep up with the linespeed set by the team leader—which may go above the formal standard timing. In other words, prerogative over work speed has been acceded to management and, where workers do not keep up, they profess their *inability* rather than their *unwillingness* (cf. Cavendish 1982); workers do not challenge management on what they should do, only on what they are able to do. This exemplifies the way in which managerial ideology is dominant at Nippon CTV (Armstrong *et al.* 1981).

There is little at Nippon CTV to indicate that Japanese manufacturing management represents a rebuttal of the Taylorist approach of dividing conception from execution. Contrary to the findings of Kenney and Florida (1993), Nippon CTV does not fit the description of an 'innovation-mediated' producer with 'the integration of innovation and production, of intellectual and physical labor' (Kenney and Florida 1993: 14), nor do the workers at the plant resemble the 'highly skilled problem solvers' promised by Womack *et al.* (1990). While management meetings at Nippon CTV may pay lip-service to the need for worker involvement, there is little to suggest this is anticipated or actively encouraged by front-line management and the team leaders. It might be argued that the restrictive and oppressive nature of control at Nippon CTV precludes the prospect of encouraging workers to make discretionary contributions.

As was detailed in Chapters 5 and 7, workers typically make no effort to contribute beyond the strict limits of their designated job task, neither do they play a substantial role in Nippon CTV's problem-solving and improvement activities. The shop-floor members make virtually no input through the formal mechanisms, and any ideas that are put forward reflect workers' beliefs that the linespeed is too high or that there are too few workers. These are ignored because decreasing the linespeed or increasing labour levels would have a detrimental impact on efficiency. The message for new members at induction conveys the necessity of 'showing willing' and following instructions while it is clear that the team leaders do not expect workers to have a regular and practical input on decisions.

Despite the description above of the ways in which management at Nippon CTV has reduced uncertainty and hence restricted workers' opportunities for informal negotiations, the process of management must still be seen as one of negotiation. While management may have secured a position of extended control, the system itself appears dependent for its perpetuation upon aspects of informal management indulgence. For instance, the information presented in Chapter 5 suggests that the senior members and off-line workers may act as a 'safety valve' to release some of the pressure put on the line workers by the formal systems. This aspect of workplace relations would appear to be commonplace (the charge-hands at Valleyco appear to play a similar, if less significant role), but at Nippon CTV the patterns of indulgence are not allowed to become institutionalized into the shop-floor *modus operandi* (cf. the concept of custom and practice, Brown 1972). Precedents by which workers may secure some counter-control through informal bargaining do not develop (cf. Armstrong *et al.* 1981). In other words, the operators may not expect or assume this indulgence to be repeated and even those most sympathetic to their situation do not allow them to 'take advantage'.

Moreover, it would appear that the intense pressure exerted upon team leaders to meet the targets set by management for their line restricts this indulgence to issues which do not directly affect the output and efficiency of operations. The clearest examples are where a senior member or an off-line worker will attempt

to ensure that their line members are not disciplined over their quality performance. This does help the individual concerned but does not have a detrimental
effect on performance. Indeed, one might argue that, once again, the impact
for management is a positive one, in this case because the system itself may
implode should too many workers be recorded as having too many defects and
hence be in need of 'counselling'.

The manner in which indulgence serves to maintain the social relations of
production may also be seen in the way that the panel shop manager collabor-
ates with her team leaders in hiding the exact batch by batch performance of each
panel line against standard times. This informal action secures the manager's
position and ensures the commitment of her team leaders. The pressure exerted
upon the team leaders by encouraging them to compete with each other is par-
alleled at the level of managers through the use of an 'Inputs and Outputs'
measurement system to record efficiency and performance in the different shops.
There is also some evidence that, away from the line, the system does rely on
some form of informality, for example, with the detail of the ins and outs or
regarding the relationship between the stores and materials handlers.

The information systems at Nippon CTV are such that some of the indulgence and 'misbehaviour' must be visible to senior management. For example,
it seems unlikely that management is unaware of the way in which the quality
test members can find some respite from the line by failing a series of good
panels or that the panel lines show variable performance against standard times
for individual batches. While the research into the management process in this
study has been focused on the shop-floor, it does seem likely that at least some
of these actions take place with the tacit acceptance of senior management. It
appears that these aspects of workplace relations may form the limits to management hegemony since, in keeping with Gordon (1976), the primary responsibility
of management remains the reproduction of the relations within capitalism.
Without this pattern of indulgence the formal systems would prove unworkable
and the pressure on the shop-floor might generate direct resistance. Laurie
Graham's (1995) ethnographic study of Subaru/Isuzu reports such occasions
when management inflexibility and intransigence prompted worker resistance.

We can demonstrate the significance of indulgence by considering the effects
of management working strictly to its own rules. During the research period, a
strict adherence to the rules for recording defects against individuals, and counselling those above a certain level, would have necessitated 'counselling' for
more than half the line. Were this to be undertaken then the disruption to production for that month would be substantial, with operators constantly away from
the line and the team leaders having to spend long periods counselling workers.
Moreover, under a management 'work-to-rule', this scenario would have to be
repeated in the following months and many of the members would have to be
formally disciplined and then dismissed under the system of performance monitoring. If the formal systems at Nippon CTV were adhered to unquestioningly
in a management 'work-to-rule' then they would result in an untenable position

for that management, who would have to either continually raise the number of defects allowed before counselling was required or constantly recruit replacement workers for those dismissed under the disciplinary system.

By comparing the hypothetical impact of management and labour 'working-to-rule' we may discern the nature of each in relation to the formal system. For management, the marginalization of uncertainty allied to the combination of qualitative and quantitative efficiency within the system means that its role is to extend control beyond that formally underwritten in order to achieve greater economic performance. These pressures are moderated by the necessity of replicating the social relations of production, which results in some indulgence from management or its agents in relation to the formal rules. Hence a strict work-to-rule would ease the pressure on labour to go beyond the formal expectations of the system, but the very nature of those formal requirements may produce intolerable pressures for workers. For workers, in 'working-to-rule', the opportunities to ease their position are almost negligible since the system itself is the primary mechanism by which their actions are secured.

WORKING HARDER NOT SMARTER

The preceding sections have discussed the ways in which management at Nippon CTV has been able to marginalize uncertainty and combine the qualitative and quantitative requirements for efficient manufacturing. It has also been noted that the workplace relations at both plants contain elements of management indulgence which are likely to be key in maintaining the relations of production. The following details the key issues regarding labour's position, particularly with a view to specifying the comparative situation of labour at Nippon CTV and to interpreting how the workers interact with their management in creating and recreating their workplace relations.

The process of management described above has clear demands of labour and certain implications for the labour process. The marginalization of uncertainty which management has secured at Nippon CTV includes (needs) a reliable and, where necessary, flexible workforce. As we have seen, the reduction in uncertainty means management is primarily concerned with securing *reliability*. Contrary to the rhetoric of highly skilled workers rotating jobs, flexibility here is typically a necessary reactive response to (remaining) uncertainty in the system, since 'spare resources' are kept to a minimum. For example, an absentee must be replaced by another worker who will need to work at a work station which is different from their usual one. Management's response to this is to seek to restrict absenteeism to an absolute minimum, in order to minimize the problem, rather than to place emphasis on coping with the problem through working flexibly. Still, workers are required to accept both functional and temporal flexibility. However, these are forms of inefficiency for management since stand-in workers are not able to work as quickly as those they replace and overtime requires the payment of premium rates. Any form of job rotation is avoided wherever possible.

As a central aspect of the management system at Nippon CTV, labour is highly restricted in its opportunities to work or act outside the formally pre-scribed procedures. As noted above, management at Nippon CTV has reduced the number of occasions when there is the uncertainty which allows workers to informally negotiate more space in their working day. In contrast, the man-agement control system at Valleyco is full of holes which workers can exploit to regain a degree of control and regulate the effort-bargain. For example, the ineffectiveness of a piece-rate system in regulating effort is clear. In addition, any informality at Nippon CTV is within a context where management ideology holds sway, so whereas workers may secure some notion of personal 'job rights' (since only experience is likely to facilitate workers in gaining the necessary speed and dexterity in any individual job) they can neither refuse a move nor engineer one.

As a result, perhaps as a function, of Nippon CTV's management system, workers' contributions to the organization rarely include any engagement in dis-cretionary activities of any form. As discussed in Chapter 7, workers who have no space during their working day are not disposed to give any extra effort. Indeed, presumably because such effort is 'unreliable', management at Nippon CTV does not actively encourage workers to do more than their formally designated range of tasks. At Valleyco, management relies on securing additional effort on occasions from its workers, most notably when the unpredictable nature of the system requires 'rush' jobs. Workers face choices at Valleyco (particularly over how fast to work) which are not available to those at Nippon CTV; the range of choice for the Nippon CTV workers does not extend much beyond whether to keep their jobs and therefore meet management expectations (cf. Burawoy 1979).

This is not to argue that worker 'misbehaviour' has been eradicated and that managerial control is complete. As we have seen throughout this book, workers at Nippon CTV actively demonstrate their resistance to management in a vari-ety of ways. Indeed, members of the shop-floor reported instances where they had successfully resisted *changes* to their labour process, most notably in avoiding the introduction of two-handed insertion. Some members also regularly avoided working overtime, against management's wishes. But these are marginal suc-cesses amid the overall picture of managerial dominance. During the research period, there was scant evidence that workers at Nippon CTV were able to exert substantive counter-control over the system. What they did achieve, through not wearing their blue jackets, through not listening at meetings and presentations, and through symbolically demonstrating their disaffection, was a *distancing* of themselves from management and its goals. In an ethnographic account of worker behaviour in an American disc-drive plant in Singapore, Chung (1994) identifies similar activities and ascribes these to the desire to secure some personal space or 'private sphere' against an intrusive management system. These empirically grounded research findings run in direct contrast to the literature's prescriptions for high commitment, mutual obligation, and reciprocity between management and labour (MacDuffie 1995; Walton 1985; Womack *et al.* 1990). They also contradict those who have anticipated that workers would internalize the goals of the organization as their own (Ray 1986; Sewell and Wilkinson 1992).

Valleyco workers also demonstrate the gap between themselves and their management in a range of ways. However, their resistance activities are such that they are able to secure substantive gains against the formal system. On various occasions, they are able to secure some control over their work pace, restrict output, build a 'kitty' and pool their work, and share the bonus across the group. Their actions can have a tangible effect on their effort-bargain and the process of management. Also, at Valleyco, resistance is not restricted to informal actions. There were examples of collective direct resistance, orchestrated by the unions at the plant. Indeed the Valleyco case is more reminiscent of the Japanese transplant researched by Graham (1995) than of Nippon CTV in this study.

At both plants in this study, workers were largely and reluctantly resigned to an uneven contest with management. However, whereas workers at Valleyco were occasionally able to secure gains over their effort-bargain, or to 'beat' the system, the situation at Nippon CTV is most accurately described as one in which workers are actively engaged in 'surviving' the system and their actions were not regularly able to secure substantive counters to management control. Moreover, Valleyco's workers regularly engaged in activities which at least partially 'moderated' their work situation, such as bluffing the timers, 'skiving for a fag', or accepting that they would not achieve the minimum bonus rate and consequently then working very slowly. Workers at Nippon CTV have adopted a 'defensive' or 'siege' mentality and seek to act in an individual and instrumental way which protects their best interests (which often match management's interests). An example is the avoidance of mistakes or defects which will be booked against themselves. Of course, it is the pressures of the system which create this environment. The contrasts in the respective workplace relations of the two plants are discussed further in Chapter 10.

THE FRAGMENTATION OF LABOUR

The cloying intensity of the manufacturing and management system at Nippon CTV makes successful collective resistance almost impossible in the plant's current context. An important element in the way the shop-floor experience is moulded in contemporary manufacturing (at least in this manifestation) is the way in which collective labour is put under extreme fragmentary pressure. The control systems and 'blame' culture result in a fracturing of shop-floor solidarity.

We see in Chapter 6 that worker peer group support is likely to be conditional. At Valleyco, workers will help and support those people who are seen as having sympathized with their own position and who have been seen to share the norm of 'fair effort', particularly over work speed. Personality clashes are also likely to shape inter-worker relations. However, at Nippon CTV and in the Peugeot cell at Valleyco, the manufacturing system has placed extra strains on these relationships by closely coupling workers' activities and requiring workers to monitor each other's quality performance. Individual workers come under pressure to 'try' because their actions have an immediate impact on other members of the line. These exhortations are not dissimilar to those of the Nippon CTV induction officer requiring new recruits to 'show willing'; they centre on the meeting of others' expectations regarding the speed of, or attitude to, work. In tightly coupled work organizations, both by working too fast (a 'flyer') and by working too slowly (a 'lazy cow'), individual workers can have a detrimental impact on their workmates' situation. The technical characteristics of JIT clearly shape the experiences of workers.

Particularly at Nippon CTV, it is difficult for workers to find ways of moderating their work effort without having a direct and negative impact on others on the line. For example, when an individual inserter cannot keep to the linespeed, their pieces are transferred to others who can; when an inserter drops pieces on to the boards as 'not connecteds' to regain a split second against the line, the end-of-line inspectors must insert those pieces; when the test gear operators record a series of good panels as faulty to free themselves from a stockpile building at their station, the technical assistants have additional boards to retest. As we have seen, this can result in heightened tension and animosity between workers.

The quality control system at Nippon CTV is particularly divisive for workers because, not only are mistakes identified and corrected, they are also individually ascribed to an accountable worker in a 'blaming process'. Mistakes do not just happen, they are someone's fault. To compound the fragmentary and divisive nature of this pressure, it is fellow workers who are responsible for designating and recording the blame. As is reported in Chapter 6, these tensions regularly informed the inter-worker relations on the line. These dynamics reflect a situation where workers are often forced to take an instrumental approach to working in their own best interests as part of a defensive survival mechanism.

However, inter-worker strife has not completely undermined the worker collective. Instead, it appears to be constituted around sub-groups on the line who deflect the worst of the pressure by 'blaming' their situation on fellow workers elsewhere on the line. Still, whereas *management* is the target for the hostility and blame at Valleyco, much of this hostility is dissipated by inter-worker friction at Nippon CTV.

A fundamental feature of this fragmentation is the appropriation of tacit shop-floor knowledge by management. The key here is the difference between the actual roles (rather than formal hierarchical positions) played by the charge-hands at Valleyco and the team leaders at Nippon CTV. At Valleyco, workers may retain and develop their own understanding and knowledge of their job to their own advantage, for example in being able to work above the job timings. This is facilitated by the charge-hands who typically identify themselves with their shop-floor workers (rather than as part of management) and are keen to see them earn a reasonable bonus. These gobbets of knowledge, the development of which is facilitated by the informal workings of a system, largely lie with the team leaders at Nippon CTV who have been incorporated into the management system. The ever-present tension to increase speed which is maintained by the team leader through 'tweaking up' the linespeed means that workers are constantly pushed to use their tacit knowledge to management's advantage. The team leader has expectations regarding the number of defects which will be recorded while working on a particular board and has developed a tacit knowledge of how fast she may expect the line to work in relation to a board's standard time. The pressure exerted upon the team leaders by the management system (see Chapter 3) is translated into a further 'closing of the pores' in the working day of the shop-floor. The informality is not eradicated but it is crowded out, even exploited, by management.

FORM AND CONTENT REVISITED

The findings of this research study provide support for the arguments that JIT and TQM may facilitate more efficient and effective production for management. However, the particular contribution of this research is in providing detailed empirical evidence on *how* this may happen and in contradicting those who have argued that under such systems workers work 'smarter not harder'. Certainly both Nippon CTV and Valleyco have various HR practices and work organization features which are different in form and structure from past practice, but with regard to content and process this research underscores the significance of continuity in workplace relations, the nature of capitalism, and the role of labour. It is content and process that must remain our primary concern in the understanding and interpretation of contemporary manufacturing.

Nippon CTV has successfully secured technical efficiency and social control with the marginalization of the effects of uncertainty, through process discipline and control, and the extension of managerial prerogatives on the shop-floor. The systemic nature of control and surveillance allows for less direct supervision and interventionist management and results in less visibility of management in the control processes. Compared to the Valleyco case and research conducted in other Japanese transplants (Graham 1995; Stephenson 1996), management at Nippon CTV is less of a target for worker discontent, there are fewer triggers for collective resistance, and the shop-floor is successfully fragmented through a TQM system that gives rise to a 'blaming culture'. The marginalization of uncertainty and informality effectively restricts worker opportunity for renegotiating the labour process and moderating the effort-bargain.

There are, however, limits to management control and both workplaces may be characterized as negotiated orders in which worker resistance and management indulgence are central features. At Valleyco the nature of workplace relations is reminiscent of numerous past studies that have reported the significance of informal negotiation and the inadequacy of bureaucratic controls. At Nippon CTV control has come at the expense of worker good will. Workers actively demonstrate their unwillingness to accept management's goals as their own and regularly resist participation in any discretionary activities. In such circumstances the unitarist managerialist approaches which propose high worker commitment and mutual obligations are inadequate and ill-founded. So too are those accounts that anticipate the internalization of management goals by labour (Ray 1986; Sewell and Wilkinson 1992). Moreover there is little to indicate that contemporary manufacturing practices (as at Nippon CTV and Valleyco) represent a break from past practice. Worker roles are characterized by a strict division of labour, a fragmentation of tasks, supervisory hierarchies, and an emphasis on physical activity. There is scant evidence of the integration of innovation and production on the shop-floor and worker involvement is predicated upon manual effort, not creativity and knowledge.

The importance of process over structure is emphasized when we reflect on the different forms of employee recognition and representation at the plants. Nippon CTV has a single union agreement and a company advisory board, and does not participate in traditional collective bargaining, while Valleyco recognizes three trade unions in traditional bargaining arrangements. However, as Chapter 8 demonstrates, despite these differences in form, the *de facto* influence of the unions is similarly minimal in each of the cases; the important caveat being that the unions at Valleyco are at least attempting to exert influence and to represent their members' interests while the union at Nippon CTV appears acquiescent and has been incorporated into the management of the shop-floor. If this is 'new' industrial relations, then it is about management circumventing and sidelining the effective articulation of worker interests rather than seeking to close the gaps between the interests of workers and managers.

Overall a complex picture emerges from the analysis of the two case plants. Certainly the management practices of JIT and TQM appear to be qualitatively different technical systems of production and their implications for workers are profound. However, the process control exerted through these systems at Nippon CTV has been experienced as intrusive, restrictive, and stressful by the workforce who are consistent in their refusal to participate in any discretionary activity such as problem solving. Consequently the dynamic continual improvement claimed for the contemporary manufacturing model is missing. The central feature is the regulation of labour in a manner which is resonant of traditional forms of control in a number of ways (see Friedman 1977). There is little to suggest that contemporary manufacturing is best characterized as 'postfordist' and that the new shop-floor is a hotbed of worker autonomy and knowledge creation.

10

A Reappraisal of Contemporary Manufacturing and the 'Japanese' Model

INTRODUCTION

The preceding chapters have portrayed two very different workplaces. While there are some similar features in the form of the two shop-floors, for example in the use of a type of JIT, TQM, and team working, the actual outcomes vary quite considerably, both for managers and for workers. There are also some key differences regarding the HRM practices of the two plants, with the Japanese transplant appearing to mirror the contemporary model of manufacturing management 'best practice', with single-status terms and conditions, highly developed communication, and partnership-based consultation with employees. However, as we have seen in Chapter 8, the shop-floor reality of workplace industrial relations differs markedly from this appearance.

The first part of this chapter compares and contrasts the workplace relations of Nippon CTV and Valleyco and explores some of the reasons for these differences. In the second part of the chapter, some broader observations regarding these findings are made. The depth and understanding that ethnographic research of this kind allows can offer the opportunity for reflecting upon wider issues within the business environment. The issues discussed include a reappraisal of the 'Japanese' model and its transferability and some observations on the position of Britain within the global economy.

CONTRASTING WORKPLACE RELATIONS

From the above discussions it seems that it is possible to characterize individual workplaces according to the ways in which management and labour actually act in relation to each other, and the formal rules and procedures, within the contested arena of the 'new' shop-floor. Indeed there have been a number of attempts to categorize 'types' of management control (Child 1984; Edwards 1979; Friedman 1977), worker behaviour (Blyton and Turnbull 1994; Graham 1994; Hodson 1995; Marchington 1992), and/or workplaces (Edwards 1986). As all manner of research has demonstrated, and as is illustrated in the two cases presented here, the workplace relations between capital and labour are predicated upon varying degrees of informality. The actions of labour at Valleyco and Nippon CTV may be categorized into three broad types of activity:

- *'Surviving' the system*, which includes workers' efforts to distance themselves from management and their attempts to escape into 'private spheres' (Chung 1994). There are a number of such examples from the two cases, including not wearing the company uniform, avoiding overtime, and not participating in any form of discretionary activity. Such activities by workers may be noted as 'resistance' or 'misbehaviour' but they do not secure substantive improvements to labour's position in the workplace, nor do they represent significant challenges to management's dominance. Another form of 'survival activity' is the practice of 'escaping into work' noted by Sturdy (1992), in which workers actually work harder as a form of distraction from their subordination—this may explain the actions of Gwen at Valleyco (see Chapter 5). Such responses are more likely to be undertaken at an individual level.

- *'Moderating' the system*. This sort of activity includes workers' attempts to secure some control over, for example, their work speed and the effort-bargain. Such behaviours as 'restricting output' (Roy 1955) and 'building a kitty' (Lupton 1963) offer workers some tangible gains against the formal system and may impact upon the system in a manner which is detrimental to management's wishes. Other action may include securing some control over the time worked through lateness, the taking of informal breaks (for example, Pollert 1981), stopping work early (for example, Cavendish 1982), and absenteeism. These activities are likely to involve individuals or small groups of conspiring workers and were commonplace at Valleyco. Some forms of sabotage may also reflect attempts at moderating the formal systems (see Hodson 1995).

- *'Beating' the system*. In circumstances where workers 'beat' the system they are able to secure significant counter-control in relation to the management system and actively to challenge managerial prerogatives in the workplace. Their action may include direct resistance to management and a refusal to undertake certain tasks and is most likely to involve groups of workers through collective action (see Graham 1994).

In capturing the dynamic interaction between workers and managers, we may also categorize managerial activity into three forms and contemplate their relationship with labour's actions. These three categories are related, but not inextricably linked, to the worker activities at Valleyco and Nippon CTV listed above.

- *'Indulging' workers*. This category of activity involves managerial behaviour which is not consistent in maintaining the formal rules and procedures of the organization. It also involves management consenting to worker 'misbehaviour'—for whatever reason (Gouldner 1955). From the evidence at Nippon CTV, this activity is unlikely to sanction a serious inconvenience to management unless workers are in a position of relative power or management is wary that a 'work-to-rule' may have serious implications for the system. It should be noted that, as with the Gouldner case (1955), and arguably at Nippon CTV, this indulgence may actually assist the organization's management in achieving its goals.

- *'Holding the line'*. This category of behaviour basically captures the activities of management in seeking to maintain its position with regard to formal rules. Management activity is constituted around following, and keeping workers to, the systems and procedures formally designated by that management. Such managerial behaviour might be characterized as a 'work-to-rule' in that management expects workers to follow the procedures but does not seek to extend its control and influence beyond that.
- *'Extending' control* may be seen as management activity which goes beyond the formally prescribed rules in seeking further effort and value from labour. This might be characterized as 'superexploitation', in which the frontier of control is extended beyond that which is prescribed and contained within the systems as they stand. In these circumstances management will go beyond the formal expectations of labour in speeding up the line, insisting that workers do overtime, or increasing workers' job tasks. The situation at Nippon CTV would appear to reflect these characteristics, and, for example, much of the management behaviour reported by Armstrong *et al.* (1981) also represents attempts to legitimize extending the frontier of control.

It should be noted that it seems likely that individual workplaces will play host to each of these forms of behaviour to varying degrees. Certainly in the cases discussed here, there are examples of each form of activity. However, as a comparative device one may identify the predominant form of behaviour for both management and labour. It seems logical to anticipate that a workplace in which management is dominant to the extent that it seeks to extend its control beyond the formal systems is likely to be one in which worker resistance has been largely marginalized to the periphery, taking the form of distancing behaviour through which workers seek to survive their everyday work experience without great expectations of securing radical and beneficial change or improvement to the effort bargain. Nippon CTV is an exemplar of such a workplace on the basis of the research evidence.

Following the logical line, one might anticipate that the middle categories of behaviour might also match up in a form of 'mutual accommodation' where workers seek to moderate the impact of the formal system and management seeks to secure its control to that level. Within such a workplace, there are likely to be certain instances or areas over which one or other of the parties may make substantial gains, but these are possibly balanced by concessions elsewhere. It seems that the situation at Valleyco might be represented thus. Management has been able to reduce inventories, improve quality, and extend its control in some parts of the plant, while at the same time many assembly workers are securing considerable gains against the piece-rate system and retaining some control over their work speed and effort-bargain.

While the management at Nippon CTV has been successful in securing control of the shop-floor and has benefited from establishing tight process control, there has been a price to pay. The restrictive and coercive pressures to conform and the high surveillance—low trust environment have led to a situation in which workers resist attempts to change the labour process, withdraw their good will, and refuse to contribute any discretionary effort. As a consequence, the dynamic of continuous improvement and increasing performance which is central to the theoretical model of best practice outlined in Chapter 1 is missing. White and Trevor (1983: 5) claim that employee relations practices in Japanese transplants aim to secure a stable workforce 'with a high level of commitment to the company' that is 'extremely cooperative in accepting change', that puts the company's interests 'level with or even ahead of its own', and which thus results in 'a high and rising level of productivity, and an altogether easier climate in which management can plan for changes in products and processes'. In the case of Nippon CTV, productivity may be high but it is much less likely to be rising when workers' resentment of their situation has led them to resist changes to work practices and to refuse to contribute to improvement programmes. It is precisely for this reason that the factory regime at Nippon CTV fails to provide evidence of the successful adoption of contemporary manufacturing best practice.

TOWARDS AN EXPLANATION OF WORKPLACE RELATIONS

A significant question is raised by the findings outlined above: why are the workplace relations of Nippon CTV and Valleyco so constituted? In responding to this question, I will reflect on key issues under four headings which appear to have played a substantial role in shaping the workplaces at Valleyco and Nippon CTV: the historical context; management and the production system; labour and the unions; and the wider environment or setting for the plants. The information contained here is consistent with an approach which builds from a shop-floor perspective and hence may not provide a comprehensive documentation of all the factors which have helped to inform the workplace relations of the two plants, particularly with regard to the external environmental factors. As Edwards (1986) notes, these influences are interactive and interdependent. However, in reflecting upon these local factors and then, in the following sections, considering the wider picture regarding contemporary manufacturing and the 'Japanese' model, it is possible to build an explanation for the content and form of these two workplaces.

Historical Context

This research has reported information from a particular period in two organizations. These two plants both have histories which are likely to have had a considerable influence over the way in which labour and management come together in the workplace. An interpretation of the situation must be cognizant of these key historical features.

The Valleyco plant has a longer history than Nippon CTV, and it is more complicated, more precarious, and less stable. The various changes of ownership at the plant (see Chapter 2) have undermined any identification that the shop-floor may have with the organization. While some of the workers are optimistic that the new owners might improve things, the shop-floor relationship is centred on individual personalities who transcend the various capital arrangements. This partly explains the conflictual nature of the workplace relations, since much of the antipathy between management and the workers is historic and personalized. This has also helped to institutionalize and perpetuate the importance of collective bargaining.

The years of antagonism are matched by years of *ad hoc* management with a 'make do' mentality. Management-driven changes regarding, for example, quality practices are undermined by management's own apparent inconsistency over time and the scepticism of the workforce. The continuing ineffectiveness of the systems in delivering what is required (acceptable quality from bought-in suppliers, reliable internal schedules, management control through piece-rates) allows workers to continue to exploit these gaps in order to moderate their work experience, for instance through taking informal breaks or through regulating effort. A number of these activities have become expected by workers as part of the plant's negotiated pattern of custom and practice.

In contrast, the workplace relations at Nippon CTV are marked by adherence to the formal systems, which were established by a management team with clear objectives that was able to utilize mature and proven technology. In effect the reopening of the Nippon CTV plant represented a 'clean slate' for management. In particular this is the case regarding labour. Management took the opportunity to select the most reliable workers and also selected the most cooperative and 'reliable' (for management) trade union to represent them. In the context of being grateful for re-employment, workers were encouraged to feel part of something, to identify their interests with those of the company, and to accept managerial prerogatives without question; management acts in accordance with its own espoused objectives. In this way, precedents are established and maintained, and new recruits are inducted into a shop-floor situation where a conflict of interests pertains but where conflict is peripheralized. It is interesting to note, however, that any reduction in 'them and us' attitudes that may have characterized the shop-floor during the start-up of the plant has failed to survive the high surveillance—low trust regime.

The history of the plants is at least a partial factor in defining what Chung (1994) called the 'factory consciousness' of the two cases, both of which reflect a resignedly pragmatic approach to resistance. In other words, workers do not feel that their interests coincide with management's but, for varying reasons, they recognize that there are limits to the extent to which they may enact their resistance and the manner in which they may do so.

Management and the System

As was discussed earlier, the management control processes and production systems at the two plants set a number of constraints and obstacles for labour. The process discipline and control which is exhibited at Nippon CTV assists management in marginalizing uncertainty and therefore restricts workers' opportunities to exploit the 'pores' in their working day through informally negotiating greater control over their situation. A key reason that workers at Nippon CTV are engaged predominantly in defensive, survival behaviour is the highly restrictive system in which they work. The choices workers face at Nippon CTV often do not extend beyond whether they should endeavour to keep their jobs through meeting management's expectations and quite how they will see through the day.

For Nippon CTV workers the problems are compounded because management itself maintains a consistent approach to its own rules and restricts any likelihood of precedents being set over the breaking or bending of rules. Management is able to achieve this as well as running a quantitatively efficient operation because the formal rules governing labour are consistent with the rational economic goals of capital accumulation (see Chapter 9). As a consequence, management does not have to become embroiled in informal negotiations over what workers should actually do in relation to the formal system.

From this basis, management is able informally to extend its control of the shop-floor, through maintaining a constant pressure to perform above the formally designated standards and through the appropriation by the team leaders of much of the tacit knowledge held on the shop-floor. Where management does indulge its workforce and accept behaviour outside the formal system, it appears that this may represent a necessary 'safety valve' to the pressures that build under the shop-floor systems. Such indulgence is not allowed to impact on the efficiency of the plant.

As discussed above, this situation stands in stark contrast to the fragmentary and *ad hoc* approach that characterizes management at Valleyco. Since the formal systems are prone to uncertainty and disruption, management is beholden to some extent to informally negotiated activity between itself and the workers. On occasions management may encourage workers to 'rush' jobs but on other occasions workers may be able systematically to withhold effort and play the system to their benefit. The management process at Valleyco has not successfully restricted uncertainty and, as a consequence, workers are able to claw back control and secure improvements to their work situation.

An important factor in explaining the situation at the two plants may be the relatively peripheral nature of innovation within the two systems. At neither plant does management expect labour to make major contributions to improving the production processes. Management does not attempt to encourage worker participation in problem solving. Moreover, from the shop-floor observations in this study, there is little evidence to suggest that coherent innovation and improvement activities are central to *management's* role in the two plants. As discussed later in this chapter, both plants have imported tried and trusted processes from outside the UK and the management role is primarily to maintain these, not to improve them. In essence these may be understood as 'branch' plants (see Milkman 1991) or 'reproduction' plants (see Kenney *et al.* 1997) rather than the 'learning factories' of postfordist manufacturing rhetoric (see Fruin 1992).

Labour and the Unions

At neither of the two plants is it likely that there will be concerted direct resistance to management and the limits to the power of collective labour would appear to be highly circumscribed. To a large extent this must be understood in relation to the role of organized labour. While both plants recognize unions, the union at Nippon CTV is not formally and directly involved in collective bargaining over issues of pay and conditions and the unions at Valleyco are clearly restricted in the extent to which they can actively resist management.

The situation at Nippon CTV arises from the history of the inception of the union at the plant. The union was selected by management because it would accept managerial prerogative; worker representation has been incorporated into the management umbrella of communication procedures. Consequently, the plant has no history of confrontational independent worker representation. Without such representation any opportunity for workers to organize any collective resistance is undermined. It is interesting to contrast this with the findings of Graham (1995) at a Japanese car assembly transplant during the start-up phase. There, injury-related grievances, in particular, provided a focal point for collective direct resistance. The prospect of collective resistance at Nippon CTV is further undercut by the intense inter-worker pressure which the systems induce through closely coupling workers and internal policing, etc. Such pressures lead to a fragmentation of the collective spirit which might otherwise be engendered on the shop-floor. As a result, workers resort to individual and marginal actions of resistance such as not listening at meetings, refusing to engage in any discretionary activities, and not wearing their uniforms. At Nippon CTV, worker resistance to working overtime was individual, whereas workers at the car plant studied by Graham collectively contested the unilateral scheduling of overtime (Graham 1995: 123–4). However, at both plants, any resistance which was more substantially linked to the effort-bargain was likely to have a detrimental impact on work colleagues because of the tight coupling of individual work stations.

During the research, workers did report their discontent and they did express their dissatisfaction with their union. However, because of the lack of organized support, this antipathy was not channelled into a constructive challenge to management. Where workers did resist, it was in an *ad hoc* and reactive way, such as in avoiding the introduction of two-handed insertion. There was no evidence that they might be able to mobilize collective resistance to a procedure which was already in place, such as the 'tweaking up' of the linespeed or the management control of when workers may take a toilet break. In part this also reflects the strength of managerial custom and practice which has been institutionalized in a workplace where management has established its systems and maintained its dominant position. In short, the precedents are set for Nippon CTV, and there is no sign of any 'deinstitutionalization' (Oliver 1992) through which the formal and institutionalized rules might be challenged and which might offer workers the opportunity of securing a greater level of *de facto* control.

For Valleyco workers, there is a history of organized and collective resistance to management and the union does independently represent the workforce. However, while workers are able to take advantage of the gaps in the formal system in moderating their situation, and this may include small groups acting together to moderate the system of control, protracted direct resistance to management with the goal of securing substantial gains is as unlikely as at Nippon CTV. This can only be interpreted in relation to the environmental context of the plant. It does seem that at both plants there is a 'factory consciousness' which is based on a degree of either resignation or pragmatic (and consequently) limited resistance. While it may not be desirable to argue that labour is solely *reactive* to management (Cohen 1987), it does appear that the combination of history, management systems, and environmental constraints represents a clear influence over the nature of the terrain of contest. To a varying degree, labour at both plants faces an uphill battle. It is the nature of the environmental context to which I now turn.

The Environmental Context

The situations at both plants represent negotiated and localized partial solutions to global problems. While at both plants there is 'imported technology', particularly at Nippon CTV, the individual workplaces reflect numerous aspects of both management and labour which pertain specifically to the local situation. A factor in interpreting these localized settlements is the context beyond the shop-floor. The most immediate factor affecting the shop-floor relationship at both plants would appear to be the local economic and labour market conditions.

In both areas, the major traditional sources of employment for working class males have been decimated by the restructuring of the British economy (see Chapter 2). In these circumstances, the role of working women has grown significantly and many of the female workers at both plants, and especially at Valleyco, are sole earners in their family. In the case reported by Pollert (1983) 'women workers put up with boring jobs because they look towards marriage and the family as escapes' (p. 103). Many workers at Valleyco, in contrast, already had families and were required to take on an onerous dual role, what Pollert calls their 'double burden', as 'home maker' and 'bread winner'; unlike the women in Pollert's case, Valleyco's female workers did not view wage labour as 'temporary'. As a direct consequence of economic restructuring, the employment of these women in areas of above-average unemployment was particularly vital. Many of the women at the two case companies could not afford to lose their jobs and would have had little chance of finding alternative employment should they have done so. Equally important, in understanding the nature of the workplace relationship between management and labour, is the fact that workers at the plants could not afford to strike. It seems highly likely that the workers' perceptions of what they might be able to achieve in resisting management was circumscribed by a concern to hold on to their jobs.

Along with the macroeconomic restructuring and recessionary pressures in the UK which are having an impact on the shop-floor, there are the product-market characteristics of the two plants—particularly the economic changes within the motor industry which have had a considerable impact at Valleyco. The 1980s brought a crisis of both production volumes and profitability in the British automotive components industry (Turnbull *et al.* 1993) and during that period the major car assemblers rationalized their sourcing and significantly reduced their supplier base (Trade and Industry Committee 1987). The outcome has been severe competition, and the major assemblers have secured a powerful market position. This consolidation of market power has basically been replicated on a global scale throughout the world motor industry (Lieuliette 1994) and commentators have linked this explicitly with the competitive pressures exerted by Japanese competitors (Jürgens *et al.* 1993).

The impact of these developments is clearly to be seen on the shop-floor at Valleyco, where major customers dominate. Indeed, the clearest example of these pressures manifesting themselves at the workplace may be seen in the way Nissan extends its market control (see Chapter 4). The importance of the dominance of the customer is compounded at Valleyco since management can call on the imperative of meeting customer requirements as a 'legitimizing principle' in informal negotiations over workplace behaviour (Armstrong *et al.* 1981). This is very effective since the shop-floor is left in no doubt over the importance of keeping customers happy (see Chapters 4 and 6). Moreover, workers were well aware of the economic recession in the motor industry as it was reported daily in the news media.

During the research period, the exhortations of Valleyco's management that workers should do whatever was necessary to fulfil customer requirements or suffer dire consequences was not likely to prove unfounded. Customer orders had dropped dramatically and if the plant had lost the Nissan business (which stayed stronger through exports into Europe) then it is likely that Valleyco would have closed the Cwmtown operation. However, the management at Nippon CTV also emphasized the significance of competing in the global market-place and the explicit link between market competition and workers' security of employment. In these circumstances, there is more evidence to suggest that these pressures are used by management as legitimation for their position and to inveigle workers into making extra effort in a manner described as 'hegemonic despotism' by Burawoy (1983). In this situation, the uncertainty implied by the global market is being used to commit workers to their own exploitation. However, the manner in which this pressure translates on to a shop-floor will depend on various aspects of the social processes underpinning workplace relations. Hence there is the need to form a detailed understanding of these localized and negotiated settlements in the face of such global pressures.

A final factor which must clearly have influenced the nature of workplace relations at the plants, especially the role of organized labour, is the UK national context for industrial relations. Various issues have weakened the position of the trade union movement since the early 1980s and there is no doubt that these have had a significant impact upon a whole range of the characteristics relevant to the union–management relationships in place (Blyton and Turnbull 1994). These range from the fragmentation and isolation of individual plants through the restricted activity of local branch and regional union organizations (as at Valleyco, see Chapter 8), through to the legislative and attitudinal backdrop which has allowed companies such as Nippon CTV to insist on selecting its own trade union and has facilitated management in incorporating that union into its own systems of control. There also appears to be a regional variation between workers' attitudes to trade unions at the two plants, with the south Wales workers articulating a greater sense of class identity and solidarity than did the workers in the south-west.

REAPPRAISING CONTEMPORARY MANUFACTURING

Having reviewed the nature of workplace relations at the plants and reflected upon the local influences on those relations, I now consider the broader issues that are influencing developments in manufacturing organizations and use the research findings reported here and elsewhere to reflect upon key aspects of contemporary manufacturing. First I consider the extent to which the situations of the two plants may be understood in relation to the concept of 'Japanization' and the transfer of the 'Japanese' model.

The Transfer of the 'Japanese' Model?

For us to consider the significance of Nippon CTV and Valleyco in regard to the 'transfer' of the 'Japanese' model, we must first consider exactly what has been introduced at the two plants and what relation that may have to the 'Japanese' model. As was discussed in Chapter 9, Nippon CTV has incorporated a form of 'internal JIT' which has a number of characteristics in common with the technical aspects of contemporary manufacturing best practice. The key characteristics of the manufacturing system at Nippon CTV are that: (a) it has a reliable and (but only where absolutely necessary) flexible internal environment; the system is founded on tight process control; (b) the management at Nippon CTV is able to run without large buffers of stock, excess labour, or time because of this tight control; (c) the system is predicated upon the tight coupling of individual workers and processes and involves the close monitoring of quality with individual accountability for mistakes.

The areas of the shop-floor at Valleyco where management has recently introduced changes to the historical systems also share these characteristics, particularly in reducing inventories, grouping workers' activities, and making the workers responsible for the self-monitoring of quality. Preceding chapters have discussed in detail the ways in which the practice of shop-floor operations is negotiated. However, as discussed in Chapter 9, Nippon CTV management has succeeded in marginalizing uncertainty and combining the control of labour with economic efficiency; this has severely restricted opportunities for substantive worker resistance. It should be noted that worker behaviour is a potential *source* of uncertainty for management and that the marginalization of the trade union is also significant in establishing management control. The situation at Valleyco is one of directed chaos in which management is struggling to maintain control of its processes and systems and where uncertainty still predominates on most of the shop-floor. Consequently, labour may still be successful in attempts to regulate the effort-bargain. However, even here resistance is likely to be covert, and the role of the union and collective resistance limited.

While the internal features of the shop-floor operations at Nippon CTV are consistent with some of the technical expectations drawn from the fundamental features of contemporary manufacturing outlined in Chapter 1, the organization has not extended its involvement in its environment to include aspects of supply chain management. Indeed, the plant management has successfully sought to decouple itself from its environment in order to secure internal stability and predictability rather than attempt to extend its control and influence into its business environment (cf. the activities of Sony described in Morris *et al.* 1993). This is most noticeable in the way in which the internal operations are buffered from market fluctuations by the inventory policy of the retail arm of Nippon CTV's business. In contrast, the situation at Valleyco is one marked by the disruptions and uncertainty caused by an unpredictable and unstable environment stemming from the unreliable supply of poor-quality materials and unreliable and varying orders from customers.

Thus, one may report a partial application of the *technical* aspects of the 'Japanese' model to *internal* operations at the two plants, with the direct investor clearly outstripping the emulator in terms of both extent and success of application. We should also recognize that the production technology at both the plants was designed and developed by the parent companies in their home countries and exported as a 'mature' technology into the UK. Likewise the product design and development was conducted by engineers and technicians outside Britain. The Nippon Denki Corporation spends more than $2 billion per year on research and development, but not in Britain.

However, when one considers the social aspects of the 'Japanese' model and the characteristics of the employment relationship for core workers in major

Japanese companies, the differences between the case plants and the model are far more substantial. The 'three pillars' of the employment relationship reported in Japan (Abegglen 1958; Dore 1973) are not to be found at either Nippon CTV or Valleyco. There is no lifetime employment—indeed, the management at both plants actively threatens workers with job losses if they fail to meet company expectations; there is no seniority basis to pay, promotion, or conditions at either plant; and there is no enterprise unionism as such, although one may argue that the AEEU is playing the role of a 'functional equivalent' (Cole 1971; Oliver and Wilkinson 1992) in the way that it is co-opted into management procedures at Nippon CTV.

Of equal importance in our interpretation of the situation for labour in contemporary manufacturing, the opportunity for worker involvement in innovation and improvement activities, which is so central to the arguments of Womack *et al.* (1990), MacDuffie (1995), and Kenney and Florida (1993), is missing. Contrary to the expectations professed by these authors, there is little or no evidence of systematic and regular job rotation, multiskilling, small group problem solving, decentralized decision making and employee participation, or 'team' working in the sense described by proponents of the model reviewed in Chapter 1. Indeed, the research evidence presented here suggests that workers are 'a pair of hands' and little more to management, and that management appears to hold minimal expectations of the input of the workforce to 'discretionary activities' beyond the Taylorist notions of task execution and compliance to managerial prerogative.

For workers at Nippon CTV the experience of work—positioned at a moving assembly line repeating endlessly the same limited cycle of standardized tasks—is very similar to that described by previous studies into working on assembly lines (for example, Cavendish 1982; Hamper 1992). Workers at Nippon CTV appear to be even more closely monitored and are held individually accountable for their performance in a more oppressive manner than that described by earlier authors. When one considers in addition that the workers at Nippon CTV do not actively participate in group problem solving and typically do not contribute suggestions, then the case reported offers some support for the 'superexploitation' thesis of Japanese management put forward by Dohse *et al.* (1985). However, these authors anticipated that the 'Japanese' model would not be transferable because 'it is only possible in an industrial-relations environment in which there are hardly any limits to management prerogative' (p. 140). The situation described in the preceding chapters does not represent a discontinuous departure from traditional manufacturing (cf. Womack *et al.* 1990), but rather an extension of the principles of Taylor through the systematic standardization and proceduralization of tasks within a context of heightened managerial dominance and control. There is no evidence from the Nippon CTV case to support the views of Ohno (1988), Shingo (1988), or Dore (1973) that the 'Japanese' model rests on a Theory Y approach to the management of labour nor to substantiate the recent claims that Japanese firms are key exemplars of those high-performing organizations which have encouraged mutual obligation and reciprocity between workers and managers through the integration of high-commitment HRM practices with the production system (MacDuffie 1995). The situation at Nippon CTV is one of high surveillance and low trust on the part of management, and of no autonomy and no discretionary effort for workers.

The findings here are similar to those of Milkman (1991) in her study of Japanese transplants in California and to the review of Japanese transplant organizations in Australia by Dedoussis and Littler (1994). Both studies emphasize that the actual operations in the Japanese transplants do not equate to the 'full Japanese' model and both associate this with cost minimization on the part of the Japanese parent. Milkman (1991: 6) notes that:

The Japanese model is transplanted rarely, and mainly in highly complex, capital-intensive operations such as auto assembly. Most Japanese-owned factories in the U.S. are branch plants of large Japanese multinationals engaged in relatively simple fabrication and assembly operations. Under these conditions, the training and other costs of implementing the Japanese model seem to be forgone, and American-style work organization and management practices prevail instead.

Dedoussis and Littler (1994: 177–8) argue that:

human resource management in [Japanese] overseas subsidiaries will be characterized by the introduction of low cost practices which can offer immediate and distinct advantages to the organization. High cost labour practices, such as tenured employment and seniority based remuneration which aim at securing the long-term presence of a loyal and committed workforce, need not be introduced to subsidiaries.

How do the conclusions of Milkman and Dedoussis and Littler square with the universalist model of Womack *et al.* (1990) and conceptions of manufacturing 'best practice'? What do our conclusions over the nature of contemporary manufacturing in these two UK-located plants tell us regarding the transfer of the 'Japanese' model and its emulation by western firms? Do these findings support those who believe that the cultural and institutional specificity of the home country will proscribe transfer overseas (for example, Ohno, in Monden 1983; Yoshino 1976; Ackroyd *et al.* 1988; Abo *et al.* 1994)? What is actually being instituted at these two workplaces and is it 'Japanese'?

A Question of Sector?

When reviewing the literature on the practices of Japanese transplants (Abo *et al.* 1994; Dedoussis and Littler 1994; Fucini and Fucini 1990; Garrahan and Stewart 1992; Graham 1994; Kenney and Florida 1992a, 1993; Milkman 1991; Morris *et al.* 1993; Rhinehart *et al.* 1994; Stephenson 1996; Taylor *et al.* 1994) it is possible to discern a consistent variation between the Japanese transplants in the automotive sector and those in the electronics sector. Indeed, this is explicitly recognized and explored in comparative studies by Abo *et al.* (1994), Milkman (1991), and Kenney and Florida (1992a).

Milkman reports that the General Motors–Toyota joint venture, NUMMI, is the exception rather than the rule in California because it has introduced Japanese practices such as quality circles and flexible team working. Abo and his colleagues attempted systematically to score the 'Japaneseness' of the transplants that they studied and concluded that some form of 'hybrid' organization is widespread. However, they note significant sector differences in the transplants that they studied and that the application of the 'Japanese' model was highest in the auto assemblers, followed by automotive parts makers. The lowest level of application was found in the consumer electronics transplants. These findings are mirrored by those of Kenney and Florida (1992a) when they compare automotive industry transplants with those in electronics.

The case studies of car assembly plants all report that the work on the line is highly routinized and standardized (Fucini and Fucini 1990; Garrahan and Stewart 1992; Graham 1994, 1995; Parker and Slaughter 1988; Rhinehart *et al.* 1994), although that description would also fit the situation at car assembly plants other than those owned by the Japanese (Beynon 1973; Hamper 1992). However, they do report the use of team working and the utilization of small group problem-solving activities as part of the plant's process of *kaizen* or continuous improvement. In this respect, then, these car assembly transplants are different from the Nippon CTV case reported here and from the majority of electronics plants researched by Milkman. It should be noted that these studies do not report complete success for management's initiatives and that they note these processes are often marked by conflict and resistance from workers. None the less, the management at these plants appears to have sought systematically to harness the 'mental' labour of the workforce to its own ends. These are the plants upon which Kenney and Florida (1993) and Womack *et al.* (1990) have based their assumptions of a universal model of 'innovation-mediated' production led by 'highly skilled problem solvers'. So, what are we to conclude from these variations between electronics and autos? Is the contemporary manufacturing model dependent upon sector, and if so, why?

Abo and his colleagues (1994) assume that the relatively high degree of 'adaptation' (as opposed to 'application') of the 'Japanese' model by Japanese transplants in the USA may be accounted for on the basis that those Japanese companies *could not* replicate their operations outside Japan because of 'the enduring importance of place in shaping the character of production innovation' (Abo *et al.* 1994: xxi). Following Yoshino (1976), Abo *et al.* are convinced that the 'Japanese' model is derived from the special characteristics of Japanese society. They claim that their research findings, in which they identify a 'hybrid' of application and adaptation as commonplace among transplants, vindicate this view. They ascribe this 'hybrid' as being the result of the 'strained relationship' between Japanese management and the American socio-cultural environment. However, that conclusion does not allow them to explain the systematic variations between the automotive and electronics industries.

Dedoussis and Littler (1994) point us to an alternative explanation: that management *chooses* not to implement the 'full Japanese' model, or at least not the model of employment relations which is to be found in major Japanese corporations for core employees. Dedoussis and Littler (1994) suggest that what we are seeing through the globalization of Japanese capital *is* the transfer of a 'Japanese' model—but it is the model which explains the employment relationship for the peripheral workforce in Japan.

In explaining this transfer of a 'peripheral model of Japanese management', Dedoussis and Littler argue that it is 'a fallacy to suppose that Japanese managers wish to totally transfer "Japanese management practices"', and that 'the rationale for the peripheral model of Japanese management is cost minimization in the context of well-developed external labour markets' (1994: 176). For the authors, then, the nature of the transferability debate is shifted from explaining the 'incomplete transfer' of Japanese management practices in terms of cultural or structural barriers (cf. Abo *et al.* 1994) to the realization 'that a different model of management is applicable. Japanese managers transfer as much as they wish, and as little' (Dedoussis and Littler 1994: 191).

While Dedoussis and Littler ignore the potential impact of contest and agency in the management process, their contribution to the 'Japanization' debate is very important. The dual nature (core and periphery) of Japanese firms' activities is now well known (Chalmers 1989; Saso 1990) and this distinction may be applied to understand the variations reported between the auto assembly operations and consumer electronics plants such as Nippon CTV. The activities of the consumer electronics transplants are labour intensive and low skilled (see Kenney and Florida 1992a; Milkman 1991) and would often be subcontracted out in Japan. Specifically, the panel shop activities at Nippon CTV in Britain are conducted in a series of small subcontractor factories lying outside the main Nippon Denki plant in Japan. Workers in the subcontractor plants, who are mostly women, are paid much less than a Nippon Denki employee and do not enjoy the benefit of secure employment. They are not expected to participate in the organization's activities through problem solving and the like. Management at the subcontractor plant is not expected by Nippon Denki to make improvements to the production processes, only to run them as efficiently and cheaply as possible. These processes are relatively simple and mature and are deemed fully rationalized by NDC senior management.

In contrast to this, the auto assembly activities of Japanese transplants are typically similar to those conducted by the Japanese parent at home. They involve more complex processes and greater levels of capital intensity and investment. Correspondingly, the managers of Japanese car transplants seek to elicit worker knowledge because they do not feel the systems have been rationalized completely. In other words, it is in more complex production processes involving newer technology for more complex products that improvements are anticipated. These processes are carried out by the parent company, which expects its core employees to contribute their ideas for improving the system in an ongoing series of innovations. On the other hand, the 'mature' technologies which management does not expect to be the source of innovation are subcontracted out to subsidiaries with lower labour costs. It is the level of maturity and complexity of the technology, products, and production processes, and the relative centrality of innovation which explain the difference in management expectations for labour. Dedoussis and Littler's (1994) cost-minimization explanation of which HRM practices are incorporated into the system appears to hold across transplants in the electronics *and* automotive sectors. Neither sector has examples which have adopted lifetime employment, seniority-based pay, and all the other elements of the 'full Japanese' model.

However, within these variations regarding the complexity of production processes and the centrality of innovation, there are key features which appear across both the automotive and electronics sectors. These are that the organizations in question have highly fragmented and standardized work procedures and have taken steps to diminish uncertainty in a context of managerial dominance. This is usually accompanied by either a non-union stance or a workplace characterized by 'passive' or 'co-operative' unionism (Garrahan and Stewart 1992; Milkman 1991; Taylor *et al.* 1994; cf. Graham 1994, 1995). This leads to the conclusion that the persistent and defining characteristic of the 'Japanese' model is the way in which management seeks to marginalize uncertainty and simultaneously to combine qualitative and quantitative efficiency. This implies that any research into contemporary manufacturing practice and the 'Japanese' model should make central an analysis of the extent of managerial prerogative.

The Transfer of Managerial Prerogative

While we may be able usefully to reinterpret the 'Japanization' debate along the lines of a core/periphery divide and the extent to which innovation is central to production, there is a fundamental feature of the process of the globalization of Japanese capital which has been ignored by commentaries on how 'Japanese' the Japanese transplants are. The key point to be understood from this study on what is being instituted on the 'new' shop-floor is that these developments reflect the dominance of managerial ideology and a unitarism which undermines workers' collective and independent rights and representation. To discuss the system as 'more or less' Japanese is to obfuscate its true significance as a system which extends managerial domination in the workplace. As such, then, the 'Japanese' model is hardly 'original', but it may be understood as a significant development in the history of capitalist workplace relations.

Much of the debate on the 'Japanese' model has understandably centred on the motor industry. However, this has actually clouded the interpretation of the practices of Japanese management since the car assemblers are atypical of Japanese investors, in having transferred production processes in which innovation is expected. While researchers such as Laurie Graham (1994, 1995) have reported that 'legitimate consensus' between management and workers was 'simply impossible' (cf. Dore 1973), the facts that the systems are not mature and fully rationalized, and that management seeks worker participation in innovation, have offered workers the opportunities for resistance which are largely absent at plants such as Nippon CTV. Graham argues that management at the plant has sought to 'harness workers' collective intelligence for continuous improvement' and that bureaucracy is reduced and authority decentralized as management seeks to gain control over the 'social aspects of production'. This situation is very different from that at Nippon CTV, although Graham also reports very fragmented jobs which are rationalized to a tenth of a second, and the difference may be ascribed at least partly to the relative levels of innovation which are expected by management. Graham reports examples of resistance by workers which include direct collective resistance through which workers won concessions. Such action is unlike anything that occurred at Nippon CTV.

If one interprets what is being transferred in terms of relative levels of managerial control, then Nippon CTV might be considered *more successful* than the automotive sector transplants, since managerial control appears more complete than at, say, the transplant researched by Graham (remembering that the success of Nippon CTV is in establishing a system which combines both quantitative and qualitative efficiency). Still, there is evidence that the Japanese automotive sector transplants have secured greater levels of control over their workforce than domestic assemblers and that the stresses and fragmentary pressures on workers which were reported in the Nippon CTV case are also present in the motor industry transplants (see Garrahan and Stewart 1992; Parker and Slaughter 1988; and cf. Hamper 1992). Moreover, Nippon CTV may be considered *unsuccessful* with regard to the contemporary model of manufacturing 'best practice' since the dynamism of innovation and improvement is missing.

There are some distinctive features of the employment relations at the Japanese transplant in this study when compared to local industry. This is in contrast to the conclusions of Milkman (1991) on the Japanese transplants (except NUMMI) in California, which she felt closely resembled American-owned non-union firms. Also distinctive at Nippon CTV is the role of the trade union, including the very nature of the single union agreement which the two parties signed, the union's active participation in management forums, and the paucity of collective bargaining activities between the union and management. The question is, however, whether these are best researched and explained as aspects of 'Japanization' or rather the further establishment of managerial prerogative within the context of capitalist workplaces.

These management–union practices and other HRM features in Japanese transplants have been characterized as 'sophisticated consultative' management (Purcell and Gray 1986) but this research suggests that, while Nippon CTV may have the formal structures one associates with pluralist employee relations, the actions and practices of management are inconsistent with that pluralism and are resonant of a unitarism which sees the 'organization's goals' as overarching and overriding in importance and seeks to deny the legitimate conflict of interests which pluralism recognizes. The Nippon CTV company handbook makes it clear that management expects the company advisory board, as the 'sole joint body', to find solutions before problems arise and hence 'conflict becomes unnecessary'.

The implication of these findings is that much of the research into the 'Japanese' model has been ill founded and, frankly, has missed the point. The culturalist and institutionalist arguments over the development of the 'Japanese' model and their conclusions on the implications thereof for industrial convergence (from Abegglen 1958 and Dore 1973 to Abo *et al.* 1994) have failed to recognize the fundamental facet of modern Japanese management and have therefore helped to promote and sustain a series of misguided interventions into the debate.

The work of a number of critical economic historians points to the fact that the post-war development of Japanese management has been a story of re-establishing managerial prerogatives. Most notably the work of Andrew Gordon (1985) has demonstrated that, between 1949 and 1953, there was a period when management, with the assistance of the state, reasserted itself and that subsequently the labour relationship has evolved 'in a context of domination by management'. Indeed, the Nippon Denki company union's own literature reports a 'red purge' in the early 1950s as the company re-established control. The comparative case studies of Tabata (1989) show how Nissan management reacted to intense competitive pressure by decimating the company union's previously independent workplace organization and establishing a workplace similar to that at Toyota, where the union accepts 'virtually unconditionally' management schemes for rationalization and efficiency improvements. This interpretation of the development of Japanese management during the post-war period is actually shared by the architect of the Toyota production system which has proved so influential, Taiichi Ohno. According to Cusumano (1985), Ohno considered his greatest achievement to be the subduing of the union at Toyota: 'despite his obvious genius as a production manager, Ohno still considered his success in controlling the union to have been the most important advantage Toyota gained over its domestic and foreign competitors' (Cusumano 1985: 307). Ohno himself commented, 'Had I faced the Japan National Railways Union or an American union, I might have been murdered' (Ohno, quoted in Cusumano 1985: 306).

This interpretation, in turn, raises the question of whether it is accurate to consider this model as 'Japanese' and whether it is helpful to talk of 'Japanization'. In an article published in 1988, Ian Graham notes that 'the concept of "Japanese production management techniques" claims political neutrality and is characterised by the ahistoricity [necessary] to qualify as a myth' (Graham 1988: 74). He argues that the linking of organizational changes to Japan presented these changes as imperative in order to compete internationally and thus secured assent for management from workers over workplace changes that might otherwise have been resisted. To Graham, the association of production techniques with 'best practice' has allowed management to secure further gains against workers. In a similar way, researching these changes as though they represent 'Japanization' may also allow for misrepresentations and misreadings.

Smith and Meiksins (1995) argue that cross-national organizational analysis must recognize that there is a *three-way interaction* which influences work in any country. The elements of this are the economic mode of production ('system'), national legacies and institutions ('societal'), and ' "best practice" or universal modernisation strategies generated and diffused by the "society-in-dominance" within the global economy at a particular period of time' ('dominance'). This represents a more sophisticated method for interpreting change in individual workplaces and recognizes the significance of capitalism in defining those changes. As Smith and Meiksins note:

Taylorism . . . was initially bounded by the constraints of American capitalism; but its diffusion transformed it into a 'best practice' which was seen as a system requirement in some economies. . . . The identification of Taylorism with American economic success made it difficult to resist. Disentangling the three influences of society, system and dominance has always been part of the critique of Taylorism as it became a dominant ideology and began to diffuse to Europe and Japan; but we could say that it was only with the emergence of other dominant capitalist states, in Europe and Japan, that such a critique has been able to separate these levels, and identify what in Taylorism is specific to America, what is part of capitalism, and what held sway only through American economic hegemony and not intrinsic qualities of Taylorism itself (Aoki, 1988). (Smith and Meiksins 1995: 263–4.)

I hope that this study has gone some way to establishing the characteristics and attributes of the 'Japanese' model and that it has made clear that the debates over the 'Japanese' model and 'Japanization' should be firmly located within the wider research perspective regarding the ongoing development of global capitalism and workplace relations.

BRITAIN IN THE GLOBAL ECONOMY: THE *MAQUILADORA* REGION OF EUROPE?

For the British economy it also seems that the findings of this study, albeit based on two plant cases, reinforce the significance of certain fundamental questions. The interpretation of these findings, in broadly following those of Dedoussis and Littler (1994) and Milkman (1991) regarding the nature of Japanese investment elsewhere, is highly significant in recognizing the impact of these investment flows into the UK. It is that Britain has appealed to the majority of Japanese firms as a low-cost location for the siting of low-complexity, labour-intensive operations. In reviewing the Japanese transplant manufacturing sector, Williams *et al.* (1992) argue that employment is restricted to low-grade assembly jobs and that the high value-added activities are retained in Japan. This coincides with Milkman's (1991) findings and she notes that:

Like those in Mexico and South East Asia, these Japanese owned plants in California are branch plants that perform relatively routinized, low skilled assembly or fabrication, while the more complex phases of the production process remain in Japan itself. (p. 72.)

This finding is highly significant in interpreting the true value of such investments and is consistent with the findings in this and other research which has studied Japanese electronics transplants (Kenney and Florida 1992a; Taylor *et al.* 1994). It is worth noting that there are 216 manufacturing enterprises in the UK with Japanese ownership and around 73,000 people are employed in these plants (JETRO 1996). While the car assemblers Honda, Nissan, and Toyota have attracted most of the academic and media attention they account directly for only about 10 per cent of that employment. Many more workers are employed in the electronics sector by companies like Nippon CTV.

The workplace situation at Nippon CTV is consistent with the findings of researchers studying Japanese transplants in Mexico and the *maquiladoras*. Shaiken and Browne (1991) studied Japanese-owned plants in Mexico and concluded that managers there 'seem to be satisfied with using traditional quality control and work organization methods' and are ignoring the techniques, such as *kaizen* and quality circles, 'that are credited with bringing their parent companies stunning success'. In other words, the flexible team working, the problem-solving groups, and the decentralized responsibility and active employee participation which are missing at Nippon CTV are missing there also.

Kenney and Florida (1992b) report that the 'Japanese maquilas occupy a special position in the global production chain of Japanese companies, providing a source of low cost labor for labor-intensive production and assembly'. It appears from this research that Nippon Denki's British operations also meet this description and that, perhaps Sony aside, this is characteristic of most Japanese investment in the UK except for the car assemblers (Morris *et al.* 1993). If the UK is to be the *maquiladora* region of Europe then the implications are profound. This research underscores that of others who have argued that the result is low-wage assembly jobs. Dedoussis and Littler (1994) and Williams *et al.* (1992) emphasize that these investments are precarious.

Underlying the peripheral model is the lack of long-term commitment to the host country of Japanese multinationals. Japanese corporations hive off labour-intensive activities to subsidiaries and subcontracting firms. In the context of the globalization of production and the overseas expansion of Japanese subcontracting networks it may be anticipated that production activities in any one host country will continue to be carried out as long as conditions remain favourable from the viewpoint of the parent corporation. This however means that the commitment of the subsidiary firm is substantially lower compared with the parent company in Japan. (Dedoussis and Littler 1994: 176.)

The 'favourable' conditions which encouraged Japanese investment to Britain included low wage levels, high unemployment, the collapse of domestic manufacturing, and state-orchestrated enmity toward organized labour underpinned by increasingly restrictive labour laws (Turnbull and Delbridge 1994). The logic of Dedoussis and Littler implies that we must retain these 'advantages' in order to continue to attract and keep this type of foreign direct investment. Furthermore, there are serious implications for the longer-term competitiveness and growth of the UK's manufacturing sector if the role of indigenous managers is merely to operate systems and technology designed and developed elsewhere. In short, if the 'thinking'—the design and development of technology and management systems—is conducted in Japan or elsewhere and a 'mature' and fully rationalized system is transferred (in the eyes of the parent company), then the role of local managers may mirror that of their workforce who operate in production systems where innovation is not central. That is, the role of local managers may be hugely circumscribed to that which involves 'maintaining' an established system. If this proves to be the case then many middle managers will find their roles increasingly subjected to the rationalization, standardization, and intensification which characterize the labour process on their shop-floor.

Bibliography

ABEGGLEN, J. (1958), *The Japanese Factory: Aspects of its Social Organization*, Glencoe, Illinois: The Free Press.

ABERCROMBIE, N., HILL, S., AND TURNER, B. (1988), *Dictionary of Sociology* (2nd edn.), Harmondsworth: Penguin.

ABO, T. *et al.* (1994), *Hybrid Factory: The Japanese Production System in the United States*, Oxford: Oxford University Press.

ACKERS, P., SMITH, C., AND SMITH, P. (eds.) (1996), *The New Workplace and Trade Unionism*, London: Routledge.

ACKROYD, S., BURRELL, G., HUGHES, M., AND WHITAKER, A. (1988), 'The Japanisation of British Industry', *Industrial Relations Journal*, 19 (1): 11–23.

AMOROSO, B. (1992), 'Industrial Relations in Europe in the 1990s: New Business Strategies and the Challenge to Organised Labour', *International Journal of Human Resource Management*, 3 (2): 173–90.

AOKI, M. (1988), *Information, Incentives and Bargaining in the Japanese Economy*, Cambridge: Cambridge University Press.

ARMSTRONG, P., AND GOODMAN, J. (1979), 'Managerial and Supervisory Custom and Practice', *Industrial Relations Journal*, 10 (Autumn): 12–24.

——, ——, AND HYMAN, J. (1981), *Ideology and Shop-floor Industrial Relations*, London: Croom-Helm.

BASSETT, P. (1986), *Strike Free: New Industrial Relations in Britain*, London: Macmillan.

BECKER, H. (1970), *Sociological Work: Method and Substance*, Chicago: Aldine.

BEER, M., SPECTOR, B., LAWRENCE, P., QUINN MILLS, D., AND WALTON, R. (1985), *Human Resource Management: A General Manager's Perspective*, Glencoe: Free Press.

BELL, C., AND ENCEL, S. (eds.) (1978), *Inside the Whale: Ten Personal Accounts of Social Research*, Oxford: Pergamon.

BELL, D. (1974), *The Coming of Post-Industrial Society*, Harmondsworth: Penguin.

BERGER, P., AND LUCKMANN, T. (1967), *The Social Construction of Reality*, Harmondsworth: Penguin.

BEYNON, H. (1973), *Working for Ford*, Harmondsworth: Penguin.

BHASKAR, R. (1978), *A Realist Theory of Science*, Hassocks: Harvester Press.

BIGGART, N., AND HAMILTON, G. (1997), 'On the Limits of a Firm-based Theory to Explain Business Networks: The Western Bias of Neoclassical Economics', in M. Orrù, N. Biggart, and G. Hamilton (eds.), *The Economic Organization of East Asian Capitalism*, Thousand Oaks: Sage, 33–54.

BLAU, P. (1974), *On the Nature of Organizations*, New York: Wiley.

BLUMER, H. (1969), *Symbolic Interactionism*, Englewood Cliffs, N.J.: Prentice-Hall.

BLYTON, P., AND TURNBULL, P. (1994), *The Dynamics of Employee Relations*, London: Macmillan.

BLYTON, P., AND TURNBULL, P. (eds.) (1992), *Reassessing Human Resource Management*, London: Sage.

BRAVERMAN, H. (1974), *Labor and Monopoly Capital*, New York: Monthly Review Press.

BROWN, W. (1972), 'A Consideration of Custom and Practice', *British Journal of Industrial Relations*, 10 (1): 42–61.

BUCHANAN, D., BODDY, D., AND MCCALMAN, J. (1988), 'Getting in, Getting on, Getting out and Getting back', in A. Bryman (ed.), *Doing Research in Organizations*, London: Routledge, 53–67.

BURAWOY, M. (1979), *Manufacturing Consent: Changes in the Workplace under Monopoly Capitalism*, Chicago: University of Chicago Press.

—— (1983), 'Between the Labor Process and the State: The Changing Face of Factory Regimes under Advanced Capitalism', *American Sociological Review*, 48: 587–605.

BURRELL, G. (1992), 'Back to the Future: Time and Organization', in M. Reed and M. Hughes (eds.), *Rethinking Organization*, London: Sage, 165–83.

CAVENDISH, R. (1982), *Women on the Line*, London: Routledge & Kegan Paul.

CHALMERS, N. (1989), *Industrial Relations in Japan: The Peripheral Workforce*, London: Routledge.

CHILD, J. (1984), *Organization: A Guide to Problems and Practice* (2nd edn.), London: Harper & Row.

CHUNG, Y. (1994), 'Conflict and Compliance: The Workplace Politics of a Disk-drive Factory in Singapore', in J. Bélanger, P. Edwards, and L. Haiven (eds.), *Workplace Industrial Relations and the Global Challenge*, Ithaca, N.Y.: ILR Press, 190–223.

CLEGG, S. (1989), *Frameworks of Power*, London: Sage.

—— (1990), *Modern Organizations: Organization Studies in the Postmodern World*, London: Sage.

COHEN, S. (1987), 'A Labour Process to Nowhere?', *New Left Review*, Sept./Oct., 34–50.

COLE, R. (1971), *Japanese Blue Collar: The Changing Tradition*, Berkeley: University of California Press.

CRESSEY, P., AND MACINNES, J. (1980), 'Voting for Ford: Industrial Democracy and the "Control of Labour"', *Capital and Class*, 11: 5–33.

CROZIER, M. (1964), *The Bureaucratic Phenomenon*, London: Tavistock.

CUSUMANO, M. (1985), *The Japanese Automobile Industry*, Cambridge, Mass.: Harvard University Press.

DALTON, M. (1959), *Men Who Manage*, New York: Wiley.

DASTMALCHIAN, A., BLYTON, P., AND ADAMSON, R. (1991), *The Climate of Workplace Relations*, London: Routledge.

DEDOUSSIS, V., AND LITTLER, C. (1994), 'Understanding the Transfer of Japanese Management Practices: The Australian Case', in T. Elger and C. Smith (eds.), *Global Japanization? The Transnational Transformation of the Labour Process*, London: Routledge, 175–95.

DELBRIDGE, R. (1995), 'Surviving JIT: Control and Resistance in a Japanese Transplant', *Journal of Management Studies*, 32 (6): 803–17.

——, AND TURNBULL, P. (1992), 'Human Resource Maximisation: The Management of Labour under a JIT System', in P. Blyton and P. Turnbull (eds.), *Reassessing Human Resource Management*, London: Sage, 56–73.

——, —— (1993), 'Diventare Giapponesi? L'Adozione e l'Adattamento dei Sistemi di Produzione Giapponesi in Gran Bretagna', *Sociologia del Lavoro*, 51–52: 119–49.

——, ——, AND WILKINSON, B. (1992), 'Pushing Back the Frontiers: Management Control and Work Intensification under JIT/TQM Factory Regimes', *New Technology, Work and Employment*, 7 (2): 97–106.

DIMAGGIO, P., AND POWELL, W. (1983), 'The Iron Cage Revisited: Institutional Isomorphism and Collective Rationality in Organizational Fields', *American Sociological Review*, 48 (Apr.): 147–60.

DOHSE, K., JÜRGENS, U., AND MALSCH, T. (1985), 'From "Fordism" to "Toyotism"? The Social Organization of the Labour Process in the Japanese Automobile Industry', *Politics and Society*, 14 (2): 115–46.

DORE, R. (1973), *British Factory—Japanese Factory: The Origins of National Diversity in Industrial Relations*, London: Allen & Unwin.

EDWARDS, P. (1986), *Conflict at Work*, Oxford: Basil Blackwell.

——, BÉLANGER, J., AND HAIVEN, L. (1994), 'Introduction: The Workplace and Labor Regulation in Comparative Perspective', in J. Bélanger, P. Edwards, and L. Haiven (eds.), *Workplace Industrial Relations and the Global Challenge*, Ithaca, N.Y.: ILR Press, 3–21.

EDWARDS, R. (1979), *Contested Terrain: The Transformation of the Workplace in the Twentieth Century*, London: Heinemann.

ELAM, M. (1990), 'Puzzling out the post-Fordist Debate: Technology, Markets and Institutions', *Economic and Industrial Democracy*, 11 (1): 9–37.

ELGER, T. (1975), 'Industrial Organizations—a Processual Perspective', in J. McKinlay (ed.), *Processing People: Cases in Organizational Behaviour*, London: Holt, Rinehart & Winston, 91–149.

—— (1990), 'Technical Innovation and Work Reorganization in British Manufacturing in the 1980s: Continuity, Intensification or Transformation?', *Work, Employment and Society*, Special Issue (May): 67–101.

——, AND SMITH, C. (eds.) (1994), *Global Japanization? The Transnational Transformation of the Labour Process*, London: Routledge.

FILIPCOVA, B., AND FILIPEC, J. (1986), 'Society and Concepts of Time', *International Social Science Journal*, 107: 19–32.

FREUND, J. (1979), 'German Sociology at the Time of Max Weber', in T. Bottomore and R. Nisbet (eds.), *A History of Sociological Analysis*, London: Heinemann.

FRIEDMAN, A. (1977), *Industry and Labour: Class Struggle at Work and Monopoly Capitalism*, London: Macmillan.

FRUIN, M. (1992), *The Japanese Enterprise System*, Oxford: Oxford University Press.

FUCINI, J., AND FUCINI, S. (1990), *Working for the Japanese: Inside Mazda's American Auto Plant*, New York: Free Press.

GARFINKEL, H. (1967), *Studies in Ethnomethodology*, Englewood Cliffs, N.J.: Prentice-Hall.

GARRAHAN, P., AND STEWART, P. (1992), *The Nissan Enigma: Flexibility at Work in a Local Economy*, London: Mansell.

GEARY, J. (1995), 'Work Practices: The Structure of Work', in P. Edwards (ed.), *Industrial Relations: Theory and Practice in Britain*, Oxford: Blackwell, 368–96.

GEERTZ, C. (1973), *The Interpretation of Cultures*, New York: Basic Books.

GILL, J., AND JOHNSON, P. (1991), *Research Methods for Managers*, London: Chapman Publishing.

GODARD, J. (1993), 'Theory and Method in Industrial Relations: Modernist and Postmodernist Alternatives', in R. Adams and N. Meltz (eds.), *Industrial Relations Theory: Its Nature, Scope and Pedagogy*, Mefuchen, N.J.: IMLR/Rutgers University Press, 283–306.

GOLDTHORPE, J. (1974), 'Industrial Relations in Britain: A Critique of Reformism', *Politics and Society*, 4 (4): 419–52.

GORDON, A. (1985), *The Evolution of Labor Relations: Heavy Industry, 1853–1945*, Boston: Harvard University Press.

GORDON, D. (1976), 'Capitalist Efficiency and Socialist Efficiency', *Monthly Review*, 24 (July/Aug.): 19–39.

GOULDNER, A. (1955), *Wildcat Strike: A Study of an Unofficial Strike*, London: Routledge & Kegan Paul.

GRAHAM, I. (1988), 'Japanisation as Mythology', *Industrial Relations Journal*, 19 (Spring): 69–75.

GRAHAM, L. (1994), 'How Does the Japanese Model Transfer to the United States? A View from the Line', in T. Elger and C. Smith (eds.), *Global Japanization? The Transnational Transformation of the Labour Process*, London: Routledge, 123–51.

—— (1995), *On the Line at Subaru-Isuzu: The Japanese Model and the American Worker*, Ithaca, N.Y.: ILR Press.

GRANT, D. (1996), 'Japanization and New Industrial Relations', in I. Beardwell (ed.), *Contemporary Industrial Relations: A Critical Analysis*, Oxford: Oxford University Press, 203–33.

GRIPAIOS, P., BISHOP, P., AND GRIPAIOS, R. (1992), *The Plymouth Economy: A Case Study*, Plymouth: South West Economy Research Centre, Plymouth Business School.

——, AND WISEMAN, N. (1994), 'Recovery in the South West?', in *The South West Economic Review*, Plymouth: South West Economy Research Centre, Plymouth Business School.

GUEST, D. (1989), 'Human Resource Management: Its Implications for Industrial Relations and Trade Unions', in J. Storey (ed.), *New Perspectives on Human Resource Management*, London: Routledge.

GUEST, D., AND HOQUE, K. (1996), 'Human Resource Management and the New Industrial Relations', in I. Beardwell (ed.), *Contemporary Industrial Relations: A Critical Analysis*, Oxford: Oxford University Press, 11–31.

HAMMER, M., AND CHAMPY, J. (1993), *Reengineering the Corporation: A Manifesto for Business Revolution*, New York: Harper Business.

HAMPER, B. (1992), *Rivethead: Tales From the Assembly Line*, London: Fourth Estate.

HANDY, C. (1984), *The Future of Work*, Oxford: Blackwell.

HARASZTI, M. (1980), 'Piecework and "Looting"', in T. Nichols (ed.), *Capital and Labour*, London: Fontana, 290–301.

HECKSHER, C., AND DONNELLON, A. (1994), *The Post-Bureaucratic Organization: New Perspectives on Organizational Change*, Thousand Oaks: Sage.

HOBSBAWM, E. (1994), *Age of Extremes: The Short Twentieth Century, 1914–1991*, London: Michael Joseph.

HODSON, R. (1995), 'Worker Resistance: An Underdeveloped Concept in the Sociology of Work', *Economic and Industrial Democracy*, 16: 79–110.

HYMAN, R. (1987), 'Strategy of Structure?: Capital, Labour and Control', *Work, Employment and Society*, 1 (1): 25–55.

—— (1992), 'Trade Unions and the Disaggregation of the Working Class', in M. Regini (ed.), *The Future of Labour Movements*, London: Sage, 150–68.

JACQUES, R. (1996), *Manufacturing the Employee: Management Knowledge from the 19th to 21st Centuries*, London: Sage.

JETRO (1996), *The Twelfth Survey of European Operations of Japanese Companies in the Manufacturing Sector*, London: JETRO.

JURAVICH, T. (1985), *Chaos on the Shop Floor*, Philadelphia, Pa.: Temple University Press.

JÜRGENS, U., MALSCH, T., AND DOHSE, K. (1993), *Breaking with Taylorism: Changing Forms of Work in the Automobile Industry*, Cambridge: Cambridge University Press.

KAMATA, S. (1983), *Japan in the Passing Lane: An Insider's Account of Life in a Japanese Auto Factory*, London: Allen & Unwin.

KANTER, R. (1989), 'The New Managerial Work', *Harvard Business Review*, 67 (6): 85–92.

KEAT, R., AND URRY, J. (1975), *Social Theory as Science*, London: Routledge & Kegan Paul.

KELLY, J. (1996), 'Union Militancy and Social Partnership', in P. Ackers, C. Smith, and P. Smith (eds.), *The New Workplace and Trade Unionism*, London: Routledge, 77–109.

——, AND KELLY, C. (1991), '"Them and Us": Social Psychology and "the New Industrial Relations"', *British Journal of Industrial Relations*, 29 (1): 25–48.

KENNEY, M., AND FLORIDA, R. (1988), 'Beyond Mass Production: Production and the Labour Process in Japan', *Politics and Society*, 16 (1): 121–58.

KENNEY, M., AND FLORIDA, R. (1992a), 'Japanese Styles of Management in Three US Transplant Industries: Autos, Steel and Electronics', paper presented at Workshop on Japanese Management Styles, Cardiff.

—— , —— (1992b), 'Japanese Maquiladoras', Program in East Asian Business and Development, Working Paper No. 44, Institute of Governmental Affairs, University of California, Davis.

—— , —— (1993), *Beyond Mass Production: The System and its Transfer to the U.S.*, Oxford: Oxford University Press.

—— , GOE, R., CONTRERAS, O., AND ROMERO, J., WITH BUSTOS, W. (1997), 'Learning Factories? A Study of the Labor-Management System Employed in the Japanese Consumer Electronics Maquiladoras in Mexico', Program on Pacific Rim Business and Development Working Paper Series, No. 15, University of California, Davis.

KERR, C., DUNLOP, J., HARBISON, F., AND MYERS, C. (1960), *Industrialism and Industrial Man: The Problems of Labor and Management in Economic Growth*, Cambridge, Mass.: Harvard University Press.

KLEIN, J. (1991), 'A Re-examination of Autonomy in the Light of New Manufacturing Practices', *Human Relations*, 44 (1): 21–38.

KOCHAN, T., KATZ, H., AND MCKERSIE, R. (1986), *The Transformation of American Industrial Relations*, New York: Basic Books.

LASH, S., AND URRY, J. (1987), *The End of Organized Capitalism*, Oxford: Polity Press.

LAWLER, E. (1992), *The Ultimate Advantage*, San Francisco: Jossey-Bass.

LEGGE, K. (1995), *Human Resource Management: Rhetorics and Realities*, London: Macmillan.

LIEULIETTE, T. (1994), 'Strategic Technology, Radical Change, Blinding Speed: Building Blocks for Survival in the Nineties', paper presented at the 'Age of Agility' Conference, Traverse City, Michigan.

LINCOLN, J., AND KALLEBERG, A. (1990), *Culture, Control, and Commitment: A Study of Work Organization and Work Attitudes in the United States and Japan*, Cambridge: Cambridge University Press.

LINHART, R. (1981), *The Assembly Line*, London: John Calder.

LITTLER, C., AND SALAMAN, G. (1984), *Class at Work: The Design, Allocation and Control of Jobs*, London: Batsford.

LUPTON, T. (1963), *On the Shop Floor: Two Studies of Workshop Organisation and Output*, Oxford: Pergamon Press.

MACDUFFIE, J. (1995), 'Human Resource Bundles and Manufacturing Performance: Organizational Logic and Flexible Production Systems in the World Auto Industry', *Industrial and Labor Relations Review*, 48 (2): 197–221.

MARCHINGTON, M. (1992), 'Managing Labour Relations in a Competitive Environment', in A. Sturdy, D. Knights, and H. Willmott (eds.), *Skill and Consent: Contemporary Studies in the Labour Process*, London: Routledge, 149–83.

MARTINEZ LUCIO, M., AND WESTON, S. (1991), 'Worker Rights and Worker Representation as an Arena of Struggle in the Context of New Strategies', paper presented at the British Universities Industrial Relations Conference, UMIST.

——, —— (1995), 'Trade Unions and Networking in the Context of Change: Evaluating the Outcomes of Decentralization in Industrial Relations', *Economic and Industrial Democracy*, 16: 233–51.

MATZA, D. (1969), *Becoming Deviant*, Englewood Cliffs, N.J.: Prentice-Hall.

MEHAN, H. (1979), *Learning Lessons: Social Organization in the Classroom*, Boston: Harvard University Press.

MILES, R., AND SNOW, C. (1984), 'Designing Strategic Human Resource Systems', *Organizational Dynamics*, Summer: 36–52.

MILKMAN, R. (1991), *Japan's California Factories: Labor Relations and Economic Globalization*, Los Angeles, Cal.: Institute of Industrial Relations, University of California.

MILLWARD, N., STEVENS, N., SMART, P., AND HAWES, W. (1992), *Workplace Industrial Relations in Transition*, Aldershot: Dartmouth.

MONDEN, Y. (1983), *Toyota Production System: Practical Approach to Production Management*, Norcross, Ga.: Industrial Engineering and Management Press.

MORRIS, J., AND IMRIE, R. (1992), *Transforming Buyer–Supplier Relations: Japanese-Style Industrial Practices in a Western Context*, London: Macmillan.

——, MUNDAY, M., AND WILKINSON, B. (1993), *Working for the Japanese: The Economic and Social Consequences of Japanese Investment in Wales*, London: Athlone.

——, AND WILKINSON, B. (1995), 'Poverty and Prosperity in Wales: Polarization and Los Angelesization', *Contemporary Wales*, 8 (Dec.): 29–46.

MUELLER, F., AND PURCELL, J. (1992), 'The Europeanisation of Manufacturing and the Decentralisation of Bargaining: Multinational Management strategies in the European Automobile Industry', *International Journal of Human Resource Management*, 3 (1): 15–34.

MUETZELFELDT, M. (1989), 'Organisation as Strategic Control', paper presented at the Third International APROS Colloquium, Canberra.

OHNO, T. (1988), *Just-in-Time: For Today and Tomorrow*, Cambridge, Mass.: Productivity Press.

OLIVER, C. (1992), 'The Antecedents of Deinstitutionalization', *Organization Studies*, 13 (4): 563–88.

OLIVER, N., AND WILKINSON, B. (1992), *The Japanization of British Industry: New Developments in the 1990s*, Oxford: Blackwell.

——, DELBRIDGE, R., JONES, D., AND LOWE, J. (1994), 'World Class Manufacturing: Further Evidence in the Lean Production Debate', *British Journal of Management*, 5 (June): S53–S63.

OUCHI, W. (1981), *Theory Z: How American Business Can Meet the Japanese Challenge*, Reading, Mass.: Addison-Wesley.

PARKER, M., AND SLAUGHTER, J. (1988), *Choosing Sides: Unions and the Team Concept*, Boston: Labor Notes.

PASCALE, R., AND ATHOS, A. (1982), *The Art of Japanese Management*, Harmondsworth: Penguin.

PETERS, T. (1987), *Thriving on Chaos: Handbook for a Management Revolution*, New York: Harper & Row.

PIORE, M., AND SABEL, C. (1984), *The Second Industrial Divide*, New York: Basic Books.

POLLERT, A. (1981), *Girls, Wives and Factory Lives*, London: Macmillan.

—— (1983), 'Women, Gender Relations and Wage Labour', in E. Gamarnikow, D. Morgan, J. Purvis, and D. Taylorson (eds.), *Gender, Class and Work*, London: Heinemann, 96–114.

PURCELL, J. (1991), 'The Rediscovery of Management Prerogative: The Management of Labour Relations in the 1980s', *Oxford Review of Economic Policy*, 7 (1): 33–43.

——, AND GRAY, A. (1986), 'Corporate Personnel Departments and the Management of Industrial Relations: Two Case Studies in Ambiguity', *Journal of Management Studies*, 23 (2): 205–23.

RAY, C. (1986), 'Corporate Culture: The Last Frontier of Control', *Journal of Management Studies*, 23 (2): 287–97.

RHINEHART, J., ROBERTSON, D., HUXLEY, C., AND WAREHAM, J. (1994), 'Reunifying Conception and Execution of Work under Japanese Production Management? A Canadian Case Study', in T. Elger and C. Smith (eds.), *Global Japanization? The Transnational Transformation of the Labour Process*, London: Routledge, 152–74.

ROSE, M. (1975), *Industrial Behaviour: Theoretical Development since Taylor*, London: Allen Lane.

ROY, D. (1952), 'Restriction of Output in a Piecework Machine Shop', Ph.D. dissertation, University of Chicago.

—— (1955), 'Efficiency and "the Fix": Informal Intergroup Relations in a Piecework Machine Shop', *American Journal of Sociology*, 60: 255–66.

SAKO, M. (1992), *Prices, Quality and Trust: Inter-Firm Relations in Britain and Japan*, Cambridge: Cambridge University Press.

SASO, M. (1990), *Women in the Japanese Workplace*, London: Hilary Shipman.

SCHONBERGER, R. (1982), *Japanese Manufacturing Techniques: Nine Hidden Lessons in Simplicity*, New York: Free Press.

—— (1986), *World Class Manufacturing: The Lessons of Simplicity Applied*, New York: Free Press.

SCHUTZ, A. (1962), *Collected Papers 1: The Problem of Social Reality*, The Hague: Martinus Nijhoff.

SEWELL, G., AND WILKINSON, B. (1992), 'Someone to Watch over Me: Surveillance, Discipline and the Just-in-Time Labour Process', *Sociology*, 26 (2): 271–89.

SHAIKEN, H., AND BROWNE, H. (1991), 'Japanese Work Organization in Mexico', in G. Szekely (ed.), *Manufacturing Across Borders and Oceans: Japan, the*

United States, and Mexico, San Diego: UCSD Center for U.S.-Mexican Studies, 25–50.

SHINGO, S. (1988), *Non-Stock Production: The Shingo System for Continuous Improvement*, Cambridge, Mass.: Productivity Press.

SHWEDER, R., AND D'ANDRADE, R. (1980), 'The Systematic Distortion Hypothesis', in R. Shweder (ed.), *New Directions for Methodology of Social and Behavior Science*, San Francisco: Jossey Bass.

SMITH, C., AND MEIKSINS, P. (1995), 'System, Society and Dominance Effects in Cross-National Organisational Analysis', *Work, Employment and Society*, 9 (2): 241–67.

STEPHENSON, C. (1996), 'The Different Experience of Trade Unionism in two Japanese Transplants', in P. Ackers, C. Smith, and P. Smith (eds.), *The New Workplace and Trade Unionism*, London: Routledge, 210–39.

STOREY, J. (1981), *The Challenge to Management Control*, London: Hutchinson Business Books.

STRAUSS, A., SCHATZMAN, L., EHRLICH, D., BUCHER, R., AND SABSHIN, M. (1971), 'The Hospital and its Negotiated Order', in F. Castles, D. Murray, and D. Potter (eds.), *Decisions, Organizations and Society*, Harmondsworth: Penguin, 103–23.

STURDY, A. (1992), 'Clerical Consent: "Shifting Work" in the Insurance Office', in A. Sturdy, D. Knights, and A. Willmott (eds.), *Skill and Consent: Contemporary Studies in the Labour Process*, London: Routledge, 115–48.

TABATA, H. (1989), 'Changes in Plant Level Trade Union Organization: A Case Study of the Automobile Industry', Occasional Papers in Labour Problems and Social Policy No. 3, Insitute of Science and Technology, Tokyo University.

TAYLOR, B., ELGER, T., AND FAIRBROTHER, P. (1994), 'Transplants and Emulators: The Fate of the Japanese Model in British Electronics', in T. Elger and C. Smith (eds.), *Global Japanization? The Transnational Transformation of the Labour Process*, London: Routledge, 196–225.

TERRY, M. (1994), 'Workplace Unionism: Redefining Structures and Objectives', in R. Hyman and A. Ferner (eds.), *New Frontiers in European Industrial Relations*, Oxford: Blackwell, 223–49.

THOMPSON, P., AND ACKROYD, S. (1995), 'All Quiet on the Workplace Front? A Critique of Recent Trends in British Industrial Sociology', *Sociology*, 29 (4): 615–33.

——, AND MCHUGH, D. (1990), *Work Organizations*, London: Macmillan.

TICHY, N., FOMBRUN, C., AND DEVANNA, M. (1982), 'Strategic Human Resource Management', *Sloan Management Review*, 23 (2): 47–61.

Trade and Industry Committee (1987), *The U.K. Motor Components Industry: Third Report*, London: HMSO.

TURNBULL, P. (1988), 'The Limits to "Japanisation"—Just-in-Time, Labour Relations and the U.K. Automotive Industry', *New Technology, Work and Employment*, 3 (1): 7–20.

TURNBULL, P., AND DELBRIDGE, R. (1994), 'Making Sense of Japanisation: A Review of the British Experience', *International Journal of Employment Studies*, 2 (2): 343–65.

—— , —— , OLIVER, N., AND WILKINSON, B. (1993), 'Winners and Losers: The "Tiering" of Component Suppliers in the U.K. Automotive Industry', *Journal of General Management*, 19 (1): 48–63.

WAINWRIGHT, H. (1994), *Arguments for a New Left*, Oxford: Blackwell.

WALTON, R. (1985), 'From Control to Commitment', *Harvard Business Review*, 64 (3): 76–84.

WASS, V., AND WELLS, P. (eds.) (1994), *Principles and Practice in Business and Management Research*, Aldershot: Dartmouth.

WAX, R. (1960), 'Reciprocity in Field Work', in R. Adams and J. Heiss (eds.), *Human Organization Research: Field Relations and Techniques*, Homewood, Ill.: Dorsey, 90–8.

WEBER, M. (1947), *A Theory of Social and Economic Organization*, New York: Free Press.

—— (1949), *The Methodology of the Social Sciences*, New York: Free Press.

Welsh Office (1994), *Welsh Economic Trends*, Cardiff: Welsh Office.

WHITE, M., AND TREVOR, M. (1983), *Under Japanese Management: The Experience of British Workers*, London: Heinemann.

WHYTE, W. (1948), *Street Corner Society*, Chicago: University of Chicago Press.

WILKINSON, A., MARCHINGTON, M., GOODMAN, J., AND ACKERS, P. (1992), 'Total Quality Management and Employee Involvement', *Human Resource Management Journal*, 2 (4): 1–20.

WILLIAMS, K., HASLAM, C., WILLIAMS, J., ADCROFT, A., AND JOHAL, S. (1992), 'Factories or Warehouses?: Japanese Manufacturing Foreign Direct Investment in Britain and the U.S.', Occasional Papers on Business, Economy and Society No. 6, University of East London.

WINTERSON, J. (1991), *Oranges are not the Only Fruit*, London: Vintage.

WOMACK, J., JONES, D., AND ROOS, D. (1990), *The Machine That Changed the World*, New York: Rawson Macmillan.

YOSHINO, M. (1976), *Japan's Multinational Enterprises*, Cambridge, Mass.: Harvard University Press.

INDEX

Index

Printed in the United States
18550LVS00002B/80